Manual of Morphops~~~, ~~~ ~~

FACES
══ & ══
CHARACTERS

Dr. Louis Corman

Illustrated with 300 drawings

Translation from the original French by Gillian Pollock
www.guid-publications.com

Edited by Natalie Pavey
www.nptranslations.com

Revised by Benoît Corman
www.benoitcorman.com

The drawings and photographs in this book are the originals taken from
Dr. Louis Corman's original work, *Visages et caractères*. The translation
into English respects the author's terminology and intended meaning.

Faces & Characters

© Presses Universitaires de France, 1985, original title: VISAGES ET CARACTÈRES

© Guid Publications, original translation into English, 2017, Faces & Characters

© Translation into English 2017, Gillian Pollock

Guid Publications
Bruc, 107, 5-2
08009 Barcelona
Spain
Email: guid@guid-publications.com

Design: Estudio Hache

ISBN: 978-84-945213-7-9

www.guid-publications.com

Contents

Foreword

If someone were to ask me, "Of everything that has helped you to understand how the human being functions up to now, if you had to pick one thing, what would it be?", without hesitation I would answer 'Morphopsychology'. As an analytical method, morphopsychology provides me with valuable information on a daily basis on how to manage my relationships with all kinds of people in all types of contexts. It reminds me not to take anything personally and to respect the uniqueness of each person. This I owe to the author of the book that you have in your hands.

Many of us try to become experts in the art of self-knowledge and understanding of others so that our lives may flow more smoothly. We wish to access our inner world to understand and accept what drives us in order to follow the path that makes us happy. To recognise and channel the conflicts that cause internal imbalance and to understand the patterns that condition other people's behaviours.

A number of different diagnostic tools in the study of the personality exist nowadays. The majority are based on cognitive concepts that generalise character typologies and behaviour patterns. However, we imagine that, in order to define our character, it is a somewhat complex process, considering that we are a blend of multiple traits combined to create something unique to each individual. For this reason, these systems – which are designed for personality analysis – are often considered unreliable because it is assumed that these systems pigeonhole people and are therefore only partially and circumstantially accurate.

How can we reach an accurate understanding of the functioning of our own psyche when it is derived from a unique and peculiar combination of traits? How can we detect if we are subconsciously attributing our own virtues and defects to others without recognising them in ourselves?

The French psychiatrist, Louis Corman, created and then directed a child psychiatric department for over 20 years in the Saint-Jacques Hospital in Nantes. He was able to demonstrate, through the rigorous application of his method, that facial traits constitute a clear and objective source of information for identifying character traits. Corman created morphopsychology officially in 1937 through the publication of his first book on the subject. He acquired a great deal of knowledge from studies that had already been done on the correlation between the face and the personality and, based on biological laws, created a method for observing and interpreting the face that enabled a very precise identification of the forces that determine our fundamental inner needs and that condition our patterns of behaviour towards the outside world.

Morphopsychology, which brings together the physical and mental processes, is based on a groundbreaking concept, as many continue to believe that our physical body is nothing more than a vehicle which functions independently from our psyche and that there is no interaction between the two entities. However, science has now been able to show us that this is not the case, that the body–mind relationship is indisputable and constant: biology and psychology go hand-in-hand. For example, who can deny the existence of psychosomatic illnesses?

Aware of the power of the multiple applications that his method provided, Louis Corman created the *Société Française de Morphopsychologie* in 1980 for the dissemination and teaching of his method. I would like to highlight a fundamental aspect of his work that Louis Corman always reiterated as a means of guaranteeing a constructive use of morphopsychology: 'Do not judge, understand'. It was, and remains, the code of ethics of morphopsychology. What does it mean? It means that morphopsychology does not exist to discredit, discriminate, accuse or seek revenge. If you come across someone teaching or using morphopsychological knowledge intended to influence court judges, criminologists or defence lawyers by identifying supposed 'faces of evil', remind them that they are breaking the code of ethics that all those who practice morphopsychology must follow.

In which situations and for whom would morphopsychology be useful?

In keeping with the code of ethics which I have just mentioned, morphopsychology is useful in any context that requires a quick and profound understanding of the functioning of the inner world of the people we deal with so that we can adapt and make the most appropriate choices:

In our family circle: our parents, partners, children.

In our social circle: our friends, neighbours, political representatives, our local doctor.

In our professional environment: colleagues, clients and suppliers.

I should highlight that, in all work where human contact is important, morphopsychology is a very valuable tool for teachers, professors, doctors, psychologists, therapists, coaches, team leaders, human resources managers, negotiators, mediators, consultants, sales people and shop keepers.

I have been teaching morphopsychology since 2011 based on the Louis Corman method, applying it in various personal situations (personal growth, personal relationships) and in my professional life (business trajectory, negotiation, creation of effective teams). I'm often asked: 'How can you possibly know so much about me by simply looking at my face?' I answer: 'It's not magic. It's a beautiful logic that is hidden in our physical forms. I use a specific method to decode it. It is available to anyone who wishes to train their sense of observation and learn the principles of morphopsychology'.

I will finish by extending my gratitude to Louis Corman for having made this method of understanding the human being available for everyone. It never ceases to surprise me in its demonstrable accuracy and value in everyday life.

I hope that your reading of *Faces & Characters*, a reference work of Louis Corman, will provide you with a new way of seeing faces. As Marcel Proust said, 'The real voyage of discovery consists not in seeking new landscapes, but in having new eyes'.

Benoît Corman
Morphopsychologist and teacher (*Société Française de Morphopsychologie de Paris*)
President, Instituto Louis Corman
Barcelona, Spain
www.benoitcorman.com

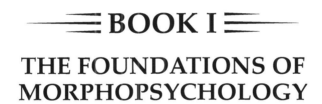

BOOK I

THE FOUNDATIONS OF MORPHOPSYCHOLOGY

CHAPTER I
DECODING THE FACIAL FORM

Since time immemorial, it has been thought that there is a direct relationship between the facial form and character traits, as well as levels of intelligence. The assumption was therefore that one's personality could be deduced from their morphology. However, this purely empirical knowledge lacked the science to support it. For it to become scientific, it was necessary to identify the laws that determine the relationship between the physical shape of the face and the psyche. This discovery is relatively recent and has laid the groundwork for a new science that I named, in a book published in 1937[1], *Morphopsychology*.

These laws are the laws of life. By going to the source of the processes that regulate our existence, we can understand the relationship between physical morphology and the psychology of character, their relationship explained by their common origin. The biological perspective must therefore be the primary point of reference for this discipline.

However, *life is essentially movement, growth and progress*. The purpose of any life science is the study of things in movement: living matter in perpetual motion. Therefore, the reader of this book must understand—right from the beginning—the crucial fact that morphopsychology is not static but *dynamic*. And particularly, this science is neither designed to study fixed nor static elements that one could understand via quantitative evaluation,

---

1: Quinze leçons de morphopsychologie, Ed. Stock, 1937.

nor is it about measuring the diameter, angle, surface or volume of a face such as in anthropometry.

On the contrary, we must consider all forms as being in a state of movement, *the result of a thrust from the depths of the living being coming up against the forces of its environment*—in some instances conjoining, in others, colliding. This is the movement that really counts, as the forms are nothing more than the manifestation of this movement, which they make visible to the naked eye.

Likewise, the psychological aspect of life derives from that same thrust from the depths of the living being and must be expressed in terminology that considers the energy, impulses and *'tendencies to'*. Again, one must not break the psyche down into fixed personality traits and limited intellectual abilities, as does psychometrics, in an attempt at definition by measurement.

Considering the dynamics of the life forces, it is apparent that the morphopsychologist is unlike any other expert: he is not like a naturalist or a physicist standing before the object studied, external to it, analysing it objectively. He himself is affected by this profound movement that he is studying; he experiences it himself and can only understand it in others based on his own personal experience. This form of understanding is called *intuition*, which is based on direct participation in the phenomenon studied. It plays a key role in morphopsychology, as it does in most human sciences such as medicine.

This means that the science of morphopsychology is also an art, and, like any art, not only requires knowledge of the laws that govern it, but diligent daily practice over a long period of time. As a consequence of this personal commitment, it is worth noting that 'the observation is only as good as the observer'. This means that the more experience acquired by the morphopsychologist, the more practiced he will be in facial analysis, finding himself engaged in enriching, meaningful situations, in whichever domain, and, as a consequence, the more likely he is to be able to really understand the psychological meaning of faces.

STUDYING THE FACE

Morphopsychological knowledge relies essentially on an accurate evaluation of the facial forms, drawn from the perspective of the *fundamental law of dilation and retraction* which is at the centre of our studies. The analysis must be methodical and include study of the *frame, sensory receptors, shape and expressions*.

The *frame*, also known as the 'large face', is a bone structure cushioned by two important muscles, the temporalis and the masseter muscles, which are in charge of the essential function of mastication. It reflects the body's structure and as such demonstrates the individual's degree of vital expansion, so that, wide or narrow, it is a crucial indicator for the morphopsychologist in understanding his personality (Illustration 1).

Illustration 1. – I. THE FRAME

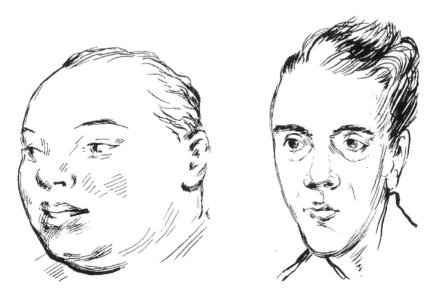

The facial bone structure, also known as 'the large face', indicates the degree of expansion of a person's vitality. The image on the left is of a short and broad face, the other long and narrow, demonstrating the opposing forces of vitality: strong versus weak.

Illustration 2. – I. THE SENSORY RECEPTORS

The receptors are very important in interactions with the environment, working together with that of the facial shape as a means of either consolidation or correction. From left to right, we go from 'open' to 'closed'. In the middle lies the structure we call 'protected'. From top to bottom, the main benchmark Types: dilation, lateral retraction, frontal retraction and extreme retraction.

The *sensory receptors* form the 'small face' within the 'large face' and are the openings through which the organism interacts with his surroundings. Their structure furthermore reveals the form these interactions take. The sensors have a particularly rich innervation, specialised in what are known as the 'senses' (sight, smell, taste) and are surrounded by small muscles (called 'platysma muscles') which ensure movement and control in interaction.

In morphopsychology, comparing the relationship between the large and the small face is important as a means of understanding the personality of any individual. Briefly, I would say that the large face represents the reserves of energy in the organism, indicating the needs and unconscious tendencies of the personality, while the small face represents interaction with the environment, indicating how someone reacts to impressions received and thereby actualizes the underlying tendencies of the large face.

The interactions the subject has with his surroundings, knowledge of which is essential in psychology, are dependent upon the structure of the frame and that of the sensory receptors. Structures that, it is important to underline, are independent one from the other and from which we can deduce the different personality types. The morphopsychologist must try to clearly differentiate between *open receptors*, *closed receptors* and *protected receptors* (half-way between open and closed), illustrated here (Ill. 2-I and II), which shows how they can appear within different types of frames.

Illustration 2. – II. THE SENSORY RECEPTORS

Expression

The face is by far the most mobile part of the body—the most expressive—due to its vitality. The frame, which is fixed, directly reflects the body's structure. On the other hand, the small face displays features that don't correspond to the body's structure and that are very expressive due to the platysma muscles—muscles which, as we have just seen, are responsible for the sensory organs' motility. As a consequence, the face is the part of the body that best distinguishes individuals and highlights their differences. There is much less diversity in body shape and therefore it is not useful as a means of differentiating between individuals. Consequently, we can deduce that those who limit themselves to the study of bodies, excluding the face, bring little to the understanding of individual personalities. Some, such as Sigaud[2], exclusively focused on the study of the physiology of organs with no claims to expertise in the psychological field and are therefore not to be called into question here. Others, such as the American Sheldon, claim the ability to determine the psychological personality according to body shape, excluding the face, and can all but fail in their attempts.

The morphopsychologist can draw two types of psychological conclusions from the study of a face: the fixed base (particularly the bone structure of the large face) and the mobile base (the sensory receptors). In the middle lies the shape which, as we will see further on, can vary from one period of time to another, even after growth has finished and the definitive bone structure is in place.

As the fixed base indicates the basic tendencies of the personality, it is important to verify if these tendencies are currently active. For that reason, we must observe the expression, which provides us with up-to-date information on those tendencies. So, for example, if there is a strong affective zone (pronounced cheekbones; large, imposing nose), which signifies a profound need for affection, but it is not expressive, and if the nostrils are heavy and do not vibrate, we cannot assume a very rich and abundant sentimental life, such as one would with nostrils that vibrate. In the same way, the presence of a large forehead can only suggest a certain level of intellect if the eyes are intensely expressive.

2: This refers to Sigaud's personal classification and is not related to the law of dilation–retraction.

Facial shape

Another crucial factor is the *contour,* the outline of the face in the way painters or sculptors understand it. In the most dynamic interpretation, *the contours represent the surface where the profound forces of the organism meet the opposing forces of the environment.* We will see that this interpretation explains the psychological significance of the different types of contours.

There are four main types, which are represented in illustration 2-III: from left to right, *round,* which indicates receptivity, the ability to learn easily; *flat-undulating,* which indicates action; *retraction-indented,* a combination of the first two types, associating receptivity and action; and *flat,* which indicates sensitivity and defensiveness. As you can see here, these different facial contours are shown with different combinations of receptors.

Illustration 2. – III. DIFFERENT TYPES OF CONTOURS

The contours of the face reveal the type of relationship that the organism has with its environment. All possible alternatives are shown—from round, which indicates openness and adaptability, to flat, which indicates closure and defensiveness. Between these two extremes are the curved and retraction-indented contours, signifying a balance between the forces of expansion and retraction.

It is also very important to consider the *tone* of the contours, which has its own meaning and which we will study in Chapter III.

The two halves and three zones of the face

When analysing a face, it should be taken into account that, in reality, it is a unified whole which cannot be deconstructed like some kind of mosaic of juxtaposed forms. The morphopsychologist must confine himself to identifying the main zones which represent the key functions.

Illustration 3. – I. THE TWO HALVES

Most faces have a certain lack of symmetry, so the psychological meaning depends on the overall harmony. Here are two contrasting cases. The photograph of the German romantic novelist, Gertrude Spörri, shows a harmonious alliance of both lateral and frontal retraction, with a slight asymmetry which, altogether, is a rich combination. Beside her is the photo of a young boy with particularly pronounced asymmetry. This indicates serious difficulties in the integration of these factors due to an unresolved antagonism of opposing tendencies.

The face can easily be divided into sections: vertically into the two *halves,* right and left, and from top to bottom in three superimposed *zones,* each one corresponding to one of the major systems of the organism (Ill. 3-I and II).

To conclude this chapter, it is above all essential that the morphopsychologist learns acute observation, both in terms of observing the whole as well as the key details.

Illustration 3. – II. TYPE OF DOMINANT EXPANSION

The notion of harmony is also important when evaluating the three zones and identifying which is predominant. When one zone is particularly pronounced, such as in the above cases, the face becomes caricature-like which can be seen as a limiting factor. These images should be compared with the more harmonious faces in illustration 12.

Taking the above information into account, it becomes possible to give a general overview of the individual's personality.

The *large face* reveals the vitality of the subject, his strength and his capacity for fulfilment.

The *small face* reveals how the individual interacts with his surroundings and the *active expression* indicates the level of vitality that the individual is currently experiencing.

The *contours* indicate the individual's level of tone and degrees of receptivity and activity.

The study of the three *zones* provides us with the dominant motivator—instinctive, affective or cerebral—and indicates in which sphere of activity the subject is most comfortable.

Symmetry or *asymmetry* offers a valuable complementary element, but its interpretation is harder, which I will show in Chapter IV.

CHAPTER II

THE LAW OF DILATION–RETRACTION

In 1937, I was able to establish the scientific basis for physiognomy and promote morphopsychology thanks to the knowledge that I had acquired of the fundamental biological law discovered by Dr. Claude Sigaud from Lyon, France, at the start of the century: the law of dilation–retraction.

Sigaud's starting point was the contrast, familiar to all, between fat and thin. Based on this seemingly banal distinction, the doctor from Lyon produced an entire doctrine around temperament. He observed that fat and thin people react differently in the face of illness. He concluded that the differing body shapes correspond to the different way the immune system functions in relation to the external environment. According to him, these morphologies show the dynamic processes that lead to a specific reaction according to one's level of sensitivity. He came to the conclusion that this was the key factor in an organism's immune system. This was how he understood it: the fat, who he called *Dilated*, are hyposensitive, with limited immune systems, absorbing, without specifically choosing to do so, everything in their surroundings, regardless of whether it is harmful and without being alerted to it at any point by their specific sensitivity. This can lead to exposure to morbidly serious problems (when the harmful element has been absorbed beyond a certain threshold). On the other hand, the thin, who he called *Retracted*, are hypersensitive, with active immune systems, which means that Retracted Types withdraw from and quickly reject any elements in the environment perceived to be harmful.

What is unique in what Sigaud did was that he showed that this retraction, which slims the body that withdraws into itself, isn't, as many would imagine, a form of atrophy or a significant loss of vitality, but completely the opposite: it is a very active defensive reaction which preserves the organism, often impeding the appearance or development of a life-threatening health problem.

Sigaud was only concerned with disease of the organs, his interest extending only as far as the morphology of the body. As I have said, he never made a connection between psychological traits and their physical correspondence to facial features. But while learning the master's doctrine from two of his disciples, the Drs. de Lambert and Thooris, I quickly came to appreciate what could be drawn from it and used in the study of faces. During that period, I was practicing *planet physiognomy*, which I learned from Gervais-Rousseau[1]. I concluded that Sigaud's theory of opposites, the *Law of Dilation–Retraction,* coincided precisely with the opposition of Jupiter and Saturn, helping to explain the character traits of these two opposing types by taking different levels of sensitivity into account, in keeping with Sigaud's doctrine.

I made rapid progress as I discovered that the relationship between a living organism and its environment was dependent upon that same sensitivity, which is sometimes open to the influences of its surroundings (the *Dilated Type,* which is *hyposensitive*), and sometimes more or less closed to it (the *Retracted Type,* which is *hypersensitive*). I deduced that Sigaud's theory of opposites corresponded to the antagonism of two primordial instincts: the *instinct of expansion* and the *instinct of conservation,* which represents the dual motion of life. From these very simple bases, morphopsychology was founded as a science.

This, nevertheless, requires an explanation. Traditionally, doctors and psychologists considered the primary vital instinct to be that of conservation, the individual defending itself from attack by the external world. However, this instinct operates above all in the elderly and sick, those whose vitality is declining and who must amass their remaining strength to remain alive. I have come to understand that the true

---

1: I published on the subject with him in Visages et caractères, Ed. Plon, 1930.

basic instinct of life isn't about conservation; rather, it is the instinct of expansion, that of the young and vigorous with an abundance of strength at their disposal who use it freely as much for growth as the performance of tasks[2].

Therefore, *this instinct of expansion is represented morphologically by dilation:* the living being nourishes itself with everything available in the outside world, developing, growing in size and weight, requiring more space to better express his vitality and radiate his strength around him.

The *instinct of conservation*, on the other hand, *is represented morphologically by retraction*, a process by which the living being, when in danger, disconnects from the environment considered threatening, withdrawing into himself and concentrating his efforts on conserving his vital life functions, those which permit him to survive. We should bear in mind that the vital energy an organism has at its disposal is apportioned according to its individual needs. By necessity, part of that energy has to be reserved for the proper functioning of the internal organs, because any malfunction whatsoever could be life-threatening. With those functions taken care of, the rest of the vital energy is available for other external activities such as those indicated in illustration 4. However, it would not be wise to use part of the essential reserves of energy for these external activities. An example will demonstrate this point: Imagine that the fuel tank of a car has a reserve tank controlled by a tap, and if the car runs out of petrol, one could, on opening the tap, carry on for several more miles. However, if there hasn't been an opportunity to refill the reserve tank in the meantime, the car will stop when it runs out of its reserve fuel. In parallel, if someone has used up all of his available vital energy and then draws on his essential reserves in order to continue his attempts at expansion, he will reach a state of absolute exhaustion that poses a serious threat to his life. It is the function of the instinct of conservation to retract when all available energy is exhausted, concentrating, as we have seen, all remaining energy within.

2: It is truly surprising that this notion of expansion, which would appear so normal, has not figured earlier in either medicine or psychology. The absolute importance of this notion came to me through the philosopher Nietzsche, who made the concept of the 'Will to Power' central to his doctrine. The depth and breadth of its possible applications drew me to adopt it and to incorporate its practical aspect into my conception of temperament and morphopsychology. There is a complete account in my work entitled Nietzsche, psychologue des profondeurs, PUF, 1983.

In amongst these two instincts' activities, two essential factors intervene: *heredity* and the *environment*.

Illustration 4. – DIAGRAM OF ENERGY MANAGEMENT

Distribution of energy resources

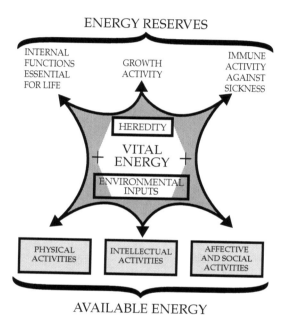

This diagram speaks for itself. It explains how energy is distributed within the organism and the rules that govern one's existence.

The effect of heredity manifests itself at birth and is unique to each individual in such a way that, in an identical environment, one will react through expansion (the hyposensitive) and the other by retraction (the hypersensitive). Should a newborn present a very specific characteristic, its most likely evolution can be predicted.

How life flourishes depends essentially on how favourable, or otherwise, the environment is, and living beings develop through expansion or retraction accordingly. It is a universal law, applicable to all living beings.

One could compare the pine trees of Landes–magnificent examples of fast growth in fertile ground, in an optimal growing climate–with the pine trees of Brittany–small, twisted, and bending trees that grow slowly because they must penetrate the rocky ground and face constant battering by strong winds; the first are Dilated and the second Retracted.

Man is like a plant: his growth depends both on his innate sensitivity and the nutrition received during his development. These two elements together, depending on the circumstances, result in either a process of dilation or retraction. It is not easy to determine which part relates to heredity and which part is acquired; they vary according to the individual and the circumstances. However, if an individual has a striking personality, his innate aptitudes will play a fundamental role and are much more determinant in the individual's character than character traits acquired growing up. This is, in itself, a sign which differentiates a great man from a normal being.

THE DILATED AND RETRACTED TYPES

For the sake of clarity, I shall first, in broad strokes, define the types of individuals wherein either the process of expansion or retraction predominates. As you will see, everything is calculated within the organism: the vital process is demonstrated equally in the biological functions and in the individual's morphology and psychological life.

1 / THE PREDOMINANTLY DILATED TYPE (Ill. 5)

Dilation is growth; that is why it is at its maximum in a healthy young baby (Ill. 5, fig. 1). It is the sign of effortless expansion, of manifold interactions with the environment. As we have already seen, the organism nourishes itself with everything that it is offered, without discrimination. Therefore, this ease of exchange also manifests itself by a relaxing of the body's internal organs, which work in harmony: circulation is fluid, blood flows easily to the skin, colouring it (the rose-pink tone of healthy babies); digestion is smooth, the intestinal function optimal; and sleep is restful. At no point is the body in discomfort and the absence of pain creates a permanent sense of euphoria, the cheerfulness of those who 'feel comfortable in their own skin'.

Illustration 5. – I. DILATION AND RETRACTION

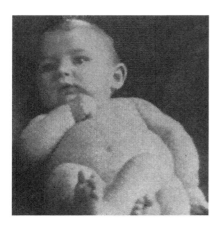

The growing baby falls in the Dilated Type category: the body and face are clearly dilated. However, it should be noted that the receptors are delicate and the expression is tonic, which predicts a greater refinement of features at a later stage.

Illustration 5. – II. DILATION AND RETRACTION

On the following two pages, you can see two opposing types of dilation and retraction in both the male and female. Dilation is featured in the illustrations on the left (in both the male and female versions): a broad frame with a round shape, wide, open receptors, which all together signify a marked predominance of expansion.

Morphologically, the predominantly Dilated Type is characterised by a solid body that is broad, thick and rounded. The bone and muscle structures are dense and the body has a certain overall stoutness that contributes to its round form. Skin and hair are light and soft to the touch. It should be highlighted that the skin covering offers little resistance to external factors: like the baby, the skin is delicate and so cuts and burns are frequent occurrences. When giving an injection, the delicateness of the Dilated's skin tissue is obvious since it is easily penetrated and there is no suggestion of pain. They are, as one might say 'made of butter'.

In the face, like the body, the forces of expansion 'work' in large format; dilation is made evident in a broad face where one can draw the frame in a circle, a large oval, or a rectangle with rounded edges (Ill. 5-II). The shape is made of large curves and soft angles (including the jawline and the temple ridge which is blurred by the roundedness of the forehead). All areas are fleshy and covered in an excess of fat. The receptors are fleshy, as well, but above all 'open'–they take up a large part of the face (large mouth with full lips, large nostrils, round eyes set well apart) –and project out from the surface of the face (protruding mouth, projected and turned-up nose and bulbous eyes). Their habitual expression is of openness, which expresses an ease in interactions with their environment. Wouldn't an observer's first impression be that the individual has an 'open face'?

Illustration 5. – III. DILATION AND RETRACTION

Retraction is featured in the illustrations on the right, in both the male and female versions. The frame is narrow and the shape is gaunt and angular, with the receptors partly closed, telling us that the instinct of conservation predominates.

Psychologically, for the predominantly Dilated Type, the factor of expansion is connected, as we have seen, to a high level of tolerance towards deviations from the norm and is at the source of a great openness which gives them the characteristic of adaptability. From there, we can deduce the entirety of their character traits and intellectual aptitudes.

Instinctive expansion. – They give in to all of their impulses and every demand from around them. They are gourmets and sensual beings, thirsty for physical contact and interaction, and desirous of the material things in life. Their actions are easy and completely uninhibited.

Affective expansion. – They have an open heart (they wear their heart on their sleeve, as we say), are welcoming, cordial, generous, easy to live with, friendly with strangers and, all in all, of good character. They like to be in a group; they are family-oriented and enjoy company. They have a lot of friends and don't like solitude. Their mood tends to be happy and optimistic.

Intellectual expansion. – They are generally open to the situation they find themselves in and easily assimilate everything that is immediately at their disposal: facts, names and numbers, for example– all practical, tangible things. They are sensorial and their understanding is more related to a flair for the intuitive rather than reason. They are well adjusted to the world around them and unhesitatingly accept the customs, fashions and opinions of others. Their conformity to traditions and rules means that they are blessed with common sense and are good at anything they turn their hand to. It is worth highlighting that this great openness to the world favours the development of their external being but not at all the flourishing of their internal life; nothing is retained at the core of their being.

2 / THE PREDOMINANTLY RETRACTED TYPE (Ill. 5)

Retraction, as I have said, should not be considered the opposite of dilation as if it concerned two symmetrical states. Retraction is not a state; it is an active process, *a movement towards*. Instead of blossoming outwards– growing and developing, expanding the vital space–the force flows back towards the interior, drawing in on itself, concentrating in the organism in order to protect the essential functions and to ensure the maintenance of life.

I must insist: retraction is not a form of atrophy, a reduction in the vitality of the organs, but a very active self-defence process, correlating to a hypersensitivity that, noting the smallest variations in the outside surroundings and the resulting minimal repercussions on the internal organs, remediates the situation by suspending all external interaction. This defence mechanism is manifested in all parts of the organism and the organ which is most directly exposed to the surroundings, the skin, is therefore the first to react.

It is worth noting that all areas of retraction have this sensitivity. They are very sensitive to even the lightest of touches and to heat and cold. While the tegument, the skin covering, of the Dilated Type is flaccid and lacking in defences, and therefore fragile, the Retracted Type, on the other hand, has a more resistant tegument. For example, when giving an injection, one has the impression that the skin fibres tighten to resist penetration of the needle, which increases pain–something the Dilated Type does not feel.

Retraction self-regulates according to the needs of its defence system by minimising interaction with an environment that it considers harmful. This is reduction, but not suppression. If retraction were the opposite of dilation, it would mean a complete system shutdown. But then life would be unviable due to the lack of interaction with one's environment.

Retraction can only be temporary, responding to a passing danger, restricted to the areas that are directly affected. It can also be resistant should the danger be permanent. The morphopsychologist should therefore understand the extent, intensity and the duration of the retraction. As it is never absolute, we must not refer to a Retracted Type but instead to a Type that is *predominantly retracted*, as I have done in the title of this chapter.

Later on, I will demonstrate the various types of retraction. But, whatever the degree, in the process of retraction there are common traits which can be used to create a broad outline of the subject. The key phrase for Dilation is *'openness and great adaptability'*; the key phrase for Retraction is *'closure and selective adaptation'*.

Dr. Louis Corman- Faces & Characters

Only adapting to their preferred surroundings, Retracted Types have a more complex personality than Dilated Types because it is dual. In their preferred surroundings, they act in the same way as the Dilated Types, in an unrestrained movement of expansion; outside of those preferred surroundings, they close down and seek refuge in their inner world. Speaking in the language of Jung, they are at the same time, according to the situation, both extroverted and introverted.

Instinctive retraction. – The word retraction means that their instincts do not operate with the same freedom of expression as we have seen in the Dilated Types. They can only operate within the conditions in which they are most comfortable but, lacking that, they tend to withdraw into themselves. This gives the Retracted Type the reputation of being less of a gourmand, less sensual and less active than the Dilated Type, which is true to a certain extent as their field of expansion is more limited.

Affective retraction. – Their feelings depend upon their chosen affinities: they choose their friends carefully and are difficult both in love and friendship. Their character is often difficult and they are cold and distant with strangers. The more pronounced the retraction, the more they limit their personal relationships, making them fiercely independent with often a preference for solitude over company.

Intellectual retraction. – Both their memory and desire for knowledge is selective: they limit themselves to certain domains but, unlike the Dilated, they study their chosen subject in great depth. They are not like the personable, sensorial, Dilated Type and intuition is not their forte. To arrive at a conclusion, they need to reflect, reason and plan. They often have a taste for abstraction and prefer general ideas over concrete facts. The selectivity in their skills makes them specialists in whichever domain they choose.

3 / MIXED TYPES (Ill. 6)

The contrast between Dilated and Retracted Types is only useful as an overarching idea and under the condition that it is not considered the last word on the subject, in the same way that the Retracted Type should not be considered completely devoid of the factors of expansion. That is why I have spoken of the 'Types of Predominance', although, for the purposes of simplification I will say Dilated or Retracted. It is important to understand that, in every case, this refers to a particular degree of predominance. Also, as we have already seen, the majority of men and women are a combination of the dilated and retracted Types, which I call *Mixed Types*.

In the practice of morphopsychology, it is important to restrict the meaning of this concept to the combinations which reflect a balance between dilation and retraction. This results in a great ability to adapt, being able to expand in one's preferred surroundings and retract in less favourable surroundings. These two types of reaction are simultaneously opposed and complementary.

Opposed and complementary: this brings us to the complexity of the human being, too frequently neglected by traditional psychology. The abundance of Mixed Types tells us that the antagonism between contradictory tendencies isn't the anomaly that it is often perceived to be, nor a pathological state, but is actually the norm, and should therefore be the subject of close investigation.

We must stress that all *great men* — those who, in their time, have left their mark through due to their creativity and originality—are all Mixed Types and the antagonisms are often quite marked. It is easy to understand why given that the Dilated Types are conservative, traditional, friends of the established order, with no desire to change the world in which they thrive. They are quite happy where they are. A form of retraction is necessary in order to create something new and original, with all that is implied by being in opposition to the established order.

Great men are never found amongst the most pronounced Retracted Types, as they live in a vacuum, outsiders in their own environment. No great work has ever been achieved without an intense participation in the world. One can therefore conclude that a person of great merit is always made up of an alliance between the Dilated and Retracted Types. There is the tendency to reconcile the revolutionary aspirations of the one with the more conservative habits of the other. The individual is not fully conscience of this combination that is part of him. Self-awareness only comes with retraction and becomes more acute as the retraction is more pronounced. A genius generally has a clear vision of the forces within him which oppose the influences of the culture he lives in. He is barely conscious of the Dilated aspect, which is a more hidden sensitivity. When he rebels against this established order through a conscious effort of rejection, he is subconsciously being held back, these same traditions keeping his feet firmly on the ground and confusing him because this is his internal need for organisation, freedom nurtured by discipline. No authentic personality can exist without the composition of the two opposing forces: adaptability and individuality.

Illustration 6. – MIXED TYPES

Dilation and Retraction is a combination found within many well-adjusted subjects, creating a Mixed Type. Various examples are shown above.

This continuous alliance within the genius also explains the contradictions in his conduct. For example, he is often made up of a curious mix of youth and maturity. Young at heart and spirit, he avidly absorbs everything (dilation) but with an infallible instinct for rejecting anything which might distract him from his objective, internally assimilating his diverse exterior world (retracted).

CHAPTER III
THE LAW OF TONICITY

The contrast between dilation and retraction, important as it may be, isn't sufficient to characterise a personality type. In order to complete the analysis, we must consider the notion of tonicity.

Tonicity refers to the level of activity of the fundamental vital functions. During the period of development, one progresses from the atonic form of the newborn to tonicity, which becomes more pronounced as the different functions become established. The nursing infant is atonic during its first months, except in the mouth area, for nourishment, which already has an active structure and function.

The general lack of muscle strength, indicating passivity, corresponds to a need for maternal protection. Tonicity quickly appears with the development of motor skills and as the baby assimilates the outside world which contains both good and bad elements. Passively absorbing the wrong thing could be dangerous so the child must learn to react and reject what might cause him harm. This is the beginning of retraction, the beginnings of an immune system. Medical experience has taught us that, once grown, if the subject continues to be of the Atonic Dilated Type, he is exposed, defenceless, to harmful influences in his environment and is therefore in grave danger. This explains why, in circumstances of very poor hygiene it is, to our great surprise, that the most beautiful dilated babies are those most affected in an epidemic.

Morphology. – Tonicity has two essential aspects. The first is the *firm structure of the facial contours*. Even though a baby has soft facial contours, due as much to the weakness in bone structure as the flaccidity of the muscles and the flesh, as the child develops, the face acquires a greater firmness, the bone structure and muscles become stronger and the overall appearance loses its plumpness.

The second sign of tonicity is found in *the relationship between the diameters of the height and width*. It is well known that, generally, small men are very dynamic, whereas tall and thin men are more languid. In the same way, tonicity is found in short faces while long faces are atonic. The following illustration clearly demonstrates this contrast by applying the method that I call '*the method of substitution*' which we will discuss at length in Chapter IV. Illustrated here are two faces where the upper part is identical: the only difference is to be found in the lower part of the face, where one has a short jawline while the other is long with blurred angles. If we cover the lower part, we can verify that the upper parts of the faces are identical. On revealing the entire face, we can see the considerable difference that this produces in his expression: the eyes are the same, but the expression is much more tonic in the first illustration than in the second.

Illustration 7. – I. TONICITY AND ATONY

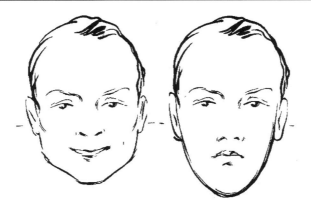

Illustration 7-1. Tonicity is a function of the length of the frame of the face. A high degree of tonicity makes the face shorter and more expressive. Atonic faces are long, with soft contours and a passive expression. (Compare the expression in these two illustrations.) To demonstrate this, I have used the substitution method explained in the text.

When a dilated face is tonic, the proportions don't change, but the contours are more clearly defined and the curves that come with dilation are flattened in certain areas. In addition, the receptors add to the level of tonicity due to the muscles that surround them, to the extent that, instead of sagging as in the case of the atonic face, they remain firmly horizontal and even lift slightly up and outwards. This can be seen in the corners of the mouth, the nostrils, the slit of the eyes and the brow line. As you can see in the faces in illustration 8, there is a marked contrast between eyes that lift at the corners and those that fall (in the style of Greuze), which are the atonic eyes. In addition, the expression shows this tonicity; it is more lively and intense.

The *Tonic Dilated Type* represents the first degree of tonicity. The second, more accentuated degree is noted by the planes and angles of tonic retraction around the face which modify the overall shape, the roundness giving way to a rectangular shape. This is referred to as the *Lateral Retracted Type*, which usually develops in adolescence, and is manifested in the body by the development of the musculoskeletal and respiratory systems: limbs grow longer and stronger, the body grows bigger and the thorax becomes longer and broader. The face also becomes longer and tonic. In addition, the development of the respiratory apparatus is marked by the development of the cheekbones which tend to give the face a hexagonal shape. In profile, the nose, still childish in structure, either concave or straight, is extended forward, making the profile more angular.

The length of the face in the Lateral Retracted Type is always moderate because if the face were any longer it would be a sign of atony. This occurs when the living form, instead of withdrawing into itself to resist external pressure, as it does for the Tonic Dilated Type, gives in to this pressure and 'slips down' in some way, becoming longer. The jaw that is tonic tends to be square and well defined while in the case of atony in the jaw region, it merges into the neck as the angle of the jaw becomes less defined (Ill. 7-III).

These scales of tonicity and atony can also be applied to both dilation and retraction, modifying the morphology and psychology of the basic type. We will see the fundamental importance of this distinction in the following chapters.

Illustration 7. – II. TONICITY AND ATONY

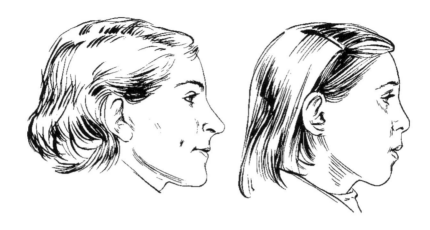

Illustration 7-II A long face is considered to be a lateral retraction, which is a dynamic process. But the degree of length is important: when it is particularly pronounced, it becomes an atonic feature which diminishes the dynamism of the Lateral Retracted Type.

Psychologically, people with tonicity are very active and not fazed by impediments that cross their path. They are tireless and tend not to be very sophisticated. Their energy reserves are high and dedicated to sporting activities. In contrast, atonic individuals prefer rest to activity, working only when necessary and tiring easily. They prefer to remain seated and rarely practice sports.

It should be highlighted that the degree of tonicity also significantly influences how the individual uses his intelligence. Not only does good tonicity confer the ability to bring ideas to fruition, as we have already said but, in addition, they give ideas clarity and precision. Atony, however, hinders achievement; thoughts remain dreams, lacking clear definition.

We do not, however, have the authority to suggest that tonicity is always positive and atony always negative. The ideal tends to be in the middle, as demonstrated in illustration 8-I. Particularly where intelligence is concerned, we know that this operates via a dual movement: in receptivity,

Illustration 8. – I. DIFFERENT LEVELS OF TONICITY

The eye must be trained to gain a fair appreciation of tonicity. In this illustration, we can see that, between the two extremes of tonicity and atony, there is a medium level of tonicity which is particularly present in the female form.

wherein we receive information, and in activity, wherein we act upon that information. These extreme levels, both acute tonicity and absolute atony, are unfavourable when it comes to exercising intelligence. An excess of tone results in intelligence that lacks receptivity: the very active wish to act upon people, things and events, to manipulate them, and not to allow these factors to act upon him in return. They are only interested in other people, things and ideas when they can be of service or have some value. They tend to be numbers people, appreciating quantity and results. I don't see them being psychologists but if they chose this profession they would be psychometricians.

On the other hand, atony favours receptivity and the passive accumulation of impressions which serve to nourish the imagination. This sort of passivity is conducive to dreaming but it means that the mind is not very practical and incapable of forming precise thoughts on any subject. Although tonicity is favourable for a logical mind and scientific reasoning, atony has improved faculties of intuition, an understanding of the intrinsic nature of things. Some intuition is always necessary for those in intimate contact with nature, such as those who work on the land or sea. This skill is useful in the human sciences where a receptive attitude towards others is necessary, such as in psychology. It is also useful in art and, as we will see, it is enough to have some tonicity in another part of the face which provides an activating influence so that this receptivity to the world of art results in a process of creation. The illustrations in 8-II show the contrast between the active expression of the logical, precise, astute individual, who is attentive to the smallest of details when studying objects, and the expression which is intuitive and calm, open to the mysterious world and everything in it.

I will complete this analysis, considering its importance, in book II where we will study how tonicity and atony affect both the dilated and retracted structures. From there I will describe the kinds of tonicity and atony for each of these types.

Illustration 8. – II. TONICITY AND ATONY

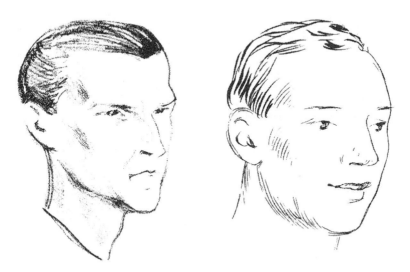

Logic and intuition. Tonicity influences how intelligence is exercised as it combines activity (high level of tonicity) and receptivity (atony). Where tonicity is high, particularly in the area of the brain, this means high levels of activity, depth of critical thinking and a logical mind. When it is only average, as in the second illustration, it suggests a high level of receptivity and is characterised by an intuitive mode of thinking, particularly prevalent in women.

CHAPTER IV
THE LAW OF EQUILIBRIUM

It is essential to understand the concept of the balanced personality. I will illustrate this point using a comparison: when a man stands on one leg, he can stay balanced in this position, but it is somewhat precarious and he is likely to fall over should something unexpected happen. On the other hand, if he is balanced and stable on two feet, it is a very comfortable position and he can stand for a long period of time without any likelihood of falling over. This is comparable to the morphopsychological Types that we have studied so far: the predominant types, *Dilated* and *Retracted*, whose balance is precarious, on one leg, remaining stable only if nothing upsets the equilibrium that they have learned to maintain. On the other hand, the mixed Types, particularly those where the forces of expansion and conservation are equally developed, find a stability that resists elements of disruption. But in order to walk, to advance, one of the legs has to leave the ground and start moving forward, putting the body in an unstable state until the foot touches ground again and re-establishes a new equilibrium. This can be called a *dynamic* equilibrium since there is movement. During this forward motion, there is a risk of falling over if a mistake is made. That's life in motion: you could say that the leg that advances represents the instinct for expansion and the one that stays behind is the instinct of conservation. If these two vital forces were perfectly balanced, man would remain immobile, as he would never have any incentive to take a step forward. In order to advance, there has to be an inequality between the forces, with one receiving the impulse to step forward, motivated by either external or internal forces, as the dominant leg (most often the right leg because it is on the most active half of the body).

This comparison gives us an idea of the conditions necessary for a balanced personality, information that we can glean from the morphology of the face. It has often been considered that the ideal lies in a harmonious facial structure, in its evenness, made up of a perfect symmetry of the two halves, evenly proportioned large and small faces and an even distribution between the three zones. It is believed that this structural harmony must therefore correspond to a superior psychology.

But this assumption ignores *the primordial law of life, which is movement.* Man is a being that walks, advances, progresses. If the present forces were precisely balanced, then there would be no movement. For there to be motion, that is to say action, there must be tension between two unequal forces, in the same way that a river can only produce the energy necessary to turn turbines if the course it runs through has sufficient differences in height.

My conclusion is that we must not be distracted by the harmony of a face, its false beauty, seductive at first sight. Neither should we consider an un-harmonious face to have a lesser value. Life itself is dynamic and obliges us to consider that morphological asymmetry is not the exception, nor an anomaly, but the norm, and a testament to the vitality of the being. In addition, we must admit that the antagonisms at the heart of an individual's psychology, which is a sign of this dynamism, are often more significant than those of the perfectly balanced personality. Therein lies the main problem for the morphopsychologist: understanding the importance of the asymmetries to establish if they destabilise the individual's personality to the point that they lead to his decline or, conversely, if they enable the subject to risk attaining a superior equilibrium which will allow him to continue evolving.

We are now going to study the asymmetries.

1 / THE TWO HALVES

Perfect symmetry between the two halves of the face does not confer an advantage because an infant starts to evolve and become active at a very early age, which creates asymmetry. The right side of the body, for right handers (particularly the right hand) takes on active functions while the left side (the left hand) remains more passive, more receptive.

This distinction can be seen in the face, as the morphology of the right side develops more tone than the left side. This is sometimes only represented in the expression (Ill. 3-I: the expression in the right eye is more intense) and can also be seen in the flare of the nostrils and a slightly raised corner of the mouth. This sometimes becomes part of the permanent shape, whereby the right side of the face has more tone and the left side is atonic. The right side is the more active side, the one which updates tendencies and looks towards the future, while the left side is more passive, receptive and backward-looking.

We can draw interesting conclusions from this rule, which, to tell the truth, are conjectures that call for verification by personal experience. If there is a reversal of this tendency, we can deduce that the subject's childhood, instead of being peaceful, may have been marked by difficult circumstances. He has had to remain alert in order to deal with it and relaxation, indicated in this case on the right half of the face, will have appeared later on. The French writer Pierre Abraham was the first to come up with the idea of separating the two halves of the face in a photo, juxtaposing the right half with its mirror image to reconstitute the entire face and doing the same with the left. This method has been used and abused ever since. The comparison between the two composite images highlights significant differences. The striking results of this exercise can be seen in the illustration, showing what we weren't initially aware of: the caricature-like asymmetry of the face of the young girl. However, this method doesn't help us much in understanding the issue; it shows frozen faces, deprived of the asymmetric movement which gives the original photo its uniqueness (Ill. 9).

Illustration 9. – THE TWO HALVES

Although it replaces a real face with a mask, this technique of creating a composition using the two halves has the advantage of highlighting asymmetry which would otherwise be harder to identify.

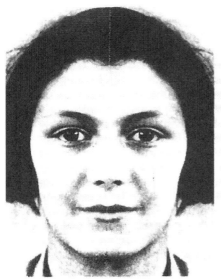
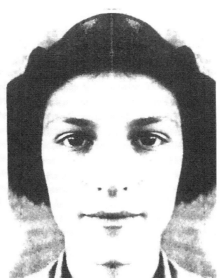

In the presence of this kind of asymmetry, the morphopsychologist must reflect upon its significance as it is clear that the more extreme the asymmetry, the harder it is for the subject to accommodate the two opposing forces that this asymmetry suggests. We must ask ourselves if such an accommodation is possible and if the subject has sufficient internal strength to make it happen.

2 / THE ANTERIOR AND POSTERIOR FACE (Ill. 10)

It is also worth noting that the front and rear parts of the face do not develop in the same way in all subjects. At the beginning of the 20th century, two physiognomists, Polti and Gary, traced an imaginary cross on the profile of the face centred on the entrance to the ear canal. In this way, they divided the face and cranium into four zones, with the two anterior segments corresponding to active aptitudes, the upper one (the forehead) representing cerebral activity and the lower segment (the jaw), physical activity. The two posterior zones corresponded to receptive aptitudes, with the imagination in the upper zone (the brain) and instinct in the lower zone (the neck). This is rightly justified, as the anterior quadrants represent movement towards the environment, with the sensory receptors, where interaction takes place, while the posterior quadrants represent the passive area, the unconscious part of the personality where the imagination and instinct are passively stored. The latter could be called a nutritive process, as much physical as mental.

As you can see in illustration 10, the man in the middle demonstrates the balance between receptivity and productive activity. As productive activity always tends to dominate somewhat, the vertical line divides the profile into two unequal parts: two-thirds in the anterior of the head and one-third in the posterior. If this balance is not maintained, it can be deduced that the dominant aptitude is activity if the anterior zone is more developed (fig. 2), and passivity-receptivity if the posterior zone is dominant (figs. 3 and 5).

In a child, both the posterior and anterior zones are equal, at least in the cerebral zone, which at this age corresponds to the prevalence of intellectual receptivity and a subconscious storing of information, which precedes and determines the subsequent thought activity (fig. 5).

Illustration 10. – THE POLTI AND GARY CROSS

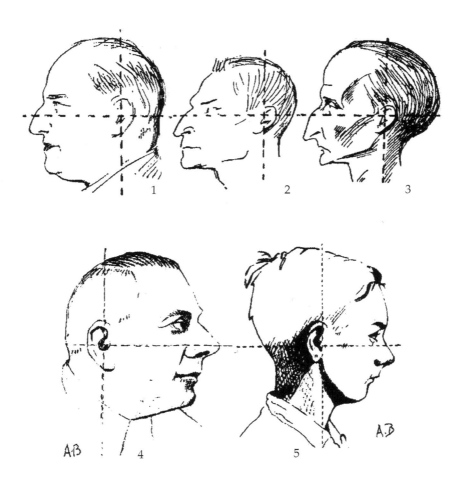

The top line of these portraits demonstrates the differences in the distribution of the 'quadrants' in different individuals. The bottom line emphasises the difference between a man of action and a child's dominant receptivity.

On the other hand, in men who are purely action-oriented, the anterior zone occupies practically the entire profile, such as the Mars Type (fig.2), a combative figure, and in this example, a great salesman, with a flair for sales which have ensured his business success.

We agree with the anthropologists who make comparisons between subjects with a broad, short skull (brachycephalic) and those with a long skull (dolichocephalic), where racial differences mean different behaviour, most brachycephalics being found in the most active and inventive races.

3 / THE TWO FACES: LARGE AND SMALL (Ill. 11)

When the large and small faces are in proportion, there is a psychological balance between the vital strength in reserve (large face) and interaction with the environment (small face). In the Dilated Type, the reserves are abundant and the receptors open, allowing for extensive interaction. On the other hand, the Retracted Type has limited reserves and, in parallel, interaction is sparing.

But in numerous cases you can find a hybrid within the structure of the two faces: the frame can be dilated and the receptors retracted, which indicates that the accumulated reserves are used sparingly, while a retracted frame with open receptors indicates that the energy expended tends to exceed the available reserves.

I call the first *Concentrated Types*, because the accumulated energy is concentrated, allowing for energetic and extended activity. However, the retracted receptors close them off, in part, from their environment in such a way that they don't allow it to influence them and are only interested in themselves. This makes them extremely proud and intolerant.

The second group, on the other hand, distinguishes itself by the tendency to react to every element in their environment. This is why I call them *Reactive Types*. They are very adaptable, but on a superficial level, and, lacking stamina, are incapable of any in-depth and prolonged activity.

I will dedicate an entire chapter to the study of these two types. Here too, the problem lies in recognizing the importance of the contrasts in the subject's structure and his ability to create balance among these contrasting values.

Illustration 11. –CONCENTRATED AND REACTIVE TYPES

The contrast between these two images is impressive: on the left, we see signs of concentration with closed receptors, while on the right, the openness of the receptors indicates a tendency to be exclusively reactive.

4 / THE THREE ZONES OF THE FACE (Ill. 12)

We have already seen that the face easily divides into three superimposed levels, each one corresponding to a specific psychological domain. In many, these three zones are evenly distributed, as much in height as in width and depth, which means that the instinctive, emotional and cerebral parts of their personality are in balance. For example, a romantic attraction is allied with sexual desire, tenderness or passion and spiritual rapport with the romantic partner.

However, when one of the zones is predominant, it means that the zone is in expansion and the others are in relative retraction. It can therefore be deduced that the specific psychological sphere corresponding to the zone in expansion plays a leading role in the life of the subject: those with predominance in the instinctive zone will always obey the call of their instincts; those with predominance in the affective zone are governed by their emotions or passions; and those with predominance in the cerebral zone are those where the mind reigns over the emotions and the instincts.

Illustration 12. – THE MAIN TYPES OF DOMINANT ZONE

In these images, in comparison to illustration 3, no single zone predominates and takes away from the harmony of the face, hence a richer psychological balance.

It is worth adding that varying types of Double Expansion also exist. For example, expansion of the instinctive-affective areas is quite frequent. These two lower zones of the face combined create an area that juts out, evoking the snout of an animal, from which one can easily suggest and draw analogies between the behaviour of this type of man and animal. Other common combinations are cerebral-affective and cerebral-instinctive. I will later demonstrate how one can deduce their psychological significance through a rigorous application of the laws of morphopsychology (see Book II, Chap. VII).

An understanding of these types of predominant zones of expansion leads us to the most fruitful area of application in the field of morphopsychology— that of identifying one's aptitudes and orientation towards a specific type of profession. The dominant zone tells us in which direction the subject is most naturally inclined, in which field his natural talents lie and where he will flourish. I will demonstrate however, that we should not focus exclusively on the dilated zones, the zones of achievement, because those in retraction are also important. They demonstrate repressed tendencies that sometimes feed the person's unconscious inner world, sometimes transferring into and nourishing the dilated zones and thereby projecting themselves externally.

5 / BALANCE IN DISHARMONY

When the morphopsychologist finds himself in the presence of subjects with asymmetry in their faces, a contrast in structure between the frame and the receptors or a predominant zone in expansion, the issue is to establish if this disharmony is a source of enrichment or a factor creating imbalance. This study is bound by three rules.

The first concerns the *degree of disharmony*. The greater the disharmony, the easier it is to conclude that antagonisms in the personality will be stronger, generating inner conflict that is difficult for the individual to master. This is the case in the presence of a very pronounced asymmetry, a marked contrast between the frame and the receptors or a particularly large expansion of one of the zones.

For example, a vastly expanded instinctive zone in comparison to the other zones, identifiable by a very large jaw, is indicative of powerful and therefore unstable instinctive urges, which could, on occasion, lead the subject to acts of uncontrolled aggression. On the other hand, it could provoke a powerful but inhibited defensive action. Or, in between the two, sublimation of these two impulses proffers great ambition on the subject to be successful in life. Through a detailed examination of his face, we can establish if his ambition is unrealistic or is backed up by real ability.

A very large forehead, for example, is not at all, as we often believe, a sign of superior intelligence but suggests an unbridled imagination that may have no practical value or perhaps an ideology or doctrine which is not based in concrete reality.

The second rule concerns *the vitality of the subject*, the power of expansion, visible in the width of the frame and the tonicity of the facial contours. The ability to integrate the antagonistic tendencies into a unified behaviour is greater if the vitality is stronger. On the other hand, this capacity is weakened in atonic subjects whereby the slightest shock creates instability.

The third rule relates to another factor of integration and that is *control*. Morphologically speaking, this can be read in the degree of retraction in the forehead and in the tonicity of the cerebral zone, particularly in the tonicity of the eyes, demonstrating a good level of self-awareness and self-control. When there is a lack of restraint—notable in the absence of retraction in the forehead, the roundness of the frame and atony of the eyes—self-awareness and self-control are weaker, the combination doesn't function or it is very fragile and the personality is in a constant state of internal anarchy.

CHAPTER V
THE LAW OF INTEGRATION

The personality of a man constitutes a whole. We talk about an 'individual', but to put it another way, do we mean an 'indivisible' being?

We should therefore understand the personality in its totality, body and soul closely associated, and do away with the notion that limits psychology to the study of 'consciousness' itself. This approach refuses to recognise the value of a science such as morphopsychology under the pretext that the bodily form is in no way related to character traits and intellectual abilities.

From the very start of this work, I have shown that the fundamentals of morphopsychology are rooted in the very source of life and that every expression of our existence comes from the combination of body and soul in the same vital impulse.

Our understanding of the world does not come naturally to us. The analytical processes we utilize to break elements down into their component parts helps us to get a better grasp on them, not only separating body and soul, as we have just seen, but also breaking the face down into its distinct parts to make it easier for us to evaluate.

Initially, it is certainly almost impossible to avoid using this method. I, myself, have resorted to these kinds of detailed analyses to decode the facial forms and their meaning. I have, however, rejected total fragmentation, a kind of mosaic of juxtaposed features. And I have shown that one must work in big groupings: the two halves, the large and small face and the three expansion zones.

I have also underlined that vitality – the essential dynamic energy – is at work to establish close ties between the different parts and therefore corrects what might appear artificial when viewed in isolation.

And so, our analytical aptitude draws us nearer to the crux of the matter by offering us a few clear, basic notions. Based on this initial impression, we can start to see the larger picture whereby *the role of intuition in our observations* comes into play. Intuition is, in fact, a perception of the whole, and our observation, too, when it is focused on a face, takes in a general image where all details are integrated into a first impression. Intuition and vision both operate in the same way and a good morphopsychologist must have both.

Working with my friend and illustrator Pazzi, I have proven that this integration of these separate parts does in fact occur by experimenting with an original study method which we have called the *substitution method*. When we look at a face, we tend to focus particularly on the eyes and the expression, believing we can read one's emotions, or even their secrets. It is said that 'the eyes are the window to the soul', but this can only be true if you use the word 'soul' in the broadest possible sense, that is, as the equivalent of the entire personality. The expression in the eyes reveals the subject's mood, which is reflected in the facial features. If these features change, the expression changes accordingly. So, if one wishes to understand the meaning of a feature, we must add it to the overall image of the face and then study the expression. However, apart from cosmetic surgery, this can't be done on a living subject. For this reason, we thought that we would experiment with the portraits ably drawn by the talented Pazzi which allow for modifications as required.

To avoid a long explanation, here is an example which will help us to understand the substitution method (Ill. 13). We have drawn two images of the same female face side by side. The first image is shown as a Dilated Type in its fullest form, with open receptors and, as dictated by her morphology, a smiling countenance. In the second image, we have simply modified the mouth by lowering the corners, expressing disappointment and bitterness. The eyes have lost their light and joy. All we have changed is the mouth; the eyes are the same in both illustrations. If you are sceptical–and you have the right to doubt (that's how strong the optical illusion is) –all you have to do is cover the lower part of the two faces with a piece of paper along the horizontal lines shown on the illustration at the level of the cheeks. In doing so, you can see that the upper part of the two faces is identical. On this basis, we can conclude that the smiling expression in the eyes in the first image is due to the raised corners of the mouth and that the sad expression in the second image is due to the drooping corners of the mouth. But how can that be, we ask ourselves, when nothing has changed in the eyes? There can be only one possible explanation: our vision does not focus on one isolated part of the face. Our gaze travels rapidly across the surface, observing each detail perceived and integrating them all, presenting them as a whole. And so, in the illustration, we visually perceive the smile or the bitterness in the mouth and apply it to the subject's eyes, where it is found reflected.

Illustration 13. – THE SUBSTITUTION METHOD

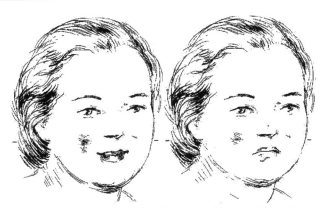

In the text, I explain the influence of changes in facial features on the personality, as drawn by the illustrator and as revealed by the expression in the eyes. As proof, one must place a piece of paper over the lower part of the face in line with the small marks placed on each side. This is also the case for illustrations 14 and 15.

And so, as I have already mentioned above, to know what a physiognomic feature means psychologically, it must be introduced, *via substitution*, to a face that doesn't already have that feature and then the expression must be studied. If you would like, for example, to know the morphological features that differentiate man from woman, all you have to do is experiment with each one of these features and, using your own intuition while looking at a face, be able to state if it is that of a man or a woman. This isn't always easy because, in both men and women, there are often certain components from the other sex that can be revealed by their morphology. The substitution method can also be applied in these cases.

Illustration 14. – THE SUBSTITUTION METHOD

In the other two illustrations, the first demonstrates a tonic structure that is indisputably masculine, notable by his strong 'man of action' jawline. In the second, we have substituted this jaw with a lower face with much softer contours and a fuller mouth. One can see that, by comparing the two, the expression changes and becomes more receptive and kinder, a clear example of a feminine element in a masculine face (Ill. 14).

Another example: if we go back to the dilated face of the young woman in illustration 13 with the gentle and cheerful expression, the introduction of a much more tonic jawline with pronounced angles and a Retracted-Indented form around the chin and the cheekbones suggests a passionate temperament, giving the expression a harder and more intense look, corresponding to a masculine element within a female face (Ill. 14).

Illustration 15. – THE SUBSTITUTION METHOD

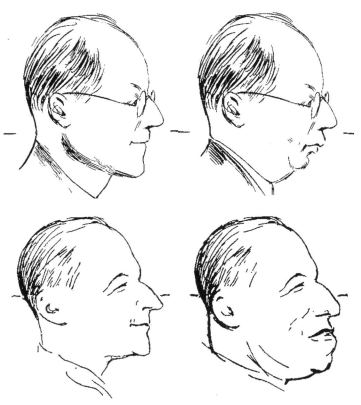

The variations in tone that we have seen in the preceding examples are relatively moderate. The result is even more striking when you put two structures side by side where the difference in tone is much greater. In the images of the two men in illustration 15, we have substituted a strong jawline and square jaw with a weak jaw with softened angles, as well as a weak, receding chin. The result is a radical change in the expression in the eyes.

Another area that deserves our attention in the above illustration (Ill. 15) is the contrasting features in the lower half of the face, 'the otherworldliness of refined forms', as the saying goes, and the material presence of heavy forms. The first image is that of a vigorous Lateral-Retracted Type with a refined chin, mouth and nose, which emphasizes the relative slenderness of the neck. In the second image, the forms are thick and heavy at the neck, jawline, mouth and nose. Comparing one to the other, the difference in the expression is striking: the half-closed eyes give the first image a spiritual expression, reflecting intelligence, refinement and good taste, while the second suggests a wily and calculating spirit, at the service of an appetite for material things, above all.

CHAPTER VI
THE LAW OF MOVEMENT

Whenever you study a face, you are generally struck first by the expressive movement of the sensory receptors which are endowed with a high level of sensitivity and motility, reflecting the dominant tendency of the personality at each and every moment in life. It is generally considered that the rest of the face is a fixed structure. But that is only partly true, and we will study the significance of transformation, which is slower and therefore less obvious and which often occurs in fixed structures, even after maturity has been reached.

FACIAL EXPRESSION

The simple Types have a habitual facial expression that reflects their dominant tendency while the Dilated Types communicate their adaptability with a happy expression, such as a large smile. For their part, the Retracted Types communicate their struggle through a tense expression, often marked by a general dissatisfaction and bitterness (Ill. 16).

The complex Types have more varied expressions, communicating their various tendencies in turn and, in this way, we know which tendency predominates. The Types that are predominantly extrovert have open receptors and a very expressive face; it is easy to read their thoughts and feelings. I've called these the Reactive Type. Meanwhile, the introverted, whose receptors are sheltered or even closed, with minimal facial expressions, may deceive an observer who is unaware of their real feelings. They may be confused with the introverted hypersensitive types who hide their moods and the phlegmatic who really are not very sensitive. In order to distinguish them, I have given the first the name *pseudo-phlegmatic*.[1]

Illustration 16. – THE DILATED VS. RETRACTED EXPRESSION

We could give these two pictures the name 'John smiling' and 'John crying'. It is usually considered that the general optimism of the Dilated Type translates into good humour, while the pessimism of the Retracted Type leads to moodiness and sadness.

---

1 - I was able to show in a study dedicated to the personality of the philosopher Bergson, how morphopsychology, through a facial analysis of this great man, has been able to redress the error made by characterology, which classified him as a Phlegmatic when he was in fact a hypersensitive introvert.

I would like to highlight that a lively expression not only suggests the extrovert vitality of the instincts and sentiments, but it also provides us with information about intelligence and drive, how quickly we make connections between the impressions we receive, the flexibility to move from one subject to another and decision-making speed. When the expressive mobility is too great, the intellect is active but at a more superficial level. This is particularly the case in Reactive Types. However, for example, in the group I call the Concentrated Type, it is a sign that the mind is not as agile but the ability nevertheless exists for both logical and profound reasoning. In the in-between cases, the retraction of the forehead brings an element of balance and reflection, moderating the active expression. Movement and control are both necessary, and one could say that, there, intelligence has no value without the combined possibility of quick thinking and reflection.

THE TRANSFORMATION OF THE FACE (Ill. 17-18)

One shouldn't believe popular opinion that once maturity has been reached, the fixed structures are immutable because during the course of life some extensive morphological *reshuffling* can take place, accompanying changes in character.

In the first place, we evolve as we age. We have seen the progressive change from atonic dilation to tonic dilation and to the lateral retraction of youth. We know, for example, that the small, concave nose of the young child changes significantly over time: due to dual frontal and lateral retraction, the nose often starts to take an aquiline shape. Taking into account this evolution over time, a valuable method of analysis has been developed based on the rule that if a subject has a facial structure representative of a certain stage in life that is not his current age, we can deduce that he has the character traits of that stage; just as a childlike face in an adult (for example, the persistence of a concave nose) suggests the emotional level of a child, the face of an old person in a young subject indicates a prematurely aged mentality. In the same way, as we will go into more detail later on, female morphological traits in a man suggest the existence of a female component, which has a great deal of influence on his psyche and, reciprocally, masculine traits in a woman suggest a virile element.

Morphological evolution, if it is progressive, may also undergo *sudden transformations* to the extent that, if the face transforms very quickly, it could change beyond recognition. For example, a typically dilated subject in childhood may, with close study, show discreet signs of retraction (for example, sunken eyes and an intense expression) which, in adolescence, then significantly retract.

The widest range of changes can occur not only during development, as we have just seen, but also *once maturity has been reached*. It is almost considered a rule that, upon aging, the face retracts, due to the predominant forces of conservation and as a consequence the face becomes smaller, closing in on itself. Having said that, there are certain adults who evolve completely differently by becoming dilated; their face gets bigger in structure (not only in the soft tissue areas), which tells us that the subject has found his path in life and has become better adjusted (Ill. 17).

Illustration 17. – FACIAL TRANSFORMATIONS: COLETTE'S CASE

If the general rule is that old age results in a retraction of the face, becoming smaller and gaunt, there are also cases where the opposite is true and the face dilates with age. This is particularly notable in the case of the great French writer, Colette. Shown above are both faces, one at 20 years old and the other at 50. This transformation can be interpreted as resulting from her sense of fulfilment after attaining her independence and becoming a successful writer.

In the second place, changes in morphology can be a direct result of events that directly affect either the physical or mental being. Physical influences can very quickly transform a face, particularly as a result of a defensive reaction to an illness, and is expressed by the transition from dilation to retraction. Take the example of this young girl, who, at 5 years old, had a strong respiratory system, evidence of which is expressed on her face by her large, thick nose. She then suffered a life-threatening double pneumonia. She survived, and you would be right to think that this is thanks to a strong retraction of the sick organ because the proportions of her nose in comparison to the rest of her face reduced in size to the point that, as an adult, we would say that she has a small nose (Ill. 18).

Emotional trauma and prolonged unhappiness can also cause major morphological changes. The middle zone of the face is the one most affected by these changes. It is very common, particularly in puberty, to see retraction in the two lateral zones of the cheeks between the nose and the cheekbones. I have called this lateral-nasal retraction, which changes the physiognomy, with a particular impact on the eyes which sink into their orbits. This retraction can have various causes, both organic and psychological. In subjects afflicted by asthma, the lateral-nasal retraction is continual and very marked but normally it is not possible to tell if the actual suffering caused by asthma is the cause or the effect of the retraction such that, in this illness, psychological and organic factors are closely related.

Here we touch on one of the most difficult problems: how to know if a deformation is the result of a pre-existing deformation which has created the functional problem or if it is a persisting perturbation of the function that has ended up creating the deformation. Clearly each case is different but what is important to grasp is that, between form and function, there is a vicious circle of reciprocal actions from which any modification we make to one of the elements naturally modifies the other. An asthmatic who is cured changes in character and reciprocally the healing of the asthmatic attacks could result in an improved psyche.

Illustration 18. – FACIAL TRANSFORMATIONS: ANOTHER CASE

Here we see a five-year-old child, whose face is notable for the size of the nose which is large and fleshy. After a serious pulmonary illness, in growing up, the face has broadened but the nose has not in proportion to the rest. It has, in fact, become slimmer and narrower, nevertheless with nostrils that flare, suggesting a permanent sensitivity. One could interpret this relative retraction of the nose as testament to the defensive reaction to the pulmonary disease. It is noteworthy that in the second photo, taken just after recovering from the disease, there has been a painful contraction of the 'upper lip nasal cavity' zone, indicating a very recent defensive retraction and a sign that another reduction will happen in this zone later on.

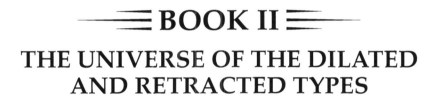

BOOK II

THE UNIVERSE OF THE DILATED AND RETRACTED TYPES

In the brief description that I have given of the Dilated and Retracted Types, I stated that we should not consider either one or the other as fixed types, characterized by unchanging traits. I also explained that the process which creates them is essentially a dynamic process, that is to say, a *tendency towards*, a movement towards dilation or retraction.

So, we must ignore statisticians when they ask for percentages of the Dilated vs. Retracted types in a particular population or race. In order to generate statistics, we would have to consider the Dilated and Retracted types as an abstraction, ignoring the individual traits within each type that make each person unique.

Avoiding categorization is impossible. I will, however, briefly yield to it by describing a type of personality as a Dilated or Retracted Type. This is a starting point, a first impression of the character which means that we will understand about 50% of the personality of the subject studied. But for the enthusiast who would like to explore further–and should–I will demonstrate in the following chapters how to create a more precise portrait through a dynamic study of the various elements within each type, a portrait which is faithful to the authentic individual.

In fact, the objective that we must set for ourselves, based on the scientific foundations of morphopsychology, is to get to the core of the subject studied. I advise enthusiasts to write short texts based on the people that they know, very precisely analysing their dominant tendencies. The great writers have left us examples whereby they have described, with a very clear morphopsychological intuition, characters that correspond to our types. The psychological richness and finesse of their portraits is of inestimable value to the morphopsychologist, as I have shown in a book dedicated to morphopsychological types in literature *(Types morphopsychologiques en literature)*, where I have borrowed from literary works from diverse eras and countries. To convince the reader of the validity of the science of morphopsychology and to illustrate the points in this book, I could think of no better way than to extract some important examples from it. I will demonstrate the character of the Dilated and Retracted Types through the traits borrowed from literary characters and I invite the reader to refer directly to the book for more information. Each of my citations has a numbered reference which refers to the specific book.

The complete list of citations is listed below.

In the book, *Types morphopsychologiques en* littérature, PUF, 1978:

1) *Colas Breugnon*, by Romain Rolland–with the characters of Colas (dilated) and Florimond (retracted).

2) *Julius Caesar*, by Shakespeare–with Cassius (retracted).

3) *Journey to the End of the Night*, by Céline–with Baryton (dilated) and

Parapine (retracted).

4) *Thérèse Desqueyroux*, by Mauriac–with Thérèse (retracted) and Bernard (dilated).

5) *Two Men*, by Georges Duhamel–with Salavin (retracted) and Edouard (dilated).

6) *Numa Roumestan*, by Alphonse Daudet–with Numa (dilated) and Rosalie (retracted).

7) *The Betrothed*, by Manzoni–with Don Abbondio (dilated) and Cardinal Federigo (retracted).

8) *The Thibaults*, by Roger Martin du Gard–with Antoine (dilated) and Jacques (retracted).

9) *The Misanthrope*, by Molière–with Alceste (retracted) and Philinthe (dilated).

10) *The Diary of a Country Priest*, by Bernanos–with the priest (retracted).

11) *Don Quixote*, by Cervantes–with Don Quixote (retracted) and Sancho (dilated).

12) *The Partisan*, by Simms–with Captain Porgy (dilated) and Dr. Oakenburg (retracted).

13) *Cousin Bette*, by Balzac–with cousin Bette (retracted).

14) *The Celibates*, by Balzac–with Abbot Birotteau (dilated), Canon Troubert (retracted) and Miss Gamar (retracted).

15) *Gone with the Wind*, by Margaret Mitchell–with Scarlett O'Hara (retracted).

16) *Tonio Kröger*, by Thomas Mann–with Tonio (retracted).

17) *Henry IV*, by Shakespeare–with Falstaff (dilated).

18) *Tartarin of Tarascon*, by Alphonse Daudet–with Tartarin (dilated).

19) *Around the World in 80 Days*, by Jules Verne–with Philéas

Fogg (retracted) and Passepartout (dilated).

20) *The Idiot*, by Fyodor Dostoyevsky–with Prince Muichkine (retracted).

21) *Le Paquebot Tenacity*, by Charles Vildrac–with Bastien (dilated) and Segard (retracted).

22) *Carrot Top*, by Jules Renard (retracted).

CHAPTER I
THE DILATED PERSONALITY TYPE

We have already seen the main qualities that characterise the Dilated Type: their openness to the world and their adaptability which encourages their development. In fact, this is evident from an early age. The Dilated are beautiful infants who grow up effortlessly, are balanced, the type of children who raise themselves. They mature early, both physically and mentally, and starting in adolescence can already be considered adults.

It is worth highlighting again that this adaptability manifests itself through a proper *integration* into their environment. It gives the impression of having a great facility for change and adaptation, even though they are in fact limited to the environment they were born into and which they have spent their entire lives in. It would be difficult for them to maintain their equilibrium outside of this setting. They are, therefore, very attached to where they were born, the part of their country and their time, respectful of traditions and customs and rarely departing from their own social group.

Body language

One's demeanour and body movements reveal the basic tendencies of the personality. The posture, gait, gestures, voice and facial expressions of the Dilated Type all reveal dominant expansion.

They stand straight, but not stiffly, sometimes leaning slightly forwards. Their gait is calm, relaxed and very different from the more rigid Retracted Type. In *The Celibates,* when contrasting the different personalities of Canon Troubert and Abbot Birotteau, Balzac describes their gaits: *'When the tall canon marched with solemn step through the naves and cloisters of Saint-Gatien, his head bowed, his eye stern, respect followed him. […] The good vicar, on the contrary, perambulated about with no gravity at all.'*

Illustration 19. – THE PREDOMINANTLY DILATED TYPE

Here are four images of Dilated Types, all of whom have in common the broad, rounded frame and open receptors.

I have already mentioned that they are of their time, that they obey what is customary, but particularly in their clothing: they follow the current fashion, passively, without demonstrating any kind of personal taste over their choice. They are very sensorial; they don't like black and white, preferring colours, inclining towards pale tones, not too bright, the most cheerful being blue, green or rose tones.

Illustration 20. – I. DILATED TYPE PERSONALITIES

Dilated Types are extroverts, always inclined to action. Here are two novelists: Abbot Prévost, more of a novelist than an abbot, the well-known author of Manon Lescaut, and Hemingway, a leading American novelist. Although one can't really compare them, they have both written action and adventure novels.

They enjoy giving hugs and handshakes and are on first-name basis with lots of people. They frequently talk with their hands and, more specifically, gesticulate when they are speaking. Daudet, speaking of his character Numa, says, *'He was superficial in voice and gestures like a tenor'*, adding that *'his greetings were accompanied by hand-shaking, embraces, and those hearty slaps on the shoulder which double the value of words that are always too cold to express Southern sympathy.'* (6)

They can't hide their emotions; their faces are open books—joy, sadness, anger, anxiety, exaltation or depression—and are all expressed openly. They smile, laugh and cry easily, in contrast to the Retracted Type. They speak a lot, and loudly, and enjoy conversation peppered with anecdotal details. Having to keep quiet goes against their nature: when Don Quixote tried to silence his squire Sancho, a Dilated Type, as we already know, his response was, *'[…] your wanting me to go with you through these desolate places day and night, without being able to talk with you when I feel like it, is burying me alive.'* (11)

Illustration 20. – II. DILATED TYPE PERSONALITIES

Extroversion also influences the social actions of industrialists, business people and politicians. Here we have Loucheur, a French industrialist and politician, who put his name to the construction of social housing after the First World War (the Loucheur Law, in 1928). Also above, Madame Boucicaut, who, along with her husband, a great businessman like herself, created the first department stores, the 'Bon Marché', combining a shrewd business sense with social awareness and great generosity, and rewarding staff with the fruits of her business.

The Dilated Type also like to sing at home, in the street or while travelling, and Captain Porgy, the Dilated Type so well described by the American novelist Simms, forced to remain quiet during his guard duty and finding this obligation difficult, says, *'Could he have talked all the while, or sung, with no ears but his own to appreciate his melodies, he would have been perfectly content […].'* (12)

In fact, there is a colourful word, 'Rabelaisian', referring to their table manners, which frequently reach the point of indecency (according to the Retracted Type).

Illustration 21. – THE CHARACTER JOHN FALSTAFF

Here we have a period engraving of John Falstaff, a comic hero from Shakespeare's plays. He is a Dilated Type, with a large torso, big paunch, a thick and short neck, large and fleshy face and a strongly dominant instinctive zone, which, as we will see, is often the case with the Dilated. This matches the temperament of a jolly fellow, a big eater and drinker, who is very fond of the ladies.

Instincts

The unrestrained expansion of the Dilated Type is due to the vigorous way in which their instinctive drive manifests itself externally.

The most developed of these instincts is the *instinct for nutrition*, an attribute linked to infancy as it is essential for growth. Even once growth has finished, we see that it remains a primordial instinct in Dilated adults. They are gourmands–big eaters and big drinkers–who love the atmosphere of banquets. Their equilibrium, their adaptability and their *joie de vivre* are all dependent upon an abundance of nutrition. Romain Rolland, in his novel *Colas Breugnon*, elevated it to a proverb: '*Stomach empty, heart heavy, belly full, heart light!*' (1) And Captain Porgy declares, '*A good dinner, I say, will sanctify a dozen sins, and here goes for one.*' He continues, '*I am convinced, however people may talk about the brain as the seat of intellect, that the brain does but a small business after all, in the way of thinking, compared with the belly. Of one thing be certain: before you attempt to argue with an obstinate customer, give him first a good feed. Bowels of compassion are necessary to brains of understanding, and a good appetite and an easy digestion are essentials to a logical comprehension of every subject.*' And he adds, not without humour, that '*A good cook is more important to the success of an army than a good general.*' (12)

In parallel, whenever Bernard Desqueyroux is sick, he believes that '*The key is for me to get my appetite back.*' (4) Incidentally, you can see in our illustrations, and it is significant, that the Dilated are often represented in the process of eating or drinking (Falstaff, Brûlebois, Porgy).

The reason for over-eating is often due to the Dilated Type's lack of sensitivity. As one said to another who was fascinated by his huge appetite, '*It's not that I have a big appetite, it's that I can still eat a lot even when I'm no longer hungry.*'

From this instinct for nutrition, we can draw the *instinct for acquisition*, the need to acquire material possessions and use them to bolster one's self worth. The Dilated Type works at earning a lot of money but they are not hoarders. Rather, they need to put their money to work, whether by spending it or putting it to use in some business. In large part, this attitude is a determining factor of their professional skills, notably their business sense. But this can also be taken to an extreme, becoming exclusively materialistic, judging everything only according to its monetary value.

They have a strong sense of their *sensuality* which appears early on in adolescence. They need physical contact and affection, delighting in the senses, such as taste, which play an important role in their life. Shakespeare gives his character, Falstaff (Ill. 21), the classical temperament of this type which gives him this irresistible fondness of sensuality. When reproached for his debauchedness, he responds by blaming his large stomach as the cause for all his actions: '*Thou knowest in the state of innocency Adam fell; and what should poor Jack Falstaff do in the days of villany? Thou seest I have more flesh than another man, and therefore more frailty.*' (17) It should be noted that they find it difficult to resist their instincts and are prone to the extremes of *mid-life crisis.*

Although inclined towards tenderness, they are sometimes a bit coarse in their amorous relationships and their lack of subtlety can shock a more sensitive partner. But their sexuality is honest, direct and without the perversions that are sometimes found in the Retracted Type.

Their *aggressive instinct* is not very well developed. Truth be told, they are predisposed to combativeness, which is a direct consequence of their large vital expansion. They tend to overcome the obstacles that block their way forward but only under the condition that the problem isn't too difficult. This is due to the fact that one of their dominant traits is restraint, or always keeping within certain limits.

On the other hand, they don't react to aggressions in their environment or direct their hostility to the individuals considered responsible. They are by nature conciliatory, always prepared to calm tense situations in their social life and forgetting any harm done. Neither are they the type to fight for a great cause or idea; they are not 'heroes', and they accuse heroic actions by others as 'folly'. Falstaff is a good example: although he likes to boast about his supposed exploits, in reality, he never puts himself in danger; declaring, '*The better part of valour is discretion; in the which better part I have saved my life.*' (17) And his friends jokingly say about him, '*He fears nothing except danger; he loves the truth, up to a point; he fights with courage but not for one second more than reason demands.*'[1] It can be said that the Dilated are those who believe, according to the saying, '*Nobody can be expected to do the impossible.*'

However, from time to time they are subject to uncontrollable fits of anger, but it is a 'blind rage' that colours their face and their words, which ends quickly and leaves no hard feelings. Ruma Roumestan, a fully-fledged Southerner, in complaining to a friend about the stubborn and vindictive character of his wife, a woman from the North, says, '*She is not like us,*

1: Unpublished translation.

among whom the greatest anger evaporates in gestures and threats, and then in the turn of a hand leaves us. They retain it! It is terrible!' (6) Also, the aggression in the Dilated Type never leads, unless by accident, to murderous acts.

Emotional life

Extroverts by nature, the Dilated like physical contact and interaction with others. We have also seen that they are insensitive to subtleties, lacking finesse in their relationships, such that, without meaning to, they come across as impolite and brazen. The German humourist W. Busch demonstrated this to us in the comic strip about a poet looking for solitude suitable for his ruminations but who repeatedly comes across a loud Dilated Type that keeps getting in the way (Ill. 27).

Nevertheless, the Dilated Type takes everything in which, from an emotional point of view, gives them the gift of empathy. They have a big, open heart, a hospitable character and are friendly with everyone. However, this ability to empathise has a flip side: they are attached to a world where everything has to go well and if something doesn't go as planned, they are incapable of adapting. In order to maintain their equilibrium, they completely refuse to deal with the situation, not wishing their optimistic view of the world to be shaken. An excellent illustration of this type of character is offered to us by Duhamel in his novel *Two Men,* in which the Dilated Edouard (Ill. 28), after encountering a neighbour suffering from an incurable disease, rejects her objections, trying with all his might to convince her that she is fine, which, in the words of the author translates as: *'Be considerate, my dear lady, be well! You know how bad I feel when someone in my immediate circle is suffering!'*[2] (5) This almost excessive sensitivity to the joy and suffering of others, and the fear of being afflicted by the same illness, causes the Dilated Type great anxiety, as we have just seen. It is for that same reason that the thought of death causes unbearable anxiety.

The Dilated are sociable, family men. They have a lot of friends and love being part of a group. They enjoy meetings, get-togethers and travelling in a group. Captain Porgy is like that, and the author says of him: *'He was*

2: Unpubl. trans.

highly delighted by the visit of the two friends, for, like most fat men, he liked company, and preferred always the presence of a number.' (12)

It is worth remembering that the Dilated lack sensitivity and that curbing their emotions favours a climate of social harmony. As we will see later in our studies of the Retracted Type, their deepest and most intense feelings arouse similar feelings in others and are often the cause of heated conflict.

They are also family men. They marry early, wishing to establish their life on a social basis, enjoying living together and loving children. Their choice of partner is not very selective; they are above all guided by tradition, the propriety of their social milieu ('avoiding unsuitable alliances') and by economic interests. They are very attached to their home and they blend their personal interests with that of the community. As Bernard Desqueyroux says during an argument with his wife, *'I won't give in to any personal considerations. I remove myself altogether; only the family matters.'*

Illustration 22. –DONA PRASSEDE

Here is a typical example of the Dilated Type, whose character will be described in detail in the following text.

It is worth noting that the sociable nature of the Dilated Type favours union and harmony in the bosom of a family where all members appear to have the same temperament. But when this is not the case, conflict can arise as, by their 'sociable nature', the Dilated can't understand, nor admit, the desire for independence from others. The novelist Manzoni (*The Engaged Couple*) describes the mother of a family, Dona Prassede, a Dilated Type (Ill. 22) with a big heart, very much the 'mother hen', never accepting and letting her 'chickens' gain their independence and live their own lives as they grew up. Manzoni humorously describes the situation: '*Besides her immediate household, […] she had five daughters, neither of whom lived at home, but they gave her the more trouble from that very cause. Three were nuns; and two were married. Donna Prassede consequently had three monasteries and two families to govern; a vast and complicated machinery, and the more troublesome, as two husbands, supported by a numerous kindred, three abbesses, defended by other dignitaries, and a great number of nuns, would not accept her superintendence.*' The novelist adds that she could not understand that others would put their independence first because she didn't have any; she was not the solitary type and was only happy in company. (7)

The Dilated are generous, giving willingly whatever they have that they don't need. But this generosity has its limits and, once that limit has been reached, their generosity lacks depth and duration. It is one of their main traits; they live in the present and express themselves freely in gestures, words and a loud voice. But in order to be able to do that, they must live in a stable situation and not be uprooted from their environment, their land. It is often said of them 'out of sight, out of mind', as they tend to forget their loved ones when they are not present.

It is also worth mentioning that they have the gift of eloquence and make frequent use of it. When they aren't able to talk, they feel ill, as we have seen in the case of Sancho above. The problem with this eloquence is that words are often a substitution for feelings and ideas. Numa, himself, says of Daudet, '*He was superficial in voice and gestures like a tenor.*' And his wife Rosalie, a completely different character, as we have already seen, fed up of him making promises that he doesn't keep, and has no intention of keeping, and tired of hearing him speaking thoughtlessly, expresses her concern out loud in front of their child's cradle: '*Will you trade in words, without troubling yourself about their worth and whether they represent your thought, if they only are brilliant and sound well?'* (6) (Ill. 32)

The dominant expansion of the Dilated makes them totally dependent upon their surroundings. Their actions are never dictated by purely personal intentions or an inner individualistic motive. They always submit to authority, keeping the strictest account of praise and blame. They are not prideful but they are vain, which means that their self-esteem depends entirely upon the opinion of others. It is one of the reasons why they search for self-worth by aspiring to official functions, honours and decorations.

Intelligence

The intelligence of the Dilated comes from their adaptability and extroversion. It is essentially an intelligence based on 'contact', grounded in concrete reality, visible and tangible beings and things. They are realists and sensorial, only attaching importance to the first thing they see, and they need to taste it, touch it, feel it and see it. Colas Breugnon, in the novel by Romain Rolland, states, '[...] *for my part I believe in life, in the light of day. I know that I live and think — very clearly too, — I know also that two and two make four.'* (1)

Due to this appreciation for objects, the Dilated have a good sense of material things, of their value and use; they like home improvements, are good with their hands and are quick to grasp what is required. They are intuitive, understanding reality without a need for reason. Edouard of *Duhamel*, a chemist, has this character trait; the author says of him, '*There are those who reason for a long time in order to understand the evidence. Edouard, on the other hand, turns his nose slightly in a clockwise direction, breathes in and click!, he knows all he needs to know.'*[3]

They adapt easily to their social and business environments. As I have said, they are of their world and time and share the opinions of their social group. They like things as they are and have no desire to change them. They are conservative, partisans of the social order, of the status quo, from which, incidentally, they benefit. They know how to work with it; they

3: Unpubl. trans.

understand the social mores and how to make the most of them. They are opportunists, taking advantage of what is available and which benefits them the most, which in general, ensures their success.

They are not men of deep reflection since, operating within a world of familiar things (from which they would not willingly depart), they analyse the situation based on their first impressions and immediately know which choice they must make. Reflection never paralyses their action; however, they may be defeated when faced with a problematic situation.

Their ideas are concrete, very similar to the facts from which they come. They are useful ideas with practical applications. The Dilated are very good at applying the knowledge they have acquired but, on the other hand, they have few original ideas or inventions.

They are very good at explaining what they want to communicate, and they talk considerably. They write in the same way. As writers, their style is natural, pleasant, generous and often a little careless, as they get carried away and forget to correct themselves.

Their knowledge is wide ranging and always falls within a very concrete domain, as opposed to the Retracted, as we will see later, who prefer to dedicate themselves to one specific subject.

They are not very adept at abstract ideas, notions that come from consolidating vast experience and which play a primordial role in scientific development. They are incapable of building theories or systems, and they defend their position by saying that they prefer facts to doctrine. And if they are scholars, they are men of experimental science, that is, factual observation and experimentation.

They are not very artistic, being too attached to material things, because they see value only in terms of something's use and solidity; in a word, in terms of quantity rather than quality. Their finances may permit opulence, a visible sign of richness, but they are not very sensitive to the finer side of luxury.

I have already mentioned that their understanding of the world is based on their extroversion which means that they give much more importance to events in their external life than that of their inner life. They believe that we are a reflection of the world we grow up in and that material and socio-economic conditions are determining factors in our personality. Their philosophy is therefore pragmatic and realist.

In their contact with others, they don't lack psychological awareness; however, they aren't very interested in delving any deeper, thus lacking introversion. I should also note that, in the same way, they lack introspection in terms of what is going on in the interior of their organism. This can often result in illness as they don't feel, or aren't aware of, the early symptoms.

Professionally, being such open people, the Dilated have a talent for adaptation which enables them to practice a wide variety of professions. Their excellent handling of the material world facilitates all manual professions, particularly technical ones, in the artisanal and industrial fields. Their sociability and sense of concrete values makes them good businessmen. As we have already seen, they are not intellectuals. Their intelligence is essentially practical which means they are best at any work which requires knowledge, know-how, memory or spontaneity, such as in teaching and the administrative professions. Their relaxed extroversion is an aid to success in journalism, acting, even singing, and in the art of public speaking and politics.

To identify their aptitudes more precisely, it is obviously necessary to study the structure of their cerebral zone.

Will

The *will to take action*, in the sense where it is the expression of the instinct for expansion, is very strong in the Dilated. As we have already seen, they are not always keen to take action because even if their expansion enables them to triumph over obstacles which hinder their progress, the obstacles must nevertheless be neither too big nor too persistent.

Their *self-control* on the other hand, is often weak. It is true that their lack of sensitivity makes them somewhat phlegmatic, based on which we can deduce that they exercise moderation and restraint. But, beyond a certain point, the high demands of their surroundings, as well as their own strong inner drive, are often overwhelming and can lead to impulsiveness. In particular, they tend to abuse the pleasures of the table and the flesh.

CHAPTER II
THE RETRACTED PERSONALITY TYPE

The Retracted Type is essentially the opposite of the Dilated Type.[1] However, I must advise the reader that the description is schematic; it provides the general static characteristics of the retracted personality but we should always keep in mind the dynamic *point of view* and consider that the very wide range of progressive retraction is punctuated by a number of quite different Retracted Types. So different from one another, that they justify a separate description which I will give in the following chapter.

Morphologically, the face of the Retracted Type presents a certain lengthening due to the retraction of the frame. The outline is more irregular than that of the Dilated, as much in the hollows and projections as in the asymmetry of the two halves, which is the norm here. The receptors are not as wide as in the Dilated; they are narrow and the openness is reduced, they sink into the depths of the face, sheltered behind the surface bone structure that frames them (*sheltered* receptors). We also note that the facial expression, instead of relaxed and smiling as in the Dilated, is serious, tense, sometimes grimacing and is often marked by a certain bitterness. (Ill. 23 and 24)

1: I have chosen both with medium tonicity. In later chapters, we will see the character traits that result from the different degrees of tonicity.

This morphology is rare in childhood as it is, when one comes across it, a sign of perturbation in the evolution of the baby before birth, which has provoked a premature defensive reaction. If the natural expansion of a child is hampered, growth does not follow the usual path: the child's health is delicate and he is sickly and frail. His appetite is irregular, his sleep troubled, his crying unceasing. He matures slowly, both physically and mentally. His mood reflects the situation: he is usually sad, grumpy and lacking in the *joie de vivre* habitual in the Dilated. Based on this weakliness, we should not assume that his vitality is also fragile because, due to the intense defensive reaction, retracted children tend to escape serious illnesses and are notably better at resisting epidemics than dilated children, although subject to frequent ailments.

Illustration 23. – THE PREDOMINANTLY RETRACTED TYPE

In the Retracted Type, you do not see a homogeneous structure as in the Dilated Type as the retraction has a distinctly acute effect as much in the lengthening of the face as in the depth; however, the outline is always retracted and the receptors sunken.

Illustration 24. – RETRACTED TYPE PERSONALITIES

The novelist Jules Renard projects himself as the hero of his autobiography, Carrot Top, whose face Pazzi drew by taking inspiration from the author's description. On the whole childlike, there are elements of retraction which are not common for someone of that age.

Here is another child of the retracted type: Jacques from *The Thibaults* by Roger Martin du Gard, where the novelist describes the contrasting character very well. Pazzi has drawn the figure according to the novelist's description: '*A stocky body with a large head, barely separated from broad shoulders; a tight jaw, redoubtable; an energetic and muscled mouth, but with a line denoting bitterness and sadness. The expression is hooded, sheltered beneath the tormented lines of the eyebrows, and a mass of unruly thick hair with a low hairline frames the face, a dark fringe brushing the forehead.*'[2] This corresponds to the description of a passionate and tormented person, the morphology of a Tonic Retracted Type.

Psychologically, the Retracted Type determines everything through the filter of *selectivity*, which makes them a more complex personality than the Dilated. On the one hand, when in their comfort zone, they act like the Dilated, adapting well, expressing their thoughts and feelings freely, achieving their objectives in life; in other words, extroverted.

But outside of their comfort zone, they retract, withdrawing from the world and experiencing internally everything that they have chosen not to in the outside world; in other words, they are also introverted. This selectivity explains why the Retracted act so differently in their social

2: Unpublished translation.

circle where they thrive, in comparison to in public where they hide behind a mask. It should be highlighted that the Retracted don't come across their preferred surroundings easily, as if it were handed to them on a plate; they have to build it themselves, patiently, as with everything considered worthwhile. It takes time. The Dilated, conversely, have no trouble finding an environment that they can adapt to; they accept it as it is and from that point on, their growth is rapid and easy, complete beings already from adolescence. Meanwhile, the Retracted grow up in a constant state of flux, like a pendulum, moving unceasingly from one point to another, never finding the perfect balance. Seeing them vacillate between one environment that is already there and their preferred surroundings, between contradicting thoughts and feelings, one thinks of someone unbalanced and might predict an uncertain future for them, but in reality, it is that perfect balance that they are looking for. Adolescent crises in particular, while frustrating, resolve themselves, in the majority of cases, as they mature and find stability from that point onwards.

The antagonistic nature of their relationships in their social life and, as a result, their relationship with themselves, is a striking feature of the Retracted personality when outside of their preferred surroundings.

Retraction, as I have said, represents a break of contact. It is all the more surprising in the case of children as it is contrary to their habitual way of being. There is an excellent example in the novel by Jules Renard, *Carrot Top,* where the young hero is described as a Retracted Type. When he plays hide and seek, Carrot Top (Ill. 24), says the author *'hides himself so well that they forget about him'*,[3] which is unusual as it is well known that young children, when clearly Dilated, aren't very good at playing hide and seek and if they are not found immediately by their playmates, the solitude in their hiding place weighs so heavily on them that they run out, crying *'Here I am!'*

As an adult, this type of behaviour is more understandable. It is much more common to be self-effacing, to have a fear of public appearances or a desire to be inconspicuous, or to refuse honours, official posts and decorations. In certain cases, this refusal is so complete that it turns into

---

3: Unpubl. trans.

an opposition to society, a rejection that can sometimes have a dramatic effect as in the case of Jacques Thibault, the character from Roger Martin du Gard's *The Thibaults*, described by the novelist as a Retracted Type who systematically rebels in his family environment, and against society: *'Ever since he was a child he has said no! He has never had any other way to express himself. No: no to life! No to the world! And here is his last refusal, his last no: no to what man has turned life into!'*[4] (8) (Ill. 24-2)

This last 'no' is a rejection of the war where, as a confirmed pacifist, his desperate efforts to try to impede the conflict results in his death. This is an extreme case, clearly, but this tendency to go to extremes is often seen in the Retracted Type.

Body language

The body of the Retracted Type betrays their difficulties in adapting. They are not flexible like the Dilated: they are continually on the defensive and hold themselves stiffly, whether standing rigidly in a superior attitude or leaning forward. They often don't know to hold themselves; they are awkward and clumsy, never knowing what to do with their hands, for example, when they are talking. Their stiffness is a reflection of their rigid mentality, which is expressed in this way. Balzac, the good morphopsychologist that he was, highlighted it in a variety of his characters, amongst others, cousin Bette and Miss Gamar, the old lady in the novel *The Celibates*. Balzac says of cousin Bette, *'she was thin, with narrow hips, long and strong arms and broad feet'* (Ill. 44), and that *'her bearing was as straight as a rod.'* Of Miss Gamar: *'she was quite tall and kept herself very straight, she walked without shifting her weight in that movement which produces such elegant undulations, so gracious and attractive in women, she moved one might say, as one piece'.* (14)

I have already compared the contrasting personalities of Canon Troubert and the Abbot Birotteau, as revealed by their gait. This rigidity can become awkward and clumsy in certain Retracted Types. (We will see later on that these are Atonic Retracted Types.) As Salavin, described by Duhamel, says, *'I was anxious about my body, I didn't know what to do with it.'*

4: Unpubl. trans.

The Retracted tend to be parsimonious in their gestures; they don't willingly embrace others and they don't like to shake hands. They are very sparing with their words and they never talk while working.

Their face barely betrays their thoughts and feelings; they don't have the degree of expressive mobility of the Dilated. They will occasionally smile, but rarely laugh, and even then their smile tends to be somewhat tense. In Shakespeare's Julius Caesar, he gives an insightful analysis of the character of Cassius, who he suspects of plotting against him, stating, '*Seldom he smiles, and smiles in such a sort, As if he mock'd himself and scorn'd his spirit, That could be moved to smile at any thing*'. (2)

And Balzac describes the face of the Canon Troubert: '*long and furrowed by deep wrinkles that contract at certain moments in an expression full of irony and disdain; but nevertheless one has to observe him closely in order to discover these two sentiments, as the Canon is usually in a state of perfect calm…. He spoke rarely and never laughed*'. (14)

Of cousin Bette, *Balzac* notes that she was not particularly neighbourly and didn't speak to anyone. The Retracted are miserly with words and quiet when not in their preferred surroundings. And they don't have any talent for singing.

The same goes for emotions: as the Dilated are so expressive, their emotions are betrayed very quickly on their faces by redness, laughter or tears, whereas the Retracted hold back their feelings, practically never openly expressing them; it all happens internally. The writer Margaret Mitchell recounts that when Scarlett O'Hara is told that the man she loves is about to marry another, '*Scarlett's face did not change but her lips went white*', adding, '*So still was her face as she stared at Stuart that he, never analytic, took it for granted that she was merely surprised and very interested.*' (15) (Ill. 45)

Tears are also quite rare in the Retracted; they hold them back, to the great surprise of those who don't understand this kind of reaction. The mother of Carrot Top, who feels no love for her child, says, '*What do you want me to do? He doesn't even shed a tear when I smack him!*'[5] (22). For them to cry, some devastating event has to occur. Such is the case for a friend of Brûlebois,

---

5: Unpubl. trans.

ironically called Lune (Moon), when, at the end of Marcel Aymé's novel, his friend is dying in hospital and the dry, phlegmatic and taciturn Lune breaks down in tears on the street.

Instincts

The Retracted are less instinctive than the Dilated, notably less fond of food and drink and less sensual. They don't give in to their instinctive desires except when they feel at ease. Their tendencies are suppressed and driven back to the subconscious when outside of their preferred surroundings. The Retracted personality is therefore particularly complex as they do not learn to master these repressed tendencies; rather, they simply shut them away. By holding back their own dynamism, their interior life becomes troubled but kept secret. This restraint is expressed in the face by a certain tension, which can be detected particularly in the receptors and, above, all in the instinctive zone: the mouth with its tightly pursed lips and lowered corners. The paleness of the face is also a sign of inhibition.

The instinct for nutrition is not prominent, unlike the Dilated. As they are so selective, the Retracted are very choosy about food. They are certainly more gourmet than gourmand. They are subject to digestive disorders, often suffering from constipation. Strong emotions, sorrow or simply fatigue can make them lose their appetite.

The aggressive instinct plays a predominant role in the Retracted Type and manifests itself in two forms. In the first place, to the extent that it is a direct expression of the vitality of the expansion, as in the Dilated, it obeys the selectivity rule and therefore manifests itself in their preferred surroundings, the environment in which they feel most at ease. In the second form, it can conversely manifest itself outside of their preferred surroundings as a means of responding to the aggressions of their environment and it is in this case that you can really use the word aggression, as it is not directed at material obstacles but at people. The Retracted tend to blame others who don't understand them and, if bullied, they will ruminate over how to get revenge. On the other hand, due to the way in which they internalize the world, this aggressiveness is not immediately expressed but will be held in for a certain amount of time until it becomes so intense that it must be discharged. The Retracted are also vengeful. It's amongst them that you find the revolutionaries, those who want to change the social order, for better or worse, sometimes creating in them the desire to violently destroy the established order and commit antisocial, or even criminal, acts.

Only amongst the Retracted will you find those capable of regicide. Julius Caesar, who intuitively perceives Cassius, the character who assassinates him, as dangerous, declares to his confidante Anthony, *'Let me have men about me that are fat; Sleek-headed men and such as sleep o' nights: Yon Cassius has a lean and hungry look; He thinks too much: such men are dangerous.'* And at Anthony's objection, he replies: *'Would he were fatter!'*

This repressed aggressive instinct is often projected outward, the subject ridding himself of his aggressiveness, after which it doesn't come from him anymore but rather from his surroundings. From then on, he complains that this aggressiveness is directed against him. Molière's Alceste declares in his *Misanthrope*, *'I hate all men!'* but, according to him, this isn't a primal hate, justifying it by pretending it to be a response to the attitude of those he considers his persecutors. (9)

Neither is the sexual instinct satisfied in the same spontaneous fashion of the Dilated. The Retracted are slower in love and more complicated than the Dilated. They don't search for direct or tender physical contact, except when within their comfort zone, modesty and reserve being an obstacle to their free expression of desire. In *The Thibaults*, by Roger Martin du Gard, the author highlights this contrast in his characterisation of the two brothers, Antoine and Jacques. The first one is a Dilated Type who became familiar with women at an early age; the second is Retracted, full of complexes and who considers carnal desire to be impure, refusing to submit to it, stating, *'I could never surrender myself to that point unless it were in a closed room, hidden from everyone's regard, and even then!'*[6] And when he has some level of intimacy with a beautiful, slightly wild, girl, who has already given herself to Antoine and who is now willing to give herself to him, the author remarks that, *'if perhaps the warmth of this female body created a physical reaction in him, he is practically unaware of it; he would die of shame and disgust at the thought of Lisbeth noticing. Being near her, he had never given her a covetous, impure glance. There was a complete disassociation between*

6: Unpubl. trans.

his soul and his flesh; the soul belonged to the loved, the flesh led its solitary life in a different world, in a nocturnal world unavailable to Lisbeth.' An allusion is made here of the solitary vice that effectively replaces sexual relations in many people whose sexuality is repressed. (8) (Ill. 24)

In their romantic relationships, their insistence on being in their preferred surroundings can cause difficulties when that need is not fulfilled. The reaction can be dramatic, hateful and potentially aggressive, even cruel, which psychoanalysis explains as a regression of sexuality to sadism which precedes it in evolution.

In others, this anxiety may provoke sexual impotence. In a woman, considering her more passive role, this impotency can go unnoticed. However, it may be expressed as frigidity which can be disconcerting for her partner. Mauriac openly touches on this subject in his novel *Thérèse Desqueyroux*, considering the issue of physical relations as essential in conjugal harmony. His Thérèse is Retracted, whose delicate disposition doesn't fit with the sensuality of her Dilated husband and who has tried to avoid physical contact right from the beginning of their marriage. The author describes her during the act as having *'teeth clenched, cold'*, and in relating her husband's complaints, that she was *'so cold, so mocking, who took pleasure in nothing.'* Later in the book, Thérèse's repugnance for physical love leads her to hate her husband and wish for his demise (Ill. 31).

Rejecting physical contact when the circumstances are not of one's choosing can create what is known as 'emotional impotence'. In his book entitled *Love*, Stendhal, a fine psychologist, dedicates an entire chapter to what he calls 'The Fiascos'. He recounts an example, according to him fairly common, of French officers in the Italian army. The local well-bred ladies, seduced by their presence, offer them a roof over their head, sustenance ... and the rest, and the soldiers, paralysed, at least at first, by the feeling of being offered something that they would not have dared to hope for.

We could compare it to the famous example of J.J. Rousseau, a writer with a predominant retraction, who relates in his *Confessions* to have been incapable of making love to the courtesan Zulietta, who was taken with him and offered herself to him. The reason was that, during the act, he discovered that she had a deformed breast. The writer adds that Julietta, aggrieved, says to him, *'Give up the ladies and study mathematics'*, an unwarranted conclusion as once the initial emotional reaction dissipates and he is in his preferred surroundings, inhibition disappears.

Emotional life

Their emotions fall in line with their retraction; they act differently in the company of strangers than those with whom they feel comfortable.

They are neither family-oriented nor social. Often, they remain single and, even when married, they try to maintain their individuality, often dreaming of freeing themselves from their family restraints. They are not at all like the family man of the Dilated Type.

They don't like socialising. As particular about friendship as they are about love, they have only a few friends and only enjoy being in small groups. If they are disillusioned or their retraction is strong, they will search out solitude. They keep their feelings very private and are more refined in their manners than the Dilated but, on the other hand, they are very sensitive and easily offended by the slightest thing, which gives them the justified reputation of being temperamental. They rarely anger; their fury is always contained, being a cold rage, as opposed to the burning ire of the Dilated. It is the same opposing retraction, the withdrawal of blood from the face versus the expansive reaction of flushed skin. In *Two Men* by Duhamel, Edouard, a Dilated Type, annoyed with his old friends who reproach him for his friendship with Salavin, departs with a slam of the door: *'The door opens and two men leave. Edouard was crimson and vocal; Salavin pale and silent.'*[7] (5)

The Retracted are not incapable of generous acts; however, they don't have the easy generosity and benevolence of the Dilated.

They are often bad-tempered and critical. There is an excellent example in *The Misanthrope*, by Molière: the hero of the piece, Alceste, constantly shows his susceptibility to pride and his passion for honesty and fairness leads him to declare to his friend, Philinthe, who is a tolerant and conciliatory Dilated Type:

7: Unpubl. trans.

Everywhere I find base flattery,
injustice, self-interest, treachery, deceit;
I cannot bear it longer; I am enraged; and my
intention is to tell the truth henceforth, to all
the human race. (9)

The Retracted are not very partial to physical contact and this difficulty is expressed as much in the psyche as in the physical body as the two are intimately connected. For example, the novelist says of Jacques Thibault, *'the drama of his life was this inability to deal with physical contact which made him unreachable'*[8] (Ill. 24). When Salavin's host invites him to sit down, *'not just on one cheek, but both'*, he replies that he rarely sits on both buttocks at the same time, and when the other asks him *'is it because you're shy?'*, he responds *'No! I just can't bear to commit!'* (5) (Ill. 28)

Thérèse, who as we have seen above, due to her pronounced retraction, finds physical contact repugnant and treats her emotional relationships likewise. It is said of her, *'She doesn't hate her husband, but what a desire to be alone! [...] If only he were gone, she wouldn't have to force herself to eat, to smile, to put on a face, to appease his gaze'*. Of course, her husband does not meet her needs in the way that she had hoped: *'She believed that there existed a place in the world where shecould be happy amongst those who understood her, perhaps admired and loved!'* (Ill. 31)

When the retraction is very pronounced, this difficulty can be so extreme as to make it impossible to enjoy the presence of others, even within their preferred surroundings. At the beginning of his friendship with Edouard, Salavin, after conversing with him makes this surprising statement, *'Leave me be now! I am happy and I need to be alone to better think of you'*, demonstrating that, in the Retracted, their emotional state can replace the warmth of one's actual presence. In relation to strangers, the Retracted are cold, distant, secretive and don't bond easily with others. We can appreciate here that when the retraction is very pronounced, the field of expansion can become so small that even minimal contact with others can be harmful, creating an intense desire for solitude, this solitude being a means of avoiding pain. We come across it frequently: in Tonio Kröger, the hero of the novel *Thomas Mann*, in which the author has most likely projected his own feelings, that solitude is inevitable. Invited to a party,

---

8: Unpubl. trans.

'*Tonio was distressed by this party in which he never really participated. He stood in a dark corner face burning, because of you, the living, the happy; and then he left...alone. He stood in front of a window, but it was inside himself that he was looking at*' (16).

In parallel, the prince Muichkine, the main character in *The Idiot*, by *Dostoyevsky*, says to a confidant, '*I am out of place in society*', and his ineptitude in his social life makes him wish he could remove himself from it: '*At other moments he felt a longing to go away somewhere and be alone with his thoughts, and to feel that no one knew where he was.*' (20) (Ill. 48)

When in love, the Retracted don't externalise their feelings like the Dilated; instead, they are very reserved and contained, as we have seen in some examples above. They tend to suppress and internalize their impulses. This can lead to an extreme transformation of sexual attraction, to the point that practically nothing of the physical reality of the object of their affection remains, only an idealised image. Tonio Kröger is in love with Imge, but he experiences this love on the inside, like a dream. He doesn't try to share it with the young girl: '*whereas fair-haired Inge, even when he was sitting beside her, seemed distant and alien and embarrassed by him, for they did not speak the same language.*' At the extreme, the ability to adapt is gravely lacking; for example, in the case of the errant knight Don Quixote and his Dulcinea. The lady that has stolen his heart certainly exists; she is a young village girl which the knight '*with whom he had been at one time in love, though, so far as is known, she never knew it nor gave a thought to the matter.*' He says to his horseman, '*I can safely swear I have not seen her four times in all these twelve years I have been loving her more than the light of these eyes that the earth will one day devour; and perhaps even of those four times she has not once perceived that I was looking at her*'. (11) Clearly an extreme case, but it helps us to see the extent to which the Retracted can be deprived of the physical contact that the Dilated have, tending to replace flesh-and-blood humans with an idealistic image that they have created. They also tend to substitute women with Woman, with a capital W, complete with all the idealistic attributes that he desires in them.

This tendency can also affect their relationship with other men. Salavin of *Duhamel*, when accused of misanthropy, responds, '*I love men and it is not my fault if I can't put up with them most of the time. When I find myself face to face with my fellows, I feel my soul contract; I can't wait to be on my own again to love men as I love them when they are not there, out of my sight.*'[9]

9: Unpubl. trans.

We can see from this how subjective the Retracted can be and how their interior life can be out of step with their external reality, that is, having a subjective opinion of a person or an object which counts more than the reality. In a conversation that Salavin has with a man he has met in *Confession at Midnight,* he states, *'Once again, please excuse me if I insist on including events that have occurred entirely inside my head.'*[10]

One can understand the difficulties this introversion can cause in terms of its integration in everyday life. *'What makes me so stupid'*, says Jacques Thibault, *'is that I can't divert my attention away from my own feelings.'*[11]

Intelligence

The Retracted also apply the law of selectivity to the intellectual domain, only paying attention to and retaining whatever interests them, rejecting the rest. Outside of their preferred surroundings, they don't entertain contact with people or things, preferring to keep a distance. They are therefore not sensorial like the Dilated; they happily substitute the real thing for an abstract idea of it.

The rule of selectivity also affects the attention span of the Retracted in the outside world. He finds it tiring when not in his preferred surroundings, to the extent that after a short while he withdraws into himself and removes himself from the world, which I refer to as *Absorbed-Distracted*.

It is also a fact that the Retracted don't have the broad field of knowledge of the Dilated; but what they lose in diversity of interest, they gain significantly in depth. They therefore tend to specialise in a field that corresponds to their own preferred surroundings.

They are not like the intuitive Dilated; they are men of reflection and logic, where everything is filtered through logical analysis. This is sometimes taken to an extreme; on the one hand, their spirit is so detached from reality, that in the extreme is atrophied; and on the other hand, reflection can become mental rumination, perplexity, and can become an obstacle to decision-making.

The imagination is also bridled and rarely given free rein. Rosalie, Numa's wife, who Daudet suggests is a woman of great integrity, logical and

---

10: Unpubl. trans.
11: Unpubl. trans.

organised, lacked imagination. He says of her *'that in M. Baudry's course, which he pompously called his "class of imagination," in which he taught style and the development of thought, Rosalie had no success, expressing every thing in a few concise words; while she herself with only half of an idea, would blacken volumes'.* (6) (Ill. 32)

Will

The *will to take action* in the Retracted doesn't have the easy spontaneity of the Dilated. It is not an automatic reaction to the demands of their surroundings; it comes from inside, from their innermost vitality. As you will see, it varies according to the level of vitality and is expressed through tonicity. It is the same with ambition: they don't have the social ambitions of the Dilated, preferring to maintain their individuality in their preferred surroundings, usually going against the current.

Their *self-control* is better than that of the Dilated: they are able to put a brake on their impulsive urges but this constraint can block the machine, creating inhibition. Under these conditions, repression can create perversions by diverting the natural course of the instincts.

This issue is tied to the question of social mores. The Retracted, even in this area, are very different from the Dilated: they don't follow the customs, the current social mores. Instead of marrying according to tradition, they are happy to marry out of their social class if they wish. In a general sense, their morality is independent: they either obey often rigid moral principles or reject all moral order, living according to their own rules, on the edges of society.

Professionally, the Retracted Type doesn't have the wide range of options available to the Dilated. They lack the expansive spontaneity which enables them to adapt to situations and people. They can't handle several tasks at once or juggle work and pleasure as they can only focus on one thing at a time. Their main occupation has a certain ascetic element, forcing them to eliminate all distraction, which, to a certain degree, is an advantage.

In a later chapter (Chap. VI), I will show the professions they are best suited for, which, as we will see, depends on the specific types of retraction. I am, nevertheless, going to give an overview here.

Retraction is a dynamic process in which the level of activity varies according to the degree of retraction, variations determining different, sometimes opposing, character traits. So, the first level of retraction has a dynamic effect, generating a reaction to the influences of the environment in someone who is of the expansive type. This results in an extroverted Type which I have called the Tonic Dilated Type (a close relative to the Lateral Retracted Type).

However, if the retraction is more pronounced, vitality withdraws in a movement of *internalisation* which is a very important factor psychologically as it determines the formation of the self.

If it is even more pronounced, the forces of conservation supplant the forces of expansion and the facial form *narrows,* indicating that the energy reserves are directed towards the *inner being.*

And the final level is the desiccating retraction, that of the elderly, a sign that reserves have reached their lowest possible level.

Illustration 25. – RICKSHAW

Marked opposing features of dilation and retraction can sometimes create a caricature-like effect. This image of a rickshaw in Saigon is striking due to the contrast between the dilated man, seated comfortably, very satisfied with his situation in life, and the man who is standing, retracted, skeletal, who earns just enough to avoid dying of hunger.

CHAPTER III
ANTAGONISMS AND THE ATTRACTION OF THE COMPLEMENTARY

Morphopsychology draws us immediately into the complexity of character as the antagonism between the forces of expansion and conservation is evident.

Mixed Types are a combination of dilation and retraction and this antagonism is easily managed by establishing a balance between the two conflicting forces. This results in flexible adaptation. On the other hand, in the extreme Types where either retraction or dilation predominates, thoughts, feelings and behaviour are opposing and incompatible. In this sense, I have already shown what is lacking in the Dilated Type: sensitivity, restraint, depth of thought, the interior life, all of which are features of the Retracted. So, the Dilated have characteristics that are missing in the Retracted: good adaptive capabilities, sociability, spontaneity of action, common sense and the ability to express ideas and feelings.

At first sight, you might think that these antagonisms are irreconcilable as the predominant tendency exists exclusively in either the conscience of the Dilated Extrovert or the Retracted Introvert. But the problem is more complex than that. We owe it to Dr. Jung for having shown us that, if the dominant tendency appears to be the sole influence on the subject's behaviour, it is because the opposing tendency, having been relegated to the subconscious, has escaped conscious control; however, this does not minimise its dynamism and influence, even though it is concealed. In the Dilated, the *conscious extroverts*, they have pushed their inner life, their subjectivity and individuality into their subconscious; whereas in the Retracted, the *conscious introverts*, this repression expresses itself in their conscious relationships with things and people.

Illustration 26. – CAPTAIN PORGY

Here we can see the contrast of a Dilated Type, Captain Porgy, leader of the 'Partisans', and a Retracted Type, Dr. Oakenburg, his comrade in-arms, one might say. The novelist Simms describes Porgy as follows: 'His skin was dark and swarthy; his eyes, black, piercing, and quick; his forehead, high, full, and commanding; his nose was aquiline; his chin bold and projecting [...].' He also gives him a very large belly. In contrast, he makes Dr. Oakenburg, described in incisive words by Porgy himself, as 'a skeleton, an inveterate naturalist, with sunken cheeks'. Nothing can demonstrate their differences better than their differing ideas of the good things in life. Paul Dauce has created the scene above, in which Porgy declares, '[...] it is throwing pearl to swine to put a good dish before such a creature as that skeleton, Oakenburg. [...] Only yesterday, we had a nice tit-bit an exquisite morsel only a taste a marsh hen, that I shot myself, and fricasseed after a fashion of my own. I tried my best to persuade the Wretch to try it only to try it and would you believe it, he not only refused, but absolutely, at the moment, drew a bottle of some vile root decoction from his pocket, and just as I was about to enjoy my own little delicacy, he thrust the horrible stuff into his lantern jaws [...].'

Illustration 27. – THE POET AND THE LOUT

This cartoon by W. Bush, a German humourist, recounts the tales of a Retracted poet, found here in the bottom corner of the image, searching for inspiration. Failing, he left for the country to find a more propitious solitude. He believed himself alone in the carriage compartment, when, at the moment of departure, a large, clumsy and unabashed gentleman, as the Dilated often are, arrives and unintentionally disturbs his peace.

To this, Jung adds another vitally important point, which is: should the repressed tendency attempt to make itself heard, as self-censure impedes it, it will try to find a way out through a *mechanism of projection* by acting out on someone who effectively takes the place of the intended subject. Clearly, the greater the similarity between the repressed tendency and the individual chosen to assume it, the easier the projection; that is to say, a Dilated Type will project his introversion onto someone introverted and a Retracted Type will project his extroversion onto an extrovert.

The inner conflict therefore becomes an external conflict which can be resolved in two very different ways. The first is that the antagonism persists and the subject doesn't understand the individual he is projecting onto. This serves to highlight the negative judgments that the Dilated and Retracted have formed about those with opposing characteristics. Literary works, of which I have made numerous references in the preceding chapters, provide us with important examples of pejorative opinions which characterize not only the subject giving the criticism but also the person to whom the criticism is addressed.

The second is that the antagonism resolves itself through mutual attraction. The subject, a Dilated or Retracted Type, is in some way fascinated by his subconscious and this fascination is reflected in the projection onto the other person. We will see that this explains how opposites often become friends or spouses.

I will study these two possibilities in detail.

1 / ANTAGONISMS

Both the Dilated and Retracted express what they don't understand in the critical judgment of their opposites.

The miscomprehensions of the Dilated Type

The Dilated are contented with their life and can't understand the gloomy pessimism of the majority of the Retracted. Colas, in the novel by Romain Rolland, states, '*I see all sorts of useless grumblers around me; they say I have picked out a queer time to shout in, that we are in a sad state now; but no state is sad, there are only dreary people, and I am not one of them, the Lord be praised!*' And talking about his son-in-law Florimond, whose personality is completely different from his own, depicts him thus: '*He is a little man, inclined to stoutness; his broad face is pockmarked, his nose red, and his little eyes dance with cunning. He is always growling and complaining of everything and everybody.*' (1)

In the same way, when Salavin, in the novel by Duhamel, says to his friend Edouard that '*he should start a new life*', Edouard, a good Dilated Type, replies, '*Start a new life? How can one live any life other than his own?*'[1] (Ill. 28)

It is this all-encompassing discontent that drives the Retracted to rebel against the established order. Plutarque tells us that Emperor Julius Caesar

---

1: Unpublished translation.

saw it in the face of the person who would be his assassin, Cassius. I've already spoken about him in Chapter II, Book II, concerning the Retracted personality Type.

We can also see it in the novel by Céline, *Journey to the End of the Night*, where the somewhat crooked but efficient director of a care home, Baryton, criticises his assistant Parapine for his lack of ability to adapt: *'He's a boy who doesn't want to adapt. He is not happy in his work; he isn't even happy in the world… and in that he is wrong, because he is suffering!'*[2] And, evoking his own ability to adapt, he draws a parallel with what, according to him, would be Parapine's reaction should the earth start to rotate in the opposite direction: *'He wouldn't be able to sleep if the earth started to rotate in the opposite direction. He would consider it some kind of unusual injustice … And do you think he would be content just to whine about it? That wouldn't be the worst of it. No! He would try to find some way to make the earth jump … just for revenge!'* (3) (Ill. 29).

The extroverted can't understand the introverted when it comes to the expression of feelings. The Dilated, who are expansive, are often theatrical in their expressiveness and can't accept the reserve and restraint of the Retracted, happily concluding that they are insensitive. When Thérèse Desqueyroux loses a much-loved aunt, her entourage, who was hostile towards her, comment on her guarded face, saying, *'Have you noticed? She doesn't even pretend to mourn!'* (4)

In a similar example, Numa, from Daudet's work, is unsettled by his father-in-law, a severe State Counsel by whom he feels judged, and the novelist speaks of *'the timid chill which the Southerner felt in the presence of this tall, silent man with a pale, haughty face, whose blue-gray eyes were Rosalie's eyes without her tenderness and indulgence, and looked freezingly down on his enthusiasm. Numa, who was wavering and fickle in character, and profuse in words, at once ardent and confused, rebelled against the logic, uprightness, and stem character of his father-in-law […].'*

Numa has the same uncomprehending reaction when his wife surprises him in flagrante delicto with another man; *'the pale face of his wife marked with an expression of renunciation, the chagrin repressed between clinched teeth and smothered sobs, rent his heart. They were very unlike his own manifestations, and the coarse sensibility which he showed on the surface.'* (Ill. 32)

2:: Unpubl. trans.

Illustration 28. – SALAVIN

Salavin, a Retracted Type characterized by atony and helplessness, is a familiar character in the work of Georges Duhamel, who describes him at length: *'the drooping shoulders, stooped, the arms a little too long, a face lost in shadow, hollow cheeks, thin mouth'*, which Pazzi has faithfully reproduced here. On the opposite side is his friend Edouard, who is described as having *'a good round figure, full and generous cheeks, a broad forehead, well-built, an aquiline nose, thick but not heavy'*.[3]

Illustration 29. – BARYTON AND PARAPINE

The typical opposites of Baryton, the director of a care home, a good businessman, optimistic, with *joie de vivre*, and his assistant Parapine, an anxious character, always rebellious. They have been drawn by Pazzi, the first as a Tonic Dilated Type (if not a little overweight) and the second as Retracted.

3: Unpubl. trans.

The Dilated are those who make emotional connections and are family men, unable to understand the need of the Retracted to live an independent life. We have seen in Chapter II how the mother of a family in the novel by Manzoni, *The Engaged Couple,* Dona Prassede, acts as protector of her family, meddling in their business, wanting to help but not understanding why the others want their independence more than anything. Independence doesn't interest her in the slightest as she is only happy in company.

In the intellectual domain, the Dilated are intuitive, often grasping ideas straight away, and think that the Retracted complicate everything. As Edouard says in regards to Salavin, *'There are those who have to reason at length before understanding the evidence.'* In the moral domain, we have seen that the Dilated are opportunists and lack firm rules of conduct. When Parapine believes he has cut his patron Baryton to the quick by accusing him of *'lacking ethics'*, Baryton replies *'that one doesn't anger over such a small thing'*[4] (3). In the same way, Numa, the opportunist, is prepared to betray the legitimist cause that he has been committed to up to that point in order to position himself in the new political regime. He doesn't understand his wife's criticism, who believes that one should always keep their promises. However, he will end up conceding to her, which will later confer a solid reputation of loyalty onto this fickle character.

The miscomprehensions of the Retracted

The Retracted also have their miscomprehensions about the Dilated, and more frequently, as their nature tends toward the critical. They are convinced that the benevolence and cordiality of the Dilated is worthless, given that they are superficial and will talk to anyone, no matter whom. They will cite the refrain 'many friends, few friendships'.

Daudet often represents men from the South of France in his work as he knows them well, hailing from there himself. His characters Numa and Tartarin, however, take sides with those who criticise the retracted, such as himself. Notably, as regards to Numa, he talks of *'this verbose race, all on the surface, superficial'*. And when this same Numa, who tends to make

---

4: Unpubl. trans.

promises that he has no intention of keeping, says, in the guise of the excuse that '*Words are all relative*', his wife, with the fastidious character of the Retracted, objects with '*Words, nevertheless, do mean something.*'[5]

Considering the Retracted's fear of contact, they consider the Dilated vulgar for their need to have a close rapport with beings and objects, their need to smell, to touch. There is a famous example from the playwright Schiller, who, despite his friendship with the illustrious Goethe, couldn't stop himself from expressing the differences in their temperaments, saying of his friend '*He touches too much*',[6] which succinctly defines both the Retracted Schiller and the Dilated Goethe (Ill. 30)

Illustration 30. – SCHILLER AND GOETHE

Schiller says of his great friend Goethe, 'He touches too much', a statement which encapsulates the contrast between the Retracted and the Dilated. Schiller is retracted, has a long face and a pronounced lateral-nasal retraction (see Chap. VII). Goethe, on the other hand, is Dilated, notably differentiated, however, by a combination of lateral retraction and frontal retraction, with very refined receptors and expansion in the cerebral zone.

5: Unpubl. trans.
6: Unpubl. trans.

When it comes to feelings, the Retracted are introverts as their inner life is more important than external events. We have already seen that they are often revolutionaries but it's necessary to understand the sense of the word: for extroverts, a revolution means to change the order of the world, particularly the social order. For introverts, revolution must start from the inside. Jacques in *The Thibaults* explains it well: '*To be a revolutionary, what is it if not, above all, an attitude that comes from the interior of the individual? Is it not having made a personal, internal revolution first?*'[7]

And this other Retracted character, Duhamel's Salavin, echoes the sentiment in *Le Club des Lyonnais*, during a meeting presided over by a supporter of revolution. Above all concerned about political efficacy, Salavin objects that changing the world is useless if one, Salavin, doesn't change himself. And asked by the other: '*Why do you want to change?*', Salavin responds: '*Because I'm a coward!*'[8]

Neither can the Retracted understand the close family solidarity of the Dilated. They don't exist as much as individuals, but more as part of a community. When Thérèse Desqueyroux is going to have a baby, her husband, the Dilated Bernard, puts the family ahead: '*He respectfully contemplated the woman who carried within her belly the source of innumerable offspring.*' And Thérèse, suffering from the impact of those words: '*I lost all sense of my individual existence; I was but a vessel in the eyes of the family; the fruit of my body was the only thing that mattered*'.[9] (Ill. 31)

The passionate Retracted Type doesn't understand or approve of the tepid conformism of the Dilated, this conformism from which they refuse to deviate, no matter the temptation. In the novel by Manzoni, Cardinal Federigo exhibits a hot and impetuous temperament from a very young age, encouraged by a zealous revolutionary of which his teachers were very critical. Complaining of their attitude, he says of them, '*[They are] cautious men, for whom extreme virtue is as bad as vice, unceasingly preaching that perfection is the balance between two excesses.*'[10] And in the opposite sense, Don Abbondio, another character in this novel–a placid Dilated Type with safety as his principal preoccupation–protests loudly when the

7: Unpubl. trans.
8: Unpubl. trans.
9: Unpubl. trans.
10: Unpubl. trans.

Cardinal attempts to give him a mission that carries a certain danger with it: *'Isn't it surprising that both saints and scoundrels have quicksilver in their veins, that they are not happy to struggle, to torment themselves, but that they want, if they can, to have all humanity join in? Isn't it inevitable that the most spirited always find me to get me involved in their affairs? Me, who would like nothing other than to live in peace?'*[11]

We have seen above that the Dilated criticise the Retracted for their superfluous logical reasoning. In return, the Retracted criticise the Dilated's need to base their arguments on facts and precise data. And so Salavin, enjoying the company of a friend who is positive by nature, saying to him, *'I'm searching'*, and at his companion's query, *'What are you searching for?'*, responds, irritated, *'Ah, you have a taste for detail. You think that I am searching for something or someone? I search in the absolute sense of the word'.*[12] (5)

I also remember a conversation between a reporter and a judge, a Dilated and a Retracted Type, as different from one another as could possibly be. The first, a great lover of all kinds of things, as he should be, manifesting a lively interest in the profession of the judge, whose daily life is immersed in peripatetic drama, listens with disappointment to the judge's response: *'Facts! Always facts! No! See, I wasn't made to be an examining judge; I would have preferred to have been a tribunal judge.'* His face clears suddenly: *'Give me'*, he says, *'a point of law!'*

I would add that the natural tendency of the Retracted to worry means they lose themselves in the depths of their problems in an attempt at unearthing the unknown. This is very annoying for the systematic optimism of the Dilated who are content with what is already known without querying it. This is clearly demonstrated in the contrasting characteristics of the Thibault brothers in the novel by Martin du Gard: Jacques, Retracted, reproaches his brother Antoine, a Dilated Type, *'of having such consummate intelligence that he has found his fulfilment in the field of scientific studies, and even worse, an intelligence that strips things of their secret value.'* And, he could only admit that Antoine *'had developed a philosophy of life based on the sole notion of activity and was content with that.'*

11: Unpubl. trans.
12: Unpubl. trans.

We must also highlight the influence of these antagonisms on married couples which, in taking of opposing stances in the most anodyne of problems, can derail a good marriage. One particularly common case resides in the different kinds of reaction to the same event. For example, a Dilated man comes home in the evening, discusses the events of his day with his wife and, as a good extrovert, now worry-free, is ready for a good night's sleep. However, his wife, Retracted, sharing his worries, as a good introvert, will continue to reflect on them to the point of keeping her awake all night.

2 / THE MUTUAL ATTRACTION OF THE COMPLEMENTARY

A popular expression says, '*Extremes meet.*' It would be more judicious to say that '*Opposites attract*', substituting the static viewpoint for the dynamic.

We have often observed friends or spouses that are together despite their opposing morphopsychological types. This will now seem less strange after the explanation, inspired by Jung, that I gave at the beginning. I will reiterate it here: the repressed tendency works from the subconscious on the conscious in a dual action: it both *confuses* and *fascinates*. When one projects, these antagonistic personalities, such as the couples that I have mentioned, are attracted to one another by the same fascination that each one draws upon from their own subconscious.

But attraction does not mean agreement. While the foundation of the couple is based on the attraction of their subconscious minds, it should be noted that, consciously, the antagonisms persist and are at the origin of their conflicts, which will inevitably lead to their breakup. One can easily see that the breakup will most often come from the Retracted. He is hypersensitive, thus more vulnerable to hostile tension, more sensitive and likely to rebel against the demands of the Dilated partner.

Pairs of friends– The friends in the novel *Two Men*, by Duhamel is an excellent example. Edouard, as we have seen, is a Dilated Type, comfortable in his own skin and a happily married husband and father. He enjoys his work, but nevertheless something is missing. One day, he sees something in the eyes of Louis Salavin, an introversion which strikes him and he proceeds to seek out his friendship. This projection also touches Salavin, as Edouard's character represents his own suppressed expansion. But discord soon arises as Edouard, in his desire to become closer to his friend, wishes to share his wealth, as he is rich and his friend is poor. Salavin cannot accept, fiercely independent as he is, to the point of accusing his friend of defiling his self, this honestly miserable self, but to which he was so attached (Ill. 29).

Illustration 31. – THÉRÈSE AND BERNARD DESQUEYROUX

In his novel, François Mauriac describes the heroine as a typical Retracted Type. Pazzi has drawn her here, inspired by the description in the novel: sunken cheeks, high cheekbones, parted lips and a superb broad forehead. On the other hand, her husband Bernard is Dilated, which the author describes with some scorn as a somewhat overweight young man who 'immediately after his first gulps, he would start to become too red […].'

Married couples – Here we have two important examples: the Numa-Rosalie couple in *Numa Roumestan* by Daudet (Ill. 32) and the Thérèse-Bernard couple in the novel *Thérèse Desqueyroux*, by Mauriac (Ill. 31). These two couples have the particularity of associating a Retracted woman with a Dilated man and, this being the case, the natural sensitivity of the woman is heightened by her retraction, which makes the relationship with a Dilated man particularly difficult, especially in the sexual arena, as we have seen. Nevertheless, the relationship works at first due to the attraction of opposites, neither aware of the reasons behind it. Both Rosalie and Thérèse try to explain what led them to get married but can't figure it out. However, we could explain it to them through deep psychological analysis.

Illustration 32. – NUMA AND ROSALIE ROUMESTAN

The hero of the novel by Alphonse Daudet, Numa, is Dilated and his wife Retracted which is the source of conflict. Paul Dance, in drawing the figure, took inspiration from the novelist, who describes '*his heavy, restless profile, very stout on account of a sedentary profession, the curve of his broad shoulders, his large face always excited, joyous and noisy, with a bright color in his cheeks, with handsome, golden-brown, and prominent batrachian eyes, and with black frizzly hair like a visorless felt cap concealing half of his forehead.*' Completely the opposite, Rosalie (drawn by Pazzi) has '*a regular face, pale complexion, with well-defined lines, calm eyes, and a color changing as a stream whose source is deep.*'

CHAPTER IV
THE UNIVERSE OF THE DILATED

As a general overview to the subject, in Chapter II I gave a somewhat schematic description of the Dilated Type. In reality, this model should be based on the analysis of the personalities of everyone of this type. We can appreciate just how diverse the universe of the Dilated is by applying both the laws of morphopsychology and our intuition.

The most important differentiation to consider is the degree of tonicity: it demonstrates an opposition between *Tonic Dilated* and *Atonic Dilated*, which will still be, to a certain extent, schematic but in comparison to my description in Chapter II, much closer to reality. We will demonstrate it by describing the careers that each member of these two opposing groups are best suited to, as well as some examples of well-known people.

1 / THE TONIC DILATED (Ill. 33 and 34)

The greater the tonicity, the more the dilated face transforms. It maintains its large frame and open receptors but the shape is modified, the roundness of dilation replaced by planes, making the flesh firm.

In detail, the firmness of the frame, more bone and muscle than fat, is marked by the prominence of the cheeks and angles of the jaw, as well as the flattening of the dilated curve at the temples and the front of the forehead. The receptors are firmer too: the mouth is less fleshy, the nostrils are less heavy, and vibrate more, the eyes are slightly oblique in shape, raised at the outer corners and with a more intense expression. The skin and hair are coarser. The Tonic Dilated are 'hot-blooded', endowed with an abundance of blood that colours and warms the skin.

Illustration 33. – I. THE TONIC DILATED

These two images clearly demonstrate the Tonic Dilated: the man's face is heavier, while the woman's is more refined and tonic. We could say that the first portrait is of a Tonic Dilated who has thickened with age, while the young lady has a very firm frame in the dilated face which accentuates the intensity of expression in all three zones.

Psychologically speaking, tonicity means activity. Receptivity gives way to activity, where all vital tendencies become dynamic. This increase in tone represents the beginning of retraction in the Dilated due to the impact of the environment. This in turn awakens the defence mechanism, which requires an active response, resulting in the rejection of external influences. I would add that this first degree of retraction does not diminish the impetus for expansion in any way; on the contrary, it makes it more dynamic.

Body language

The Tonic Dilated stand very straight, sometimes rigidly proud. Their walk is rapid and decisive and their step firm. They are always on their feet, preferring it to being seated, even for relaxing tasks such as writing. They gesticulate a great deal and shake hands warmly, even crushingly. They are quick at whatever they do. They are noisy, tending to slam doors. They will bump into people and are quite inconsiderate in their relationships. They speak loudly and powerfully with a tendency to rant. They will happily sing while working. In their conversations, they can't be bothered to construct long sentences but express themselves in short sentences: a subject, a verb and, if necessary, a complement. They write like they speak, briefly and forcefully, in the style of a popular newspaper. In fact, many of this type are to be found running popular newspapers. There is a great similarity in Danton's address to the armies of the Revolution, '*Audacity, more audacity and always audacity*', and the title of the journal, *J'accuse*, in which Clemenceau intended to summarise the courageous intervention of Zola in the famous Dreyfus affair.

Illustration 33. – II. TONIC DILATED MEN

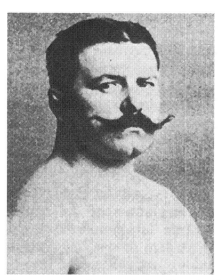 

Above are images of two men, both with broad and heavy faces and firmness in the flesh, indicating good tonicity. The first is Jules Rosset, a champion weightlifter, who has a harmonious face with a well-defined broad forehead which helps us to understand why, after his sporting career, he became a businessman. The second is a composition by Pazzi depicting Colas Breugnon, a character from the novel by Romain Rolland who we have already mentioned.

Instincts

The Tonic Dilated have the same instincts as the Dilated Type, but are passionate in a way that makes them dynamic and impulsive, although lacking the ability to maintain their impulses for long periods of time.

They have a vigorous constitution with excellent blood circulation and are not afraid of harsh weather, fresh air, strong winds or cold (and they will happily wash in cold water).

Their fiery temperament fits in well in a lively, noisy environment. They love crowds, public meetings, the hustle and bustle of the street and stormy winds. Daudet's Numa is of this type; when his sister-in-law, also a passionate extrovert, talking frankly about Rosalie, describes her strong dislike of the wind, saying that it scatters her ideas and stops her from thinking, her sister-in-law claims that she finds the wind to be exalting and intoxicating, leading Numa to cry out in agreement.

There are strong elements of aggressiveness and sensuality in the Tonic Dilated which are expressed impulsively. They don't have much self-control in these areas.

They have a well-developed instinct for action and make the most of their vitality; they are great workers, pioneers and men of conquest, made for combat, not for patient action.

Emotional life

Their feelings are strong and ardent, but short-lived. They are more passionate than tender.

As family men, they are kind and generous but they want everyone to share in their need for movement and action. They will lose their temper with any of their children who may have a tendency towards laziness or dreaminess. For them, laziness is the mother of all vices.

As men of society, they don't always have the qualities of moderation and kindness of the average Dilated as their cordiality is strongly affected by their need to manipulate people, demonstrating their authority over others in a somewhat brutal fashion.

Nothing shows the influence of tonicity on character better than the opposing characteristics of tonic and atonic subjects. In a short novel,[1] I described the woman seen here as a vigorous and combative saleswoman. She is married to a man who is also a good salesman, but who is a bit more atonic, making him more placid, measured, and who, humorously, paints a picture of their compatibility by how their car is driven (she is the driver of course!), saying: '*Adèle has her foot on the accelerator and I have mine on the brake!*' (Ill. 34).

Illustration 34. – TONIC DILATED WOMEN

These two portraits, drawn by Pazzi, represent the two feminine types that I have labelled the 'Sanguine Type' and the 'Phlegmatic Type', borrowing from the work of Le Senne. You can see that in a similarly dilated frame and very tonic shape, one has open receptors which confers on her the ability to adapt to the world (the first type) while the other has sheltered receptors, indicating a greater concentration of energy that aids in the selection of their aims in life (the second type).

In Vildrac's work, *Le Paquebot Tenacity*, are two opposing characters: Bastien, of the Tonic Dilated type, and Segard, who is a weak, indecisive dreamer. The day after the war, the two companions decide to improve

---

1: 'Portraits of Women' from the second volume of the *Manual de morphopsychologie*, Ed. Stock; reproduced in my work *Caractérologie et morphopsychologie*, PUF, 1983.

their circumstances by immigrating to Canada. Who has made the decision? That's too easy; Bastien makes it on his own and Segard accepts it passively. With their journey delayed, each one reacts differently: Bastien hops about with impatience, while Segard hangs about. When they meet a young woman they both like, Segard puts things off and contents himself with dreams of his love, while Bastien leaps into action, seduces the young woman and leaves with her without the slightest hesitation (20).

Intelligence

Essentially, the Tonic Dilated are the same as the Dilated already described, that is to say, down-to-earth, sensorial, pragmatic and in general open to all areas of practical life: commerce, industry, technical work. They have few big ideas but tonicity has the dual effect of making those ideas clear, well-formulated and immediately able to be put into practice without further reflection. They are therefore very good at improvisation, letting their intuition guide them and without planning ahead. They are only interested in the present and the immediate future in the sense of whatever it takes to ensure that any action is efficient. They don't like looking backwards, towards tradition, and they are not suitable for working on long-term projects either. They are unimaginative and are not at all open to abstract ideas, theories or systems, nor introspection.

Will

Their *will to take action* is intense and impetuous. No sooner said than done, they are tireless men of action, assisted by their robust temperament. However, they lack persistence and perseverance.

Self-control is not one of their strengths. They are very impulsive, finding it difficult to hold back their instinctive urges, and are subject to fits of anger to the point of blind rage. Their defect is the inability to resist the need to take action; they are addicted to action, lacking restraint and patience.

Professions – The Tonic Dilated are happy wherever they are needed and adapt easily to different social situations. They are spontaneous and decisive.

They are suited for manual work where strength and speed is needed but not so apt for work that requires patience. In sports, they prefer intense activities such as races (100 or 200 metres), weightlifting, shotput and discus, or team sports such as rugby, and nautical sports.

In commerce or industry, they are successful due to their business sense and their dynamism, particularly when required to innovate and forge ahead. They are seen in all kinds of positions, from street peddlers (because they are down-to-earth), to the highest positions including chief executive.

As a profession, they will always be practitioners, consumed by their need for action. For this reason, they tend to be happier as surgeons than as doctors, lawyers rather than counsellors or magistrates.

In art, they are realists, inspired by the beings and objects around them. They enjoy working with colours and painting nature. They are not really musicians but are talented singers, and can be found particularly amongst the singers that are called 'realists', who have a talent for moving and energizing their audience.

As writers, they are excellent, particularly in social dramas and action novels, rich in tales, where facts take centre stage and where there is no reference to the psychology of the characters. Having their feet firmly on the ground makes them born storytellers.

Their temperament in politics is along the lines of the general populace, as we have seen–quick to lash out and in the improvisation of their responses and actions–but they are hardly ever found among those who govern with authority such as men of State.

2 / THE ATONIC DILATED (Ill. 35 and 36)

The Atonic Dilated are completely the opposite of the Tonic Dilated.

Morphologically, their body is soft, their muscles flaccid, their joints are loose and their excess weight is flabby which creates a roundness that lacks firmness. Both their circulation and blood flow are poor, which is evident by their pale and permanently frigid extremities, particularly the hands. Their face has a dilated frame and the receptors are open which classifies them as Dilated. But there ends the resemblance with the Dilated Type previously described. The shape of the face is soft due to the sagging of the skin (jowls, double chin, bags under the eyes). The receptors also lack tone: the mouth has soft and pale lips, always slightly open due to the lack of tone; and the nose is fleshy with heavy nostrils that barely vibrate. The eyes are round and angled à la Greuze, framed by sagging eyelids (the top as well as underneath), and the expression completely lacking in radiance.

Psychologically, the general expression on this face is passive and apathetic, like someone half asleep. It betrays the lack of tone and provides us with an indication of the general levels of vitality. The Atonic Dilated need to be in a protected environment, which is limited to a small circle: mother, family, home–where they feel safe, as we shall see.

Body language

Atony is visible in their body posture, gait, gestures, voice and expression. The Atonic Dilated's posture is poor; standing is tiring, and they are always looking for somewhere to sit down. The hero of the novel by Marcel Aymé, Brûlebois, fired from his position as a civil servant for being slack at his job, doesn't even try to find another job, and it is said, *'horrified at the thought of being fatigued, he has tried to remain seated as much as possible during his lifetime, and has found that elbows on the table is by far the best position'.*[2] (16) (Ill. 36)

Their gait is nonchalant; they drag their feet and, when in a group, they are always last. They hate long walks. Kipling imagined, in one of his tales, a fat boy in a boy scout group who turned out to be unfit for any of the camp activities. In desperation, they relegate him to the stew pots as he had a certain appreciation of the aroma of whatever was cooking and liked tasting the dishes. They attribute this phrase to him, one which is appropriate for an Atonic Dilated: *'The very worst use you can make of your feet is walkin' on 'em!'*

2: Unpublished translation.

Illustration 35. – ATONIC DILATED

The Atonic Dilated have the same frame as the Tonic Dilated but the shape is soft, the receptors sagging and the expression in the eyes is passive, sleepy. Portraits 1 and 2 are typical examples. Number 3 was drawn by Dauce to represent the priest of Tours from the novel by Balzac and it is barely a caricature. Number 4 was also drawn by Dauce to represent Daudet's Tartarin, an extrovert who is much stronger in his imagination and discourse than in action.

Illustration 36. – I. ATONIC DILATED CHARACTERS

Here is Sancho Panza, Don Quixote's squire, represented here by Gustave Doré, a touch exaggerated. Completely the opposite of his master who deprives himself of food and sleep in order to pursue his noble adventures, Sancho's principal concern is to eat well and sleep well. In contrast to the knight's flamboyant spirit, he opposes both his good sense and need for security.

Their gestures are slow and lack confidence. They tend to drop things and are quite rightly called clumsy. Their voice is weak, often drowned out, unable to shout an order or to sing. Their expression lacks intensity: it is vague, like someone half asleep, and they have trouble paying attention for any length of time.

Their clothing is generally very informal. They prefer the comfort of oversized clothes and they are not particularly conscientious about personal cleanliness, nor that of their home.

Illustration 36. – II. ATONIC DILATED CHARACTERS

Here is Brûlebois, hero of the novel by Marcel Aymé. He is anything but heroic, this 'hero'. He is happiest, like Sancho, when he is idle and has a bottle in his hand. He is a good-natured soul.

Instincts

The lack of tone makes them instinctively passive. Their dominant instinct is the *instinct of nutrition* and they have stayed in the passive oral stage of the suckling infant. They are gluttons and big drinkers, always in the process of digesting something. As they have barely passed the oral stage, their sexual evolution is incomplete. At the slightest problem, they regress back to the oral phase which takes the place of sexuality. The Atonic Dilated are barely attracted to the opposite sex and usually don't marry. Marcel Aymé's Brûlebois is a typical example. The novelist says of him, *'the call of the flesh hasn't tormented him for a long time; he has been too busy with his bottles'*.[3] (Ill. 36-II)

3: Unpubl. trans.

In the same way, the *aggressive instinct* is very weak and superseded by the need for security. Sancho, the potbellied squire of the adventurous Don Quixote, enjoys, above all, a good meal and a good night's sleep and disapproves of his master's aggressive undertakings. When reproached for his cowardice, he responds, *'Señor, to retire is not to flee, and there is no wisdom in waiting when danger outweighs hope.'* So, when he finds himself face to face with the esquire of a gentleman that Don Quixote had challenged to a duel, notwithstanding the custom that the esquires, in parallel, confront each other, he says to the other, *'I can tell you, señor, I am not going to fight; let our masters fight, that's their lookout, and let us drink and live; for time will take care to ease us of our lives'.* (Ill. 36-I)

Manzoni, the Italian novelist, presents us with a character of this type from his book, a priest called Don Abbondio, explaining, *'By keeping aloof from the overbearing, by affecting not to notice their acts of violence, by bowing low and with the most profound respect to all whom he met, the poor man had succeeded in passing over sixty years without encountering any violent storms.'*

Emotional life

The emotions of the Atonic Dilated are also affected by this same passivity. It's true, they are not without their own qualities. They have passive virtues: they are good-natured, gentle, tender and patient. They don't make much noise and never argue.

But their social adaptation is limited, as we have seen, to a small circle of protection where they wish, above all, to find security. Balzac in *The Celibates*, provides us with a remarkable example of an Atonic Dilated in the personality of Abbot Birotteau, saying that he *'was all expansion, all frankness; he loved good things and was amused by trifles with the simplicity of a man who knew no spite or malice'*, but that he *'had no experience whatever of the world and its ways [...]; and must be regarded as a great child, to whom most of the practices of social life were utterly unknown.'* (Ill. 35)

I have said that their emotions are fragile. They themselves fear any experience that forces them to come out of themselves and engage in life. Of this same abbot, Balzac says he lives *'a colorless barren life in which strong feelings were misfortunes, and the absence of emotion happiness.'* (Ill. 35)

The Atonic Dilated are completely absent of ambition. They enjoy, above all, their creature comforts and hate stress.

Intelligence

Intelligence in the Atonic Dilated is typically like that of young children, characterised by malleability, ease of assimilation and a memory that records everything. It is worth noting that they take in the world on a subconscious level, without reflexion or choice. The imagination is vast and full of fantasies but they remain in this dream state, due to the fact that their atony prevents them from putting them into action. We have seen that a feature of good tonicity is that it ensures that ideas are formed with clarity and can be translated into action; here both things are lacking.

Will

The *will to take action* is profoundly deficient in the Atonic Dilated. They are born lazy, incapable of anything other than a routine job, done at a slow pace, tiring quickly whenever faced with any difficulties. Things go steadily downhill for them and, little by little, they may reach the point of becoming tramps.

Because of their lack of activity, they tend to go for the easy solution and, morally speaking, their actions may verge on fraud.

They have poor *self-control* and, although their instinctive urges are weaker than the average Dilated, they tend to let themselves be seduced by gluttony or their sensuality. Above, I introduced Daudet's Numa as a Tonic Dilated Type; but, in moments of tiredness or at critical times in his life, his tonicity suddenly lessens and, without any reduction in his instincts, his ability to control them decreases. The novelist writes about him, '[…] *his face showed lassitude, betraying in the corner of his mouth and eyes a nature at once weak and violent, with all the passions and nothing to resist them.*'

I would like to underline that in the cerebral zone (a uniformly round forehead, round and drooping eyes), atony indicates weak self-awareness and therefore a lack of self-control. When this is very pronounced, an overdose of instincts may occur: a lack of structure in life, lack of rest, abuse of all sorts, alcohol, drugs and their life itself could be in danger. The possibility of this happening is most likely when there is a combination of this atonic cerebral structure with elements of tonicity in other zones (for example, a strong jaw), indicating powerful urges.

Professionally, the range of possibilities for the Atonic Dilated is limited by the lack of tone. They would prefer a sedentary position, without any intense activity whatsoever, and no responsibility; in a word, subordinate posts.

They are not strong enough, nor adept enough for manual work. Standing or walking makes them tired, as we have seen. If necessary, with training, they can acquire certain abilities for repetitive tasks.

In commerce and industry, they are only suitable for work as maintenance workers and guards.

As they have an ability for intellectual assimilation, they are suitable for certain professions, for example, teaching, where their calmness, patience and deliberateness can, up to a certain point, compensate for their lack of dynamism.

They have no aptitude for the sciences. However, they would have artistic talents if they knew how to use them. We should, therefore, remember that when the atony is not generalised, but rather compensated by better tone in other parts of the face, they could be talented actors or singers.

They have no aptitude for management; they are made for subordinate positions. However, where the atony is partial and the morphology in other parts of the face is tonic, it can bring moderation and prudence to the dynamism of the original type and turn into a positive attribute. We see it, for example, in certain heads of industry (see Chapter VIII, Bk. II).

CHAPTER V
THE UNIVERSE OF THE RETRACTED

In the morphopsychological analysis of the different types of retraction, it is also important to take tonicity into account (Ill. 37).

There really isn't a strict dividing line between the dilated and retracted types. Where there is movement, and harmful elements in the environment are rejected, this always results in a movement towards retraction. The planes on the face of the tonic dilated, as we have just described, indicate this very early stage of retraction and, as we will see, is very close to the type I call the *Lateral Retracted Type*, the retraction having a dynamic effect on both which promotes extroversion (Ill. 38 to 40).

The true dividing line lies between the extroverted and introverted types, which is the result of a much more pronounced retraction. I call this the *interiorising retraction* (Ill. 41 to 43).

This cutoff point is very clearly defined, both from the morphological and psychological points of view. Here we enter a new area, where the qualities associated with character and intelligence are more mature, preparing us for more complex personalities.

A *second cutoff point* can be found where the retraction is more advanced. In the interiorising retraction, there is a balance between the different forces of expansion and retraction which is reflected in the differing reliefs and indents in the shape of the face. It is demonstrated psychologically by the harmonious alliance between extroversion and introversion, adaptation and individuality.

But, if the forces of retraction dominate, leaving the forces of expansion very little room, individuality takes priority over the ability for adaptation. This translates morphologically into a significant reduction in the reliefs of the facial shape which become flattened. This is *extreme retraction*, which is expressed in two different types of facial shapes depending on the degree of tonicity. When atony takes the place of tonicity, there is a significant reduction in expansion, expressed by the complete suppression of the previously dominant reliefs and indents of the face. There is sagging rather than indents, marked by soft pleats, which is a sign of a lack of tone. As in the Dilated, we can have two opposing extremes–the Tonic Retracted and Atonic Retracted Types–but, here, the complexities of the combinations of dilation and retraction force us to introduce additional set points between the two extremes.

THE TONIC RETRACTED TYPE

We have just seen that we can distinguish between three principal variants of the Tonic Retracted Type based on the degree of retraction: *lateral retraction, frontal retraction* and *extreme retraction* (in its first variant).

1 / THE LATERAL RETRACTED TYPE (Ill. 38-39-40)

Due to tonicity in the facial shape and open receptors, the Lateral Retracted Type is similar to the Tonic Dilated Type in that they have in common the dynamic characteristics of retraction and are both extroverts. However, the Lateral Retracted Type differs from the Tonic Dilated Type in that they are more dynamic and they are essentially men of action.

During childhood development, they are more advanced than the oral stage of the Dilated: the stage of the adult child and adolescent. There are some children, boys or girls, whose lateral retraction develops very early and imprints its dominant tendency on their character. They learn to walk and run early; they can't sit still for a minute; the boundaries of the house are too small for them; they need a garden or, even better, as Dickens wrote, *'the key of the street'*. Outside they're like dogs, running everywhere. They hate quiet games. At school, they are unlikely to be good students as they hate the long hours of immobility and will often play truant. But, in their everyday lives, they prove to be resourceful at an early age: during school breaks they play the role of teacher or group manager, and they take first prize in gymnastics.

Illustration 37. – THE THREE TYPES OF RETRACTION

These portraits of women represent the three degrees of retraction: dynamic (lateral retraction), frontal and extreme retraction (see text).

Morphologically, retraction lengthens the body due to the development of the locomotive apparatus: the arms and the legs. In addition, in order to ensure that there is sufficient energy for activity, the heart and the lungs, producers of oxygen-rich blood, also develop, resulting in a lengthening of the thorax. They tend to be thin, particularly in adolescence.

This evolution is made evident in the face by its lengthening which, it should be underlined, remains moderate as tonicity belongs to short facial shapes. (Long facial shapes are always a sign of atony.) The facial shape also has more accentuated planes than those of the Tonic Dilated. When seen face on, it has a rectangular shape, but the development of the respiratory zone results in more prominent cheekbones, usually transforming the rectangle into a hexagon. The receptors are open, like the Dilated, with the particularity of belonging to the projecting part of the face, where the characteristic profile has the two lower zones protruding out while the forehead is clearly sloping backwards. This structure evokes an animal's muzzle, a dog or horse for example, and we will see that the psychology of the Lateral Retracted is similar in a number of areas to that of the animal species.

Psychologically, tonic retraction, along with open receptors, preconditions the very active responses to the demands of the environment which results in the key characteristic of the Lateral Retracted: *the need for movement.*

This is where they are different from the Tonic Dilated. First, they are more selective: while the Dilated are well adapted to a social life, well integrated in groups and are family men, the Retracted only have relationships within select groups, rather than in the company of big groups or at large events. The Retracted choose to keep the company of friends who share the same interests as them in adventure, travel, hunting and sport.

Second, their emotions are predominant which makes them passionate, even more so than the Tonic Dilated, and their actions more intense.

Third, their need for action differentiates them from the Dilated; they act on the environment they find themselves in, they travel a lot and, if they are somewhere that doesn't appeal to them, they will go and look for somewhere better.

Illustration 38. – LATERAL RETRACTION

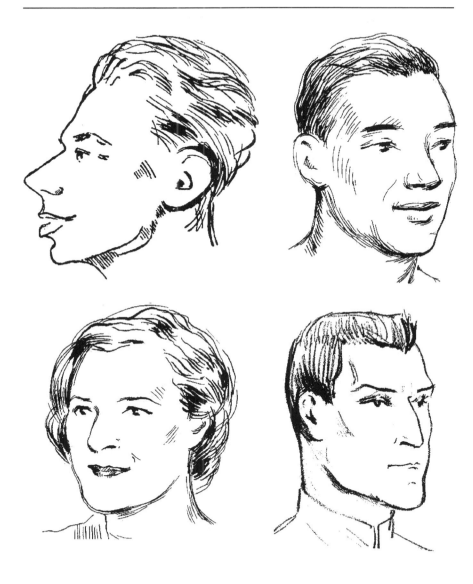

What these portraits have in common is the length, tonicity of the frame and sloping lines of the profile. These are the main characteristics of lateral retraction.

Illustration 39. – I. LATERAL RETRACTED TYPE PERSONALITIES

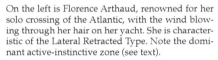

On the left is Florence Arthaud, renowned for her solo crossing of the Atlantic, with the wind blowing through her hair on her yacht. She is characteristic of the Lateral Retracted Type. Note the dominant active-instinctive zone (see text).

On the right is the American novelist Virginia Andrews with characteristics that contrast with those of Florence Arthaud. The cerebral zone is the predominant zone in this case, emphasised by a retraction of the eyes which transforms the dynamism of the Lateral Retracted into that of reflection and writing.

This irrepressible need for movement and constant need for action makes its mark on all areas of their life.

When it comes to their *physical life*, they don't know the meaning of rest. They are never seen sitting down and never stay in one place for more than a minute. As men of perpetual motion, they can't stand enclosed spaces: home, offices, museums or libraries. Finding themselves in prison would be intolerable and result in repeated attempts at escape, the kind of exploits which make history. They need large, open spaces, fresh air and nature and they undoubtedly identify with wild animals: they hate the thought of being in enclosed spaces.

They are great travellers: explorers, missionaries, sea, forest or mountain adventurers. They are quick to act. They enjoy speed: horses, cars and planes. They are smart but not apt for tasks that involve sitting down and that require calmness and patience.

Illustration 39. – II. LATERAL RETRACTED TYPE PERSONALITIES

Common in sportsmen, lateral retraction is particularly evident in the champion cyclist Merckz and in the champion boxer Georges Carpentier. Kaiser, founder of the *'Terre des hommes'* movement, has a significant cerebral expansion which confers on him a sense of idealism.

Illustration 40. –LATERAL RETRACTED TYPE PERSONALITIES

Lateral retraction is a dynamic process that can be found in all areas of human activity. A good example of the characteristic profile can be found in the great singer, Maria Callas, on the left, one of the most beautiful voices in the world. And another, as evidenced by the length of the frame and open receptors, is the filmmaker Walt Disney, who became famous for transforming fairy tales into animated film.

Body language

Their gait is alert, decisive and lighter than the Dilated Type. They take great strides when walking, often giving the impression that they are running. This is their eternal need to advance towards the future. They never sit down and if you want to interview them, you have to walk with them or catch them between flights.

They stand erect, their gaze straight ahead. Their gestures are sweeping and confident, their handshake vigorous and their voice strong. They dress well, albeit somewhat informal, preferring clothes that are not restrictive (sports apparel, for example). They like to be seen and wear bright colours, loud even, particularly red.

Instincts

They are extroverted like the Dilated in that they are spontaneous, frank and direct, the difference being that they are more passionate than instinctive.

They are aggressive. On the one hand, they have an impetuous dynamism which leads them to confront obstacles with the express aim of overcoming them and, because of that, are regularly successful in their ventures. On the other hand, they enjoy a fight, being quicker on the attack than on the defensive, but they are not nasty, and always respectful of the rules of fair play.

Their *sexual instinct* is equally passionate and quick to be awakened. They are always on the lookout for new adventures and they lack constancy (like Don Juan).

Emotional life

They have the ardour and impetuosity of the passionate extroverts. They are single-minded; they love or hate unreservedly. They don't need company but they do need companions for adventures and sport. They play by the rules and are fair in combat. They speak frankly, saying what they think and expressing their opinions freely without holding a grudge. They are spirited and impulsively generous. Courageous, too; their bravery in combat is legendary. They are always moving forward and aspiring to surpass themselves, believing that 'fortune favours the audacious', which is often true in their case.

We should emphasise that the family structure is too restricted for them. They feel imprisoned and, as a result, leave home at an early age to travel the world.

Their will is not as strong as their physical courage: if they can't surmount an obstacle the first time, they will often admit defeat. As the emotional zone is their most open zone, their obstacles tend to be their sadness, disappointments, loss and thwarted love. They may commit suicide or their vitality gives them the motivation to head off on an adventure, sometimes distinguishing themselves by their feats, when they simply wanted to escape from themselves, to leave their sad self behind them.

Intelligence

They are also dynamic in the intellectual domain, reacting immediately to any problem and taking action (sloping forehead). Like the Dilated Type, the Lateral Retracted Type is *sensorial* as they are only interested in concrete things, anything that has a practical use. Their dominant sense is not that of taste, unlike the Dilated, but the olfactory sense, which makes them very intuitive.

Their instincts guide them much more than reason. They are quick to assimilate the details of a problem and resolve it through trial and error; they can't think through or work methodically on a problem nor think ahead. They have the know-how rather than the knowledge. As they are constantly active, they don't tend to spend time in contemplation nor are they very introspective.

Given the above description, you might wonder whether their intelligence is of any value at all. The answer is that they are spontaneous, quick thinkers who go by pure sensorial intuition. On this subject, we shouldn't be a slave to the commonly held view that the understanding of problems is the sole terrain of the brain and therefore can only be read in the cerebral zone. The entire body, particularly the sensory organs, contribute to comprehension of the problem. In this case, it is the olfactory organ.

Their dynamism also affects their view of the world. They are not at all attached to tradition: they are people of the future, progressive, even revolutionaries. Their imagination makes them resourceful and their practical side never fails them. Even so, their impulsiveness gives them a 'transformative' imagination, which means that they live the event before it happens and therefore embellish it with all their heart's desires. This makes them somewhat vain and conceited. They can be deceitful and even liars due to an excess of imagination. And, due to a lack of ideas, they may have an ideal which they will put at the service of their passion.

Will

Their *need for movement* is intense and impetuous; you will never see them at rest. They love action and adventure, above all, making quick decisions and acting on them without hesitation. They tackle and overcome obstacles ... or they mess up. Their 'go for it' temperament sometimes takes them too far.

They lack self-control. They don't control their instincts or their need for action. They are impatient and practically never think before they act. In the same way, they believe that all change is progress and that it is the solution to all problems.

Professions

Their great need for action and movement dictates the type of profession that they choose.

They have a talent for manual work, particularly that which requires quick reaction times, improvisation skills and agility. At the same time, they practice almost all sports, either individual or group, often turning it into their profession. They excel at races. They also particularly like horses and equestrian sports.

In the technical professions, they are suitable for all occupations, from labourer to engineer. To give their best, there must be a great deal of activity involved, for example, working on a building site, and certainly not in an office. As we have already seen, their skills are not suitable for tasks that require calmness and patience.

They are only happy in commerce and industry in positions where their spirit of adventure is given free rein. They need activity but not as shop attendants, more likely as hawkers and sales agents. The opportunity to travel abroad makes them even happier. Their business sense and taste for negotiation is nowhere near as developed as the Dilated Type. Rather, they bring audacity and boldness to projects. It is worth highlighting that, in a period of economic growth, whose conditions are suited to their daredevil temperament, they can become very successful very quickly. On the other hand, in a period of recession, they are often doomed to fail as they are not blessed with the qualities of prudence and restraint which are needed in such times.

They are often found in professions related to nature and animals, such as agriculturalists, foresters, farmers and vets. They also like professions that offer adventure, for example as journalists or war correspondents who report from abroad.

Their aptitudes are more practical than intellectual. They don't make good students but their mental adaptability and good memory means that they are able to assimilate all the required knowledge to pursue self-employed professions. Their need for physical activity dictates their choices: they are only apt for activities that require displacement from one place to another, travelling and, above all, the need to use their improvisation skills. They aren't at all suitable for a desk job in an office or laboratory. They can be doctors, lawyers or engineers but only if they can be physically active in their jobs. As doctors, they prefer to be generalists and in direct contact with patients where they can improvise and regularly perform small surgeries or, even better, as surgeons or doctors without borders, working abroad. Working as an engineer on a construction site would be ideal, but not in the office. As lawyers, they would rather be in the courtroom eloquently defending a cause, much more than as counsellors working in a law office.

They are often found in the artistic professions as dancers, film actors (more so than theatre) and even singers.

They could be writers of short novels where they can easily describe the action and scenery of each situation. They are more successful writing for comics or cartoons.

Their dynamism gives them an interest in political activities. They are leaders and know how to talk to the masses, to be passionately convincing: they are popular orators. But in this field, too, they are the first to lead the charge and get others to follow. However, considering that they are true leaders, they lack the ability for reflection and organisation which are indispensable characteristics for someone in a position of authority.

2 / FRONTAL RETRACTION (Ill. 41 to 43)

The difference between frontal and lateral retraction is very important for the morphopsychologist as they relate to very different personalities, complete opposites in a number of areas. Frontal retraction assists the development of the instincts, intuition and reflection–all important factors from a psychological point of view.

From a **morphological** point of view, we should make sure that, in describing frontal retraction, we distinguish it from lateral retraction. As it has opposing characteristics, it is marked by a different facial shape wherein the reliefs of expansion alternate with those of retraction in successive dilated and retracted zones. There is a general straightening which erases the 'muzzle' of the lateral retracted, particularly visible in profile. This makes the profile vertical, at the same time as it reduces the openness of the receptors (protected receptors). In comparison to the Lateral Retracted Type, the forehead straightens and traces a slight curve where three superimposed zones can be distinguished. I call this morphology *frontal retraction*, in the sense of the crest of a wave or the frontline of an army (Ill. 41).

Psychologically, frontal retraction has an *interiorising* influence. Since the retracted zones are very easily influenced by the outside environment, external influences trigger a retraction and the received impression impacts all prior impressions, all of the experiences that make up the individual. Here is where the 'I' is formed and *reflective thought* is born.

In order to understand the personality of the Frontal Retracted Type, we must compare the interiorising process with that which we have already seen in the Dilated and the Lateral Retracted. Due to their dominant extroversion, the Frontal Retracted lack an individual personality and a sense of 'I', as they follow the ideas and words of the general order. They are happiest in the bosom of safe company where no threat, friction or communication problems exist and they can allow themselves to be drawn into it where, reflecting their facility for adaptation, they feel completely secure. The Lateral Dilated and Retracted types aren't interested in studying the world around them; they limit themselves to living in it, adapting and reacting to it.

On the other hand, due to their tendency to interiorise, the Frontal Retracted hold their words and actions in check, detaching themselves from the interaction to view it from a distance and, from this perspective, access an objective knowledge of people and things. In this sense, *experience is contrary to knowledge.*[1] Reflection is only possible by taking a step back. It must not be taken to an extreme, as one might otherwise lose all contact with reality and start to believe in a purely abstract world. This is what happens when the retraction is very pronounced (withered retraction).

Illustration 41. – FRONTAL RETRACTION

These two pairs of images clearly show the characteristic movement of frontal retraction which is that the receptors move from open to protected while the profile straightens.

1: 'One thinks according to one's experiences' [unpublished translation], wrote Valéry, completely in line with the notion of the biodynamics of morphopsychology.

The Frontal Retracted are people of moderation. It is worth noting that, in order to be a good morphopsychologist, you have to be more or less this type, as experience demonstrates that it is impossible to judge those with whom we identify too much (the close personal contact of the Dilated) or those with whom we have absolutely no affinity (those with extreme retraction).

The protection of the sensory receptors creates a process of perception which is different from that which we have seen up until now in those who are extremely sensorial due to their open receptors. The protected structure facilitates the selection of impressions from the environment as the receptors can open or close whenever they wish, thereby selecting or rejecting.

This is where the concept of the preferred surroundings makes most sense. We have seen above that the open receptors of the Lateral Retracted prevent them from being able to make such a choice. They are all-or-nothing types, forced to either accept everything or reject it all. As a consequence, if they feel uncomfortable and in an environment which they consider hostile, they have no choice but to go and look for somewhere else that suits them better.

The key difference with the Frontal Retracted is that they can create their own preferred environment out of the one they find themselves in by choosing what to keep and what to discard. They have the same facility for adaptation as the mixed types that we saw earlier (who are similar in appearance to the Frontal Retracted).

As you can easily imagine, there are many different levels of frontal retraction that differ according to the intensity; that is, according to the degree of reliefs, how vertical the forehead is and how closed the receptors are. The morphopsychologist must avoid becoming attached to an overall schematic description of these factors. He must analyse each case individually according to the points that I have just described.

However, in this long process, we should add more precise details and to that end I will contrast two groups of frontal retraction: those I have named 'balanced' and 'indented-retracted'.

The Balanced Frontal Retracted Type has a classic facial shape with balanced reliefs flowing smoothly into the curves. As a result, the character is very measured. The regulation of instincts, thoughts and emotions is smooth and deliberate. Moderation, reflection and serenity dominate their behaviour.

The facial shape of the Indented-Retracted is, on the other hand, uneven and full of reliefs which give the face a tormented morphology. Psychologically, it is the result of a strong tension between opposing zones. The character is therefore distinguished by powerful antagonisms of impulse and withdrawal. The facial shape is, as I have already established, characteristic of passionate temperaments as conflict has the effect of magnifying thoughts and feelings.

Illustration 42. – FRONTAL RETRACTED TYPE PERSONALITIES

The woman in the photo on the left shows a straightening of the lines, evoking what is often called a 'Greek profile', and we can see the significant development of the nose allied with a general lengthening of the face which is known as 'lateral retraction'. This lateral retraction, however, characterized by impulsivity, is moderated by the restraint that comes with retraction of the forehead. The second example, the author André Gide, also has strong elements of lateral retraction (the forehead and the ear are clearly sloped), but the retraction of the forehead dominates, conferring on the author a talent for literary criticism and as an essayist.

A / BALANCED FRONTAL RETRACTION (Ill. 42)

While the reliefs are spread evenly across the whole face, the forces of expansion and retraction are balanced, resulting in a great facility for adaptation (Ill. 43).

It is very unusual for this level of equilibrium to develop in childhood as expansion predominates at that age, as well as the need to advance slowly and to gain control of this expansion gradually, as noted in our general study of retraction. Children of this type are very mature from a young age. They have a great command of their instinctive life, a thoughtful intelligence and a happy balance between social adaptation and their individuality. These are the children we would call 'sensible': their education is very straightforward and they know what they want to do with their lives very early on. But it could be said that they will always have missed out on the zeal of childhood passions and journeys into the world of dreams.

Body language

Their attitude, gait and gestures are all measured. They never react impulsively to events; instead, they react calmly and in good time. Their gait is serene, never rushed. They tend not to hug or shake hands as they prefer to keep their distance when outside of their preferred surroundings. They are reserved and can often appear cold. They understand what is or isn't the done thing and are always dressed properly and conservatively. They will think about and reflect on what they are going to say before saying it, unlike the Dilated and Lateral Retracted who often speak first and think later.

Instincts

Their instincts are well developed but reined in and carefully measured in order to avoid potentially harmful excesses. They are especially careful not to let their sensuality take over and are loyal to their loved ones.

Their instinct for aggression is well developed but they control it well by keeping a good distance from potential violence.

Emotional life

Their emotions are controlled by their *chosen affinities*. They do not follow the crowd, keeping their distance and only showing warmth towards their closest friends and family. They are thoughtful and, with reason as their guide, they will not abandon their own. They are generous but prudent. They keep their word and respect their commitments. Love, as in friendship, is not taken lightly and they are loyal to a select few.

Their conduct is always measured. They avoid reckless activities and anything that would scare them. They are wise and careful, which frustrates more passionate and extreme people.

They are attached, but not excessively, to their independence, knowing that they can't completely ignore their fellow beings and that they must help one another. They are moderately ambitious, too, but never aim for anything out of their reach. They achieve what they want through hard work.

Intelligence

Their intelligence is a happy balance between the concrete and the abstract. On the one hand, like the Dilated, they accept facts as they are but work them out in their mind. They respect the ideas and customs of tradition but they are attached to their own beliefs and attempt to reconcile the two. They are capable of conceptualisation without losing sight of the practical side of things. Their judgements are based on moderation: they aren't as optimistic as the Dilated or as critically pessimistic as the Retracted and people tend to trust their opinions. They are neither imaginative nor inventive: their balance keeps them in the status quo, lacking the edge that is often the motor for creativity.

Will

Everything about them radiates balance. They are not particularly determined but they have a certain amount of self-mastery.

They live by their own rules which support their *will to take action* but they know how to adapt to circumstances. They are firm but flexible, without being especially stubborn, and never aim for anything that is out of their reach.

They have good *self-control* but are not rigid. They are neither impulsive nor inhibited and are considered wise and self-disciplined, which confers on them a certain authority over others.

Professionally, the ability to adapt makes them suitable for many different professions. Of course, it depends on the structure of their cerebral zone which determines the level of mental activity we may expect in the person.

In general, they succeed at whichever career they choose precisely because they are not impulsive and only make such decisions after careful consideration.

In all sectors of activity, they are able to provide practical solutions to general ideas which means that they don't generally stay in subordinate positions for long. Their natural, unforced authority makes them able leaders.

Illustration 43. – FRONTAL RETRACTION

Here are four examples of a clear frontal retraction. In all of them, we can see the same straightening of the profile and the same protected sensory receptors.

147

B / THE INDENTED RETRACTED TYPE (Ill. 44 and 45)

We know that facial shape shows us how vitality flows from the external being to the interior and vice versa. When the curves of the face lengthen in a smooth movement, like in the Balanced Frontal Retracted Type, it is a sign that, in parallel, the psychology is balanced. On the other hand, when the curves cross, creating ruptures in certain areas, as in the Indented-Retracted Type, it is a sign of a fierce conflict of tendencies which sometimes create blockages, sometimes explosions.

This facial shape may be identified by a deep crevasse on the forehead, as opposed to the flatness of balanced frontal retraction. This I have named the 'stop line' because it is effectively a brutal retraction. The stop line imposes itself between the orbital area, which gives us perception, and the rounded upper zone of the imagination, disassociating one from the other and creating a blockage in the normal route of initial impressions to final decisions. In the same way, in the middle zone, the regular curve of the aquiline nose–which indicates a measured impetus toward advancement and containment in the balanced individual–is replaced by an angled and hooked nose, a sign of two tendencies that have violently clashed. In the lower zone, we often see a contrast of a jaw that juts out, pushing the instinctive impulses outwards, and the mouth, which goes inward and is tightly closed, tending to shut down all impulses or, at least, contain them (Ill. 44).

This structure is extremely unusual in infants, usually appearing during adolescence. It is more pronounced in men than women, to the extent that, when it is so strongly marked in a woman, we should expect that its impact is powerful.

Psychologically, the result is a personality torn between opposing tendencies which engender powerful internal conflicts. The morphopsychological study of these personalities cannot limit itself to the analysis of the elements of conflict but, in order to have psychological value, it must determine if this conflict results in an unbalanced personality or if a balance can be found and how it might be achieved.

However, the conflict between these antagonistic tendencies is the source of great dynamism and one can say that, in general, the Indented-Retracted are passionate; they feel great love and hate, and live, not in peace and calm, but in drama.

Illustration 44. – THE INDENTED-RETRACTED STRUCTURE

Whether the face is long or short, broad or narrow, the indented-retracted structure is characterised by a battered facial shape, full of reliefs and indents in violent opposition.

Their morphology clearly shows how their passions differ from the Tonic Dilated or Lateral Retracted. The latter are extroverts and, due to their open sensory receptors, they react strongly to the influences around them, which means that their passionate impulses, however intense they may be, are momentary and pass quickly once the influences are no longer there. The passionate impulses of the Indented-Retracted, on the other hand, increase in intensity as a result of their deep inner forces and the concentration of the inner being (the indents); restraining the impulse increases its intensity. They are like the tiger's leap, powerful and lightning-quick, following a long and patient wait. The difficulty lies in knowing whether the leap has been correctly calculated. If the beast impulsively attacks its prey or hesitates and waits too long, in both instances he loses the prey he is after. Later on, I will explain how to try and solve this problem.

Body language

Their attitude, gait and gestures are all marked by this fierce passion. Through simple observation, one can already imagine where their equilibrium lies. Some demonstrate a restless agitation: their gait is uneven–sometimes fast, sometimes slow–depending on how they feel at the time. Their voice is blaring, eyes flaming, their impulsiveness dominating. Others, on the other hand, are quite rigid, their natural spontaneity is blocked, their gait is stiff, their gestures are controlled and contact is silent. The first dress very colourfully and conspicuously while the second dress more sternly, in sombre colours.

Instincts

Their instincts are no more important than other types with the same tonicity but they are galvanized by the heat of their passionate temperament. It could be said that it is the flame of passion that they look for and that they need, more than the attraction to the subject of their passion. In other words, they love the idea of love more than the object of their affection, which explains why they are often unfaithful.

Their sexual instinct is quick to ignite and remains ardent in conquest and seduction.

Their aggressive instinct is strong: they look for a fight, wanting to win at all costs, keen to vanquish or to dominate.

These instincts don't necessarily show themselves with as much force as one might expect. Their intensity can also put a powerful brake on the personality, paralysing their external manifestation, and can repress or sublimate these impulsions. At one point or another, it may provoke a complete change in character, which is often spoken of as 'conversion': a period of freedom from instincts which follows a period of restraint and sublimation.

Emotional life

Their feelings are almost always magnified to the point of passion. They can't live without passion in their lives and must create drama out of otherwise dull situations. ('They make a mountain out of a molehill.')

They are very passionate in love but their feelings are fierce rather than tender. As we have already seen, the object of their passion is less important than the heat of their own feelings. They are extreme in everything and can be jealous beyond reason. Their friendships are also ardent, exclusive and not easily shared.

Their fierce passion means that they lack sentimentality, which they find alarming in sentimental types. In Margaret Mitchell's novel, Ashley, the sentimental character besotted with Scarlett, a passionate type, admires her 'passion for life', which he lacks. He doesn't want to marry her, preferring the sweet Melanie, and offers the explanation: '*You would want all of a man, Scarlett, his body, his heart, his soul, his thoughts … And I couldn't give you all of me … And I would not want all of your mind and your soul. And you would be hurt, and then you would come to hate me—how bitterly!*' (Ill. 45)

For some, this ability to switch so easily between their impulse for expansion to that of retraction explains their mood changes. And when frustrated or feeling criticised, they tend to turn their back on love, the positive affirmation of the bond with their partner, towards hate.

They are difficult, as quick to be excited about something as they are to reject it. They can create discord in a group as their actions motivate others to act with passion, the result being that their social relationships are tempestuous.

Illustration 45. – I. INDENTED-RETRACTED TYPE PERSONALITIES

Here we have Jack Palance, the actor, an Indented-Retracted type well chosen as the actor in *Desperado*. And next to him, Scarlett O'Hara, drawn by Dauce according to Margaret Mitchell's description in the novel *Gone with the Wind*. A fiercely passionate character where it is said that, *'In her face were too sharply blended the delicate features of her mother, a Coast aristocrat of French descent, and the heavy ones of her florid Irish father. But it was an arresting face, pointed of chin, square of jaw. Her eyes were pale green without a touch of hazel, starred with bristly black lashes and slightly tilted at the ends. Above them, her thick black brows slanted upward'.*

Intelligence

They have the same intellectual aptitudes as the Frontal Retracted Type: both concrete and abstract, oriented towards the practical and at the same time capable of theorising. This varies according to the general structure of the face and especially the structure of the forehead. Each case must be analysed individually.

What particularly characterises the intelligence of the Indented-Retracted is that their passion dominates. On the one hand, this gives ideas their own brand of dynamism, passion, enthusiasm and impulsive action. They are able to complete tasks swiftly. On the other hand, they may be blind to reason and lacking in objectivity. Their judgments are therefore based on partial information and are often critical. Their thoughts are so intense that their verbal communication is extremely energetic which can make them eloquent. They have a powerful imagination and will often transform real life into a version of their overriding passion.

Will

Their *will to take action* is strong, fuelled by the heat of their passion. They need to achieve. They are talented trainers and chefs with the ability to make people obey their will with a simple look. This will is a function of tonicity: it should be considered that where this is lacking, at least in certain areas of the face, their energy can vanish, leaving them for a time incapable of completing their work.

Their *self-control* varies, as we have already seen. For some, their passion is a struggle in which they concede to impulsive acts. In others, this same excess of passion can lead to self-protection; the passion is restrained and channelled. Sometimes it is completely blocked, bestowing a coldness on them which can lead to a misinterpretation of their true character.

Performance

As I said at the beginning, the morphopsychologist must particularly concern himself with a broad summary of the antagonistic tendencies in the Indented-Retracted Type since how the subject creates his equilibrium, his unity, will affect how he manages his life.

Knowing how he achieves this equilibrium remains, in many ways, a mystery. Does unity, a highly desirable quality, arise from an internal organic adjustment that happens independently of the will of the subject? Or is it the result of the soul's desire for harmony? I, myself, believe that it is the result of both. Nevertheless, essentially the dominant passion imposes one single path for the different tendencies of the personality.

Sometimes it is an affirmative passion such as strong faith, a burning love or great enthusiasm for an idea. Sometimes it is a negative passion, such as hate or a desire for vengeance.

We have an example of the first case in Cardinal Federigo, a character in Manzoni's novel. His faith is so strong that he has no fear of death and he devotes his body and soul to the battle against the plague which ravages his town.

For the second case, I will cite cousin Bette, who Balzac calls this *'woman of fire and brimstone'* as he recounts her life, a life consumed by hate in the service of an unceasing desire for vengeance, rekindled by disappointment and shattered hopes. Pazzi has drawn a lifelike portrait based on the description in the book (Ill. 46).

We can also see this unity of personality created through a fanatical ideology which inhibits all other intelligent thought. Regicides belong to the Indented-Retracted Type: I have already given the example of Cassius, Julius Caesar's assassin.

We must return to the issue of the unifying action of the dominant passion. In studying the history of distinctive personalities, we often learn that during a period in their life–usually adolescence–they are torn between two opposing passions which have affected their equilibrium. One day, they discover for themselves the destiny that secretly awaits them: the dominant passion which will give their conduct a perfect unity. Some pertinent examples are the 'conversions' of saints. I prefer to refer more to the present day, to recount the case of Florence Arthaud, the yachtswoman who made a heroic solo Atlantic crossing. She explains in her book, *'The sea has forced discipline on me, which I hated, and order, as it was difficult to find someone as messy as me; it has made me sociable where before I was wild; it taught me respect for all beautiful things where before I had been dismissive. It knew how to calm the impulsiveness of a young contestant and made me a responsible woman. I was hot-headed, aloof, to avoid saying I couldn't care less; the sea has instilled in me the value of action through reflection and respect for things well done. In a few years, it has made me what my teachers would never have been able to make of me.'*[2] *(The fiancée of the Atlantic)* (Ill. 39 and 45-II)

Professions

It is not only the indented-retracted structure that determines aptitude for a particular profession. Everything depends on the base on which

---

2: Unpublished translation.

the structure is built. Aptitudes for professions will be similar to that of the Dilated Type, the Lateral Retracted Type and the Frontal Retracted Type, depending on which dominates, but they are distinguished by the intensity of the passion which takes over, affecting their professional conduct. This is completely opposite to the structure of the Balanced Frontal Retracted Type. The involvement of emotion is not without its difficulties in relationships with work colleagues, bosses and the general public, as it is contrary to the objectivity that is usually necessary in these relationships. Everything depends, therefore, on the equilibrium of the personality as we have already seen in the section on performance. Where equilibrium isn't achieved, no matter the individual's level of intelligence or aptitudes, their adaptation can be compromised by sudden impulsive acts or blockages. If, on the other hand, unity has been possible, focused on the dominant tendency, the individual becomes master of his choice of profession, his relationships and the way he manages his work, which makes him more efficient.

Illustration 45. – II. INDENTED-RETRACTED TYPE PERSONALITIES

 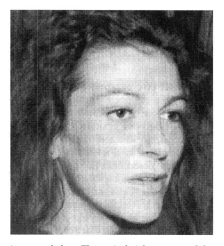

This facial structure is quite rare in a woman but it exists nonetheless. The tonic facial structure of the singer Barbara is therefore associated with a large expansion in the emotive zone which emphasizes her passionate temperament.

This same passion can be found in the yachtswoman Florence Arthaud who has two dominant zones, the instinctive and the emotional (see text). (*Photo C. Binet*)

Illustration 46. – TWO EXAMPLES OF PASSIONATE TYPES

Here are two more passionate types, characters from novels. The first one, the wife of Colas Breugnon, is completely the opposite of her dilated husband (Ill. 33), who he calls, ironically *'the graceless Marie'*. The author describes her as having *'a skinny body with hard, small, dark brown pupils'*,[3] her grumpy, obsessive and hyperactive character fitting well with her morphology.

In the second portrait is cousin Bette, by Balzac, drawn by Pazzi as she is depicted in the novel: the figure of a thin country peasant, narrow hips with long, strong arms, large feet and as rigid and unyielding as a pole, accompanied by a long sallow face with hard lines, dark eyes with a hard expression, thick charcoal eyebrows gathered together in the middle like a blossoming bouquet of flowers and dark, shiny hair. We know her story already: that of a bitter woman, whose passion is directed towards vengeance for the humiliations she has been subjected to during her life.

In this area, both the scientific and intuitive sides of morphopsychology are indispensable in determining the aptitudes for certain types of employment. There is a wide range of possibilities: at one extreme, the mediocre professions of those Indented-Retracted Types who are unstable, inconsistent, disorganised, dominated by their passions, incapable of following orders or any set organised conduct; and, at the other extreme, the Indented-Retracted Types who are capable of excelling in the creation of great works and are suited for senior positions in all domains.

3 / THE EXTREME RETRACTED TYPE (Ill. 47, 48, 49)

The more the retraction is pronounced, the slimmer the body becomes, closing in on itself. The bone structure is narrow and the joints are slender (as one can easily see in the wrists and ankles), the muscles are slim and long, with delicate skin and fine hair.

3: *Unpubl. trans.*

156

The face is small with a narrow frame: the jaw has delicate contours, the chin is pointed and the neck, slender. The receptors have a fine structure and they can be dry, which indicates a tendency toward defensiveness: the slightest impression causes a reaction–not of openness such as in the Dilated Type–but of closure. The eyes are not very round and are sheltered in their orbits, tightly surrounded by the eyelids which makes them look small and lustreless. They react as a means of self-preservation and in a blink of an eye they shrink further into themselves. The nose is slender and dry and sometimes as narrow as the blade of a knife; the nostrils are fine and dry and, at the slightest disagreeable odour or unfortunate emotional contact, they tend to curl in and attach themselves to the nostril wall, closing the nostril opening. The mouth is narrow with thin, firm lips 'zipped tight'.

This type of retraction is not natural in the young as it goes contrary to the concept of growth. If found in a child, it is a sign of an unhealthy hereditary condition whereby the body must put all of its defences to work from an early age in order to stay alive, as an old man would. The refining retraction gives the child the face of an old man, a face that is 'well lived in', as they say, an accurate observation but a bit cruel.

Illustration 47. – I THE EXTREME RETRACTED TYPE

Extreme retraction creates faces which are completely the opposite of dilated faces. As we can see here, these two portraits coincide precisely with the classic opposition of the Mercury type versus the Earth type in planetary typology.

The problem with this morphological type is that expansion, which is part of growth, is severely hindered; the retraction condemns the individual to a life of frailty within a limited, protective comfort zone. These surroundings involve maternal protection, the home and the comfort of the family. A child of this type is fearful of anything that forces him to leave this area of protection and the smallest changes in his life's circumstances cause suffering. He dreads playing with other children. Having to go to school creates anxiety, as does leaving home, moving home or travelling. Later, he will make efforts to establish family, social, and professional environments which he will not want to leave. He is a sickly child, subject to frequent illnesses which impede his development. However, he escapes serious illnesses, particularly infectious diseases and survives epidemics to which more robust children succumb. This proves the defensive value of retraction.

Illustration 47. – II. THE EXTREME RETRACTED TYPE

Here are two faces of the pronounced retracted type. The woman has a narrow frame, with an even narrower nose and mouth and, as often happens, this is compensated for by a cerebral zone in expansion. The expression in the eyes, however, betrays the lack of vitality and the predominance of ideals. In the man's face, the pronounced retraction has reached an extreme in a face dominated by lateral retraction.

Tonicity and atonicity

It is very important, early on, to distinguish between the different degrees of tonicity. Faces that show extreme retraction have good tonicity in all zones, with skin closely adhered to the bone giving firmness to the facial shape. In this case, their psychology is defined by their tonicity.

On the other hand, there are faces that are atonic and fall under the Extreme Retracted Type but, instead of having an aesthetic, flat facial shape, it is soft, not only in the frame but also in the receptors. This second version is a sign of an exhausted defence system that relies only on the hypersensitivity of retraction; that is to say, there is no energy left to cope with events in the way that the Extreme Tonic Type still can. Their only remaining defence is to turn into themselves and take refuge in their inner world. I will cite the Swiss writer Amiel (Ill 48) several times as she clearly illustrates an extreme example of the Atonic Retracted Type. To support my perception, I can do no better than to cite the words of the author himself who was acutely aware of the profound reasons for his inability to write, revealing them in his work *Amiel's Journal* in these terms: '*You have no fight left, neither against sickness, nor against man, nor against nature. You try to exist with the minimum friction*'. This explains the exhaustion of the Atonic Retracted Type extremely well: exhausted, not in the way of a man who is about to die, but in the way of one who abandons the fight in a hostile environment for being too unequal and who, with a parsimonious prudence, uses their feeble resources to stay alive.

The morphological differences between the Tonic Retracted and the Atonic Retracted are well demonstrated in illustration 47-II.

Body language

Their habitual form of expression lacks vigour. As opposed to the Dilated, they fear everything 'normal': informality, bad manners, intimate contact, noise and loud voices. Everything in them expresses fragility and restraint: their gait is light, their gestures discreet and their style is a bit awkward. They are careful in their use of language, sometimes to the point of eloquence.

They are uncomfortable outside of their comfort zone. Those of the Tonic Type appear distant and cold. Their aristocratic reserve creates a barrier between them and others, at the opposite extreme of the easy familiarity of the Dilated.

Atonic Types don't govern themselves so well; they are intimidated and never know what to do with their body, particularly their hands. As a result, they tend to be clumsy in company. The country priest (Ill. 49), who demonstrates this extreme brand of timidity, relates in his personal diary, *'Just as I was finishing my meal, in came M. le Curé deTorcy. I could scarcely move for sheer surprise. When at last I stumbled to my feet I must have looked quite wild. In getting up I knocked over the bottle with my left hand and sent it crashing.'* This priest is a particularly typical example of an Atonic Retracted Type but literature provides us with many other examples, such as Salavin by Duhamel (5) and Segard by Vildrac (21).

The Retracted Tonic Type is always formal, with immaculate and well-fitting clothes. On the other hand, the Atonic Retracted Type is generally inactive and doesn't shave or devote much time to their personal hygiene. Their awareness of this adds to their fear of appearing in public.

Psychologically, they are completely different from the Dilated Type and as far as you can imagine from their 'nature': their appetite for pleasure, their emotional and instinctive expansion and their need for human contact. They are often spoken about as 'spirituality in its refined form', reflecting the detachment from material things which is a defining feature of extreme retraction. While the Dilated Type is unsophisticated and lacking in sensitivity, enjoying nature in its purest form–fresh air, wind and water–unafraid of life's hard knocks, even violent ones, the Extreme Retracted Type is delicate, avoiding direct contact with nature and hating violence. They have to create a protected environment that meets the demands of their sensitivity. Their problem lies in creating that environment to their liking. The Tonic Type manages it: he looks for refined, worldly company which is easier to find in the city than in the country, enjoying the somewhat artificial atmosphere of salons where it is easy to keep a distance between them and others, a polite barrier to society. It is harder, however, for the Atonic Type to find their place in the world. They are timid and awkward, easily discouraged and ready to turn into themselves, into that ivory tower which is the secret 'I'.

Illustration 48. – EXAMPLES OF THE EXTREME RETRACTED TYPE

The Swiss writer Amiel is drawn here by Pazzi based on a portrait showing an indented-retracted facial shape with a strong cerebral expansion and refined receptors. This explains both the keen intelligence and the lack of ability to bring ideas to fruition.

The Prince Muichkine is the main character in Dostoyevsky's novel The Idiot and is described by the author as being 'quite tall, with refined traits, sunken cheeks and large blue eyes [..] the hair is fair and he wears a goatee.' This portrait has been drawn by Glazounov and is a perfect representation of the character in the novel.

Illustration 49. – EXAMPLES OF THE EXTREME RETRACTED TYPE

The first figure is Salavin whom we have already mentioned (Ill. 28), drawn by Berthold Mann. Here is a personality that has clearly turned in to itself: obsessive, fastidious and powerless to act, as Duhamel described him.

The second figure has been drawn by Dauce to imagine Bernanos's country priest. The author describes him: '…. my face drawn and more yellow each day, with its long nose and double furrows descending on either side of the mouth', '...my sorry countenance: it can get no thinner.' This corresponds to an anxious, fastidious character who, despite his profound religious faith, is unable to realise his idealistic objectives.

Instincts

Their instincts are kept in check which explains their lack of vital expansion, their difficulties with personal contact and their fastidiousness for quality.

Their *instinct for nutrition* is not well developed: they don't eat or drink much. They tend to be very restrained and sober. The Tonic Type is a gourmet demanding high quality food. The Atonic Type doesn't care nor give much thought to food to the extent that the 'country priest', typical of this morphological type, is happy to eat anything: '*just bread, fruit and wine*'.

Their *instinct for acquisition* is poor, making them unsuitable for business. The Tonic Type, however, does have the facility for creating and maintaining a strict economic regime. The Atonic Type doesn't have this ability, sometimes spendthrift and other times afraid of running out of money.

The *aggressive instinct* is very different between the two types. The Tonic Type is very aggressive; however, it is repressed so that it does not show outwardly. It accumulates internally until it either explodes in a sudden act of aggression or is expressed in, for example, a bad mood, being critical and ironic or judging others negatively. (They can be spiteful.)

The Atonic Type is even more repressed and, along with their lack of ability to act, they live in an almost constant feeling of impotence. They suffer in silence, unable to respond. Their usual reaction is to retreat, running from any obstacles that they feel incapable of dealing with.

I should point out that there are differing degrees of atony and differences between the constraints of the environment. For example, Jacques Thibault, a character in the novel by Martin du Gard, is not completely atonic but his instinct was repressed at an early age by the crushing authority of his father and, for that reason, cedes to the pressure. He confides to one of his friends: '... *the need to run away, to free myself by breaking away, it's a terrible thing. It's like a sickness.*'[4] Once, after running away, his father punishes him by putting him in total isolation in order to '*break his will*'. He gives in

4: *Unpubl. trans.*

and, over time, finds a soothing state of torpor in his solitude which, little by little, takes away his desire to leave (Ill. 24).

It is at this point that we discover a tendency to turn against oneself. This is one of the most common effects of suppressed aggression, particularly in the Atonic Retracted Type. They don't lash out but, rather, take it out on themselves through a type of masochism which can become an unhealthy need for self-destruction. The country priest provides us with a great example: in spite of his elevated moral position, the priest finds himself paralysed in his efforts to do good by a permanent sense of self-doubt and, analysing it, he comes to understand that '*to doubt oneself is not to be humble, I even think that sometimes it is the most hysterical form of pride, a pride almost delirious, a kind of jealous ferocity which makes an unhappy man turn and rend himself.*'

The *sexual instinct* isn't very well developed. It is usually impossible for this type to be involved with someone on a romantic level, except within the privileged conditions of their own preferred surroundings, as it would appear to be a risky enterprise bringing with it the risk of losing their individuality. This may create a phobia of physical contact. Extreme retraction can inhibit sexual maturation and hold the individual back in one of the early stages. The Tonic Type tends to remain in what the psychoanalysts call the 'anal stage', whereby, at the slightest difficulty in a romantic relationship, it can turn into an aggressive relationship, manifested directly through acts which may be sadistic or, more indirectly, by verbal criticism or rejection. An indirect expression of rejection can be impotence in the man and frigidity in the woman.

The Atonic Type tends to stay fixated on the oral stage of the infant and return to it when they are disappointed in their romantic endeavours. Their sexual relations are based on a need for protection and they tend to look for a father or a mother rather than a lover. We have already come across this situation in the Atonic Dilated Type but the difference with the Dilated Type is that this need for protection is accompanied by dependence, whereas the Retracted Type is paradoxically associated with a fierce desire for independence. There are two famous examples: the genius musician Chopin in his relationship with the novelist George Sand.

The Retracted Atonic Type tends to sublimate his instincts. Instead of creating action through combativeness and sexuality, they give free rein to their fantasies–a source of solace in what they consider to be a disappointing reality. In Vildrac's novel, Segard explains his admiration of his friend Bastien's decisiveness, a Tonic Dilated Type: *'Bastien is stronger than me, he can decide for himself; he has made decisions for me and I prefer it like that…. above all, I don't make plans; me, I make dreams.'*[5]

Emotional life

Their emotional life is dependent upon the limits of their preferred surroundings which restricts their relations to a tight family circle or a few friends. Even within their preferred surroundings, they are very withdrawn, not very warm, nor very sociable and their individualism takes priority over belonging to a group. Their sensitivity makes them very perceptive and preoccupied with how others feel. But this brings with it the desire that others, in return, show them the same sensitivity. This makes them difficult characters, frequently bad tempered. In other words, their hearts are almost entirely closed, coming across as dry, cold and egotistical which is true as a defensive reaction but doesn't exclude the fact that they can be charitable and generous when they don't feel the need to be on the defensive.

Whereby dynamism makes the Tonic Dilated and Retracted Types passionate beings, the Extreme Retracted Type lacks emotional expansion and is always quick to turn into himself. He dreads, both in friendship and love, any action by the other that feels a bit too intense. In the same way, they fear the slightest internal upset and can become afraid of their own feelings as they may be contrary to the internal peace that they so desire. This, of course, is particularly evident in the Atonic Type. Duhamel's Salavin is a remarkable example of this morbid, excessive sensitivity in that friendships represent great suffering for him. He says, *'to have a friend, a true friend, is too difficult, too complicated, too dangerous'*; of joy: *'one should never feel joy, the departure of joy leaves a too cruel suffering'*, of good luck: *'"rest now", says his mother, "good luck tires you more than suffering"'*, and of success: *'in failure, there is a sweetness that you cannot imagine'.*[6] (Ill. 28)

5: *Unpubl. trans.*
6: *Unpubl. trans.*

The minimisation of their emotional zone tends to lead them to crave solitude. Many remain single. The Tonic Type actively searches out this solitude and, as we have seen, constructs it in his daily life by building a barrier between him and others. For the Atonic Type it is a refuge, an escape from emotional relationships. Salavin hates contact with others and, as a result, is accused of misanthropy. He responds: *'I like men. It's not my fault that I can't put up with them most of the time. Ever since I came across my kind, I have felt my soul contract. All I wish is to recover my solitude in order to like men as I like them when they are not there, when they are not under my feet.'*

While the Tonic Retracted Type's moods are generally cold and lack vivacity, those of the Atonic Type are often marked by sadness. When atony is combined with extreme retraction, it becomes almost impossible to manage everyday situations and increases the need for refuge in the face of difficulties. Salavin, having lost his job, has no energy to start looking for another one; in fact, he drifts along, getting bogged down in inaction. On meeting an old companion who has become a beggar, *'he contemplated the poor wretch with a poignant interest, and there grew in his heart an indescribable desire to be this man, so alone and so low, that he no longer feared abandonment nor a fall from grace.'*

Here we touch on a key trait in their personality which I touched on at the beginning: the predominance of introversion over extroversion and self-absorption at the expense of relationships with the outside world. Some will go to the extent of saying that their self-interest is their primary objective. Ashley, one of the characters in Margaret Mitchell's novel, is completely aware of this, saying that Scarlett never felt the need to become anything, just wanting to be herself. And he explains to the passionate Scarlett, whom he loves but does not wish to marry because, he says, he has always tried to run away from people and situations that are too real, that he prefers the shadowy theatre of his dreams.

Intelligence

Extreme retraction closes the mind to concrete, sensorial and living reality, replacing it with the abstract reality of ideas. The Tonic Type's ideas are precise, clear and active; their intelligence lies in analysis, logic and important detail. There is finesse in their solutions and their responses are quick. But it is a cold intelligence and it tends to be separate from all vital attachments. They are analysts and calculators, deprived of intuition and imagination.

The Atonic Type can assimilate the world with great flexibility but their perceptions and ideas are vague and they lack the energy to bring them to fruition, which results in a tendency to fantasize and daydream.

In the Tonic Type, thought is clear and there exists the possibility of future projects. But this possibility is lacking in the Atonic Type as their thoughts constantly take them back into the past, to memories, to a time when they were happier, to the detriment of their current advantageous situation.

It is clear that in morphopsychology, nothing is certain without taking the structure of the forehead into account as this area is important for the evaluation of aptitudes.

Will

As extreme retraction is the opposite of dilation, the natural inclination to take action that we see in the Dilated, which comes directly from the power of their vital expansion, is lacking. And correlatively, they have no great ambition for social success. The need for security in the Tonic Type leads them to attempt to control what is perceived to be a hostile environment. Out of this comes a type of will which may be called 'reactive' because it is a reaction to the lack of impulse for expansion, keeping them constantly on edge.

In the Atonic Type, the will to take action is weak and they tend to put everything off until tomorrow. Their sensitivity leads to suffering and they resent the gap between their desires and their ability to realize them. Amiel has bitter experience of it and records in his diary: *'I have never been able to give up on anything, nor to accept anything less; my ideals have inhibited my ability to live and I have never been able to satisfy my ambition to the level of my secret desires.'*[7]

7: *Unpubl. trans.*

The Tonic Type has good *self-control* due to an acute sense of self-awareness which blocks all expansive spontaneity and imposes extremely strict rules of conduct.

The Atonic Type is the same, except that they are often unable to follow their self-imposed rules which makes them feel completely impotent and therefore inhibited.

Professions

For their lack of contact with concrete things, the Extreme Retracted Types have no manual skills. However, the Tonic Type, although not working directly with objects, are excellent at handling instruments and, due to their sensitivity combined with good tonicity, they are adept and suitable for professions in industry and artisanal work.

Atonic Types are not good with their hands and therefore make poor technicians.

As neither like nature and the countryside, they are not suitable for any professions in this area.

They are not very sporty and they don't play team sports; however, Tonic Types may achieve success in certain individual sports where their sharp perception and quick reactions are important, such as fencing and dance. The Extreme Retracted hate all water sports, including swimming.

They are not very suitable for commerce as they are not particularly interested in business and contact with the public is difficult. The Tonic Type, however, can work in extremely specialised fields which require finesse and a good sense of aesthetics; for example, jewellery, art and haute couture.

They have an aptitude for professional work where intellect is prioritised over any contact with reality. This includes activities such as working in research, laboratories or a library, working with documentation, in banks or in scientific research. However, they are mediocre practitioners in all other domains.

In whatever they do, they completely lack the spontaneity of those who are able to improvise as they need to reflect, calculate and make plans. As such, they are well adapted to be technicians where this expertise is required.

While the Tonic Type is quick and able to cope with work that requires speed, the Atonic Type is slow (inhibited) and is generally an office worker who enjoys the enclosed environment of a work space, a laboratory or library.

Their sensitivity and appreciation for quality give them a certain attraction to art. The Tonic Type is adept in various practical artistic fields. As writers, they have a flair for the succinct but are excellent in carving out their own style. They don't write major works as they lack imagination but they can write short stories or, even better, literary essays.

The Atonic Type is more of a spectator than an actor in every field. For example, they may be fans of art or art critics. As writers, they are not very productive and their tendency to turn into themselves usually confines them to purely autobiographical works such as personal diaries, as we have seen in the exemplary case of Amiel.

CHAPTER VI
REACTIVE AND CONCENTRATED TYPES

In my first work about morphopsychology as a science (*Quinze leçons de morphopsychologie*, Ed. Stock, 1937), I outlined the difference between 'action' and 'reaction', an opposition that is already well understood by psychologists. It is the difference between action that emanates from the organism's profound vital resources and a simple reaction which is a response to events in the environment.

What morphopsychology teaches us is that the power of action is related to the structure of the facial shape, as we have already seen, which tells us the extent of the reserves of energy that the subject may have at his disposal. On the other hand, a reaction is dependent on the receptors which react directly to external stimulants. The two tend to work together and when the subject is affected by an external event, it normally calls on internal reserves for support. We have already established that this is usually the case from the morphopsychological studies completed up to now. As such, the Predominantly Dilated Type, particularly where there is tonicity, is prepared for action due to the tonic expansion of their facial shape and, at the same time, due to their open receptors, is ready to respond to the demands of the environment.

However, there are situations where the two are disconnected. In some cases, the individual acts independently of any prompting or coercion and is not influenced by external stimuli and, in others, the individual reacts exclusively to external events. This may depend on the circumstances, but it also depends on the individual's facial structure.

Referring to the *Manuel de morphopsychologie*, published in 1947, I was able to identify these two types of opposing structures and define their essential characters through a rigorous application of the laws of this science as well as day-to-day experience.

A narrow and slim shape (i.e. the shape of the 'large face') indicates minimal energy reserves, while well-developed receptors (within the 'small face') indicate an overriding tendency to react (as opposed to act). I call this the Reactive Type. (Ill. 50-51)

In the opposite sense, a large frame suggests abundant energy reserves, while small and narrow receptors indicate that individualistic action dominates. There is minimal or no reaction to external events. I call this the Concentrated Type as the lack of reaction means that received impressions accumulate and concentrate internally over time (Ill. 52).

1 / THE REACTIVE TYPE (Ill. 50 and 51)

Before going into detail, I should clarify the difference between the reactive tendency and the Reactive Type to avoid any confusion. The reactive tendency, as we have just seen, is common to everyone and is the visible manifestation of the individual's adaptation to his surroundings. As such, open receptors are all the more important (in both the Dilated and Lateral Retracted Types). However, we should reserve the title of Reactive Type to those with the exclusive tendency to react since deliberate action, which originates internally, plays a very small part.

The Concentrated Type is rare in childhood while the Reactive Type is very common. This corresponds to the requirements for growth at this age, which entails receptiveness to the environment in order to nourish the child who hasn't yet had time to create good reserves of energy. The result is that a young child's morphology is comprised of a small face which is more developed than the frame and the reactive tendency completely dominates. Ideally, as dilation develops, vital energy accumulates in the organism. When the Reactive Type is particularly pronounced during the entire period of development, it suggests an excessive level of excitability to external stimuli and therefore a dangerous tendency to exhaust energy resources, which, in one way or another, will impede the growth and development of intellectual and emotional maturity.

Illustration 50. – I. EXAMPLES OF THE REACTIVE TYPE

When the reactive tendency is very pronounced, the face is very open and the expression lively. Face on, the receptors occupy most of the face at the expense of the frame. In this young woman, this tendency is most pronounced in the cerebral and instinctive zones. In the man, it is pronounced in all three zones, and I have observed that black people tend to have broad receptors.

Morphologically, the facial shape of the Reactive Type is narrow; however, the small face is spread out, occupying almost the entire surface of the face due to the open receptors which, from face on, are broad and stand out in profile. They have large eyes which extend out to the temples; the nose is broad, above all at the level of the nostrils; the mouth is big; and the smile is so broad it reaches the ears. The combination of these factors gives the impression of an 'open face'.

Illustration 50. – II. EXAMPLES OF THE REACTIVE TYPE

This famous, young black singer is characteristic of the Reactive Type due to the size and openness of the receptors. The great actor, Fernandel, is a Lateral Retracted Type with this tendency. We should note that in both examples there are slight signs of atony at the level of the mouth in the singer and in the length of Fernandel's face, which is unusual in a Lateral Retracted Type. This gives them both the flexibility to adapt, which is important for their artistic perceptiveness.

In addition, the receptors are very expressive. The mouth quivers and moves unceasingly, from a smile to a pout or to the drooping of the corners in disappointment. The nostrils move constantly. The eyes are lively, rarely fixing on one thing for any length of time; they move from object to object depending on whatever attracts their attention.

We should also note the characteristic shape of the eyebrows, which, at some distance from the eyes, form two arcs clearly separated by a smooth zone and tend to raise up, wide and high, creating several horizontal wrinkles. It's a surprised expression, but also one of dispersion, the opposite of concentration, which lowers the brows towards the eyes, bringing them closer together and creating vertical lines at the root of the nose (Fig. 1, Ill. 51).

In profile, the facial shape is marked by a complete absence of frontal retraction. The receptors stand out on the face: the eyes protrude from the surface, the nose projects forward and the mouth juts out further than the chin, with the lips in relief.

This morphology gives the character the impression of freshness and youth, like the Reactive Type in children. I should point out that this structure is the prerogative of childhood since, at a young age, the receptors are naturally open and the facial shape hasn't yet broadened, as this comes in later development. As we will see, Reactive adults retain many psychological traits from childhood.

Illustration 51. – THE PROFILE OF THE REACTIVE TYPE

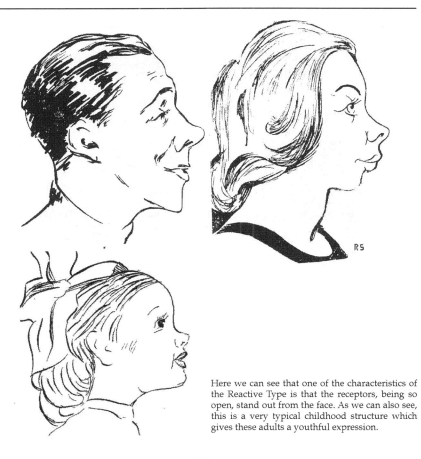

Here we can see that one of the characteristics of the Reactive Type is that the receptors, being so open, stand out from the face. As we can also see, this is a very typical childhood structure which gives these adults a youthful expression.

Psychologically, the exclusive tendency to react impacts their whole personality. On the positive side, this is useful as the individual is open to every impression from their environment, making them very adaptable and flexible when dealing with change. This also makes them spontaneous and mentally sharp.

On the negative side, they lack substance and the ability to act by making decisions informed by personal desire. They are inconsistent as they react to the constantly changing elements of their environment, like a cork bobbing on water, constantly being pushed right and left. They lose themselves in so many things that they are unable to complete any task that requires focus and consistency.

It is worth adding here that there is a fundamental, organic law of economy of effort: for there to be balance, the resources used up by the reactive tendency must not exceed the reserves available, as indicated by the facial shape. For example, the Dilated Type is balanced but when the face is narrow, energy reserves are limited. As a result, the reactive tendency may lead to exhaustion, which can be life threatening. This risk can be avoided if the face is closed, as in a retracted facial shape, which is often the case in the Reactive Type. In this case, the impressions of the environment only affect the receptors but don't penetrate any deeper since the retraction of the frame impedes it. This results in superficial reactions which don't engage the core reserves. It is typical of the Reactive Type to be superficial, which may be considered pejorative, but we can now appreciate that it is a form of self-protection.

We can assume that the Reactive Types have a rounded outline within a narrow frame (Ill. 2), and that they therefore don't have this form of self-protection. They are more vulnerable to exhausting their reserves (as they can't control them) and, as a result, tend to have a fragile temperament and are particularly susceptible to illnesses, especially tuberculosis.

Body expression

The Reactive Type is very active and needs to be in a stimulating environment in order to feel 'good'. They prefer city life to the solitude of the country. Their attitude and bearing demonstrate this need for activity: they are never still, walking quickly or slowing down according to what attracts their attention, or not, in their surroundings. They gesticulate a great deal, particularly when speaking. Their face is very expressive and reflects the stimuli that surround them which means that they have a broad range of expressions: happy, sad, emotional, fiery. They are very talkative, speak quickly and loudly and the spoken word often takes the place of thought. They want to look good, dressing carefully and in style.

Instincts

At first sight, it would appear that they live a very rich and instinctive life, appearing to be men of action, gourmands, sensual. The truth is that they are always active and that they enjoy good cuisine and the pleasures of the flesh. But, as we have seen, their activity is a result of their reaction to external stimuli and, lacking this, the Reactive Type lets himself go, becomes indolent and lazy, like a young girl of this type who excuses her laziness during the day by claiming exhaustion and yet can dance all night when she finds herself in a happy and stimulating environment.

Reactive Types are similar to the Nervous Type in character, which can be defined as emotional–inactive. This means that activity only takes place when external stimuli match their sensitivity. We can't say that they are totally inactive as, in a stimulating professional environment, they are capable of fulfilling the required tasks.

Nevertheless, their sensuality is not the manifestation of a powerful instinct because they react to whatever is around them and flit from one thing to the next. They are more epicurean than sensual. The moralist Chamfort was clearly thinking of this type of person when he defined everyday love of his era: *'Love is the exchange of two fantasies and the contact of two skins'*. There is something of this in the Don Juan type but it doesn't imply increased virility; their relentless quest is due to the fact that they are fundamentally incapable of sustaining love over a period of time. The writer Colette offers the good example of one of her friends, famous for his womanising and who couldn't resist his impulses. She wrote of him, *'He looked very anxious when we met, aging in a quarter of an hour and rejuvenating in five minutes. Youth and age emanating from the same source: a look, a mouth, a female body. In thirty-five years of a well-managed job and uncontrolled pleasure, he hadn't had time for a rejuvenating rest.'*[1]

1: Unofficial translation.

In addition, their aggressive instinct is not designed for sustained effort, originating from a deep internal force. Their aggression is reactive and vanishes as soon as the provocation stops. This subliminal aggression arises out of ambition but not from any deep desire to succeed. It is stimulated by outside factors: someone else's success, the desire for praise, the challenge of overcoming an obstacle or the desire for reward.

Emotional life

Their emotional life has the same characteristics as their instinctive life. Reactive Types are hyper-sensitive and they are affected instantly by everything around them. They are extremely sensitive to external influences, to the point of being happy when the sun shines and sad when it clouds over. They can go from joyful at hearing good news to sad at the slightest setback. A compliment flatters, a reproach saddens and a kind word comforts them. They quickly become emotionally attached, being sympathetic to the other's emotions and sad, too, when someone is unhappy. They are kind and friendly, helpful, welcoming and generous. They are very pleasant when everything goes well but, within all that, they lack depth, they withdraw with the same ease that they become attached. For them, out of sight really does mean out of mind.

It is worth mentioning that these character traits make them perfectly adapted to today's society where precisely every deep connection or every passionate expression of feelings is not considered politically correct. And, they need this superficial life: where excitement, frivolity, witty comments and variety reign, and where gossip eclipses all serious conversation. This is what they call 'being alive'.

Reactive Types are vain in the sense that they lack depth and personal conviction. They only appreciate something based on how others appreciate it, resulting in an incessant need to please and to be the centre of attention. This desire to be admired also leads them to exaggerate their talents.

They are extremely emotional and can't avoid reacting emotionally. They turn red or pale, laugh or cry or tremble with emotion. They are so emotionally overwhelmed by any slightly dramatic situation that they lose their self-control. Don't count on them to help out when you're sick or injured! They panic at the sight of blood and the spectacle of death horrifies them.

You might think that this level of anxiety doesn't fit with the easy-going, friendly character which I described above but it only appears to be a contradiction on the surface. In the family environment and when everything is going well, the Reactive Type is very adaptable. But they can't handle upsets, disappointments or even flat-out fatigue. They can suddenly get irritated and bad-tempered. This fragility is described extremely clearly by Chesterton in his analysis of Charles Dickens who is a typical example of the Reactive Type: *'Dickens had all his life the faults of the little boy who is kept up too late at night. The boy in such a case exhibits a psychological paradox; he is a little too irritable because he is a little too happy. Dickens was always a little too irritable because he was a little too happy. Like the over-wrought child in society, he was splendidly sociable, and yet suddenly quarrelsome. In all the practical relations of his life he was what the child is in the last hours of an evening party, genuinely delighted, genuinely delightful, genuinely affectionate and happy, and yet in some strange way fundamentally exasperated and dangerously close to tears.'*

Intelligence

In the sense that intelligence is a doorway to the world, the Reactive Type is intelligent, curious about everything, has the gift of repartee and a powerful memory which helps them to retain what they want to learn with minimum effort. They are essentially sensorial, perceptive through intuition rather than reflection and they have a gift for improvisation.

But the price of these gifts is that the Reactive Type prioritises the impression of the moment and, as impressions are fleeting, it makes them dispersed; nothing a long-term effect. They can't concentrate on anything for any length of time. They lack reflection so that they either understand the problem immediately or they never will. They like the gossip columns and are slaves of the day-to-day. They are not good at general concepts or synthesising them and not very adept at creating a concrete plan of action. They are not at all practical and lack the Dilated Type's common sense. At least they are shrewd and resourceful but they don't have the real gift of inventors. They aren't very imaginative but their direct contact with reality gives them certain artistic gifts, principally in the fields of form, rhythm, sound and colour.

Will

Despite appearances, they don't have any great inclination for action due to their lack of internal strength. As we have already seen, they yield to exterior stimuli and their activity is reactive which means that they lack constancy and perseverance. For example, if they fail at something they get easily discouraged. They can't handle long-term endeavours. We have already seen that the same happens with their ambition to improve their position and to achieve their objectives.

Their self-control is not well managed: not only do they yield to external stimuli but they can't resist their own impulses or control their energy resources without risk of exhaustion.

Professions

As the Reactive Type is flexible and adaptable, they are apt for a number of professions. However, they need variety as they get bored quickly when faced with a monotonous task. They have to work under specific conditions because they get discouraged if they can't easily solve problems that arise.

They lack the strength for physical activities such as professions where they must physically manage material. That is why you rarely find this type working in the country, on ships or as labourers. In addition, their natural vivacity excludes them from work that requires patience or a slow-paced rhythm. In certain circumstances, they can be good technicians as they are spontaneous and resourceful when dealing with anything new but they are incapable of learning the automatic responses that are necessary in a lot of tasks. Furthermore, if they have any difficulties in managing them they become nervous and clumsy.

Their enthusiasm and agility make them suitable for all sports that don't require strength. They can be found practising, for example, dance and artistic ice-skating. They are often impetuous and have trouble controlling their energy. Their principal defect is that they are emotional and lack detachment which can often mean that they lose their composure when the objective of the competition is important.

They are valued for their speed of reaction, their easy sociability and their lively and diverse intelligence. They can be found everywhere.

In commerce and industry, they excel as salesmen and traders, and as secretaries and hostesses. As they have a wide variety of aptitudes, they can be useful as the boss's right hand man.

As they are so sociable, they are adept at any profession that requires this talent, such as teachers and organisers. Their youthful character puts them on a level with the children and adolescents but, in certain social professions, being so emotional can be a handicap if they can't keep it under control, such as in nursing or the first aid professions.

They are excellent in those professions that require being in touch with reality such as journalism or fashion.

They can be found in diplomatic careers, in sub-positions such as the ambassador's secretary. Their talent for languages is extremely useful and suitable for professions such as an interpreter.

They work well in the self-employed careers as they have a great capacity for research. Once settled in their career, they adapt easily. Nevertheless, they lack constancy and the ability to achieve their objectives.

They have artistic abilities and are gifted in dance, song (more operetta than opera) and for playing musical instruments. They make good actors due to their ability to improvise, their good memory, verbal skills and their capacity to easily change personalities. The advantage is that they don't enter into their roles too deeply and are able to, from one day to the next, return to their own personality or change roles. They are certainly more comfortable in comedy than drama.

The Counter-Balanced Reactive Type (see Ill. 78)

The law of equilibrium is one of the essential laws of life and so any extreme tendency, dangerous by its very nature, will always try to compensate in an opposing movement in order to maintain equilibrium.

The exclusive tendency to react, which is the main characteristic of the Reactive Type, is life-threatening in the long term due to the total exhaustion of vital forces. It is important as much for the doctor as the psychologist to assess which compensatory mechanisms can be used to avoid this situation.

I have already mentioned that the retracted facial shape provides a certain amount of protection as it impedes the impressions in the environment from penetrating and consuming the individual's core energy. On this basis, I have interpreted the superficial character of the Reactive Type as a type of defence system.

Withdrawal

There are, however, other compensatory mechanisms. Under the title 'Withdrawal', I have described the most frequent compensatory mechanism, which is essentially withdrawal from the situation. In the first chapter, we saw that the instinct of conservation comes into play when there is an excess of energy consumption. By closing the tap on the reserve tank, those reserves that are essential to the correct functioning of the vital organs, and which cannot be put to any other use without risking serious consequences, are protected. The example of the Reactive Type is significant as they are unable to manage their energy use to keep it within the limits of their needs. They are more likely than other types to waste energy. Children are a good example of this, as they belong to this type: they use up their energy without taking into account its limits and they can't stop themselves when the surroundings over-excite them. For example, during a lively evening, they are exuberant and appear inexhaustible, insisting that they are not at all tired, with the result that they must be forced to go to bed. You might imagine that sleep would be impossible but, surprisingly, it's completely the opposite: removed from the excitable environment, they fall into a deep sleep in a matter of seconds.

Sleep, for the Reactive Type, just like anyone else, is the perfect compensatory reaction, as energy consumption stops and energy recovery takes place. In general, sleep represents the most efficient method of withdrawal as it allows for recovery of the energy equilibrium. The degree of exhaustion can be so great that it actually inhibits sleep. This is explained by the fact that sleep is an active defence mechanism whose regulation requires a certain amount of reserves so that if one has gone beyond the limit of energy expenditure, there isn't enough energy left for sleep, resulting in insomnia.

This is a constant danger for the Reactive Type as many of them don't know when to stop, whether at work or involved in some other activity, and can develop neuroses as a result. Their inability to remove themselves from the influences of their surroundings can end up in taking one type of pill to sleep and another to keep them awake. They need to learn the art of rest and the art of sleep by creating moments in their daily routine to pause and remove themselves from the excitement of the surrounding environment and retire into themselves, being quiet and suspending all reactions for a time.

I should emphasize here the difference in behaviour between the Reactive Type and the balanced Frontal Retracted Type. The latter type is measured in everything he does and, at any given moment, is able to manage energy expenditure according to the reserves available. The Reactive Type is incapable of this kind of restraint, expending energy without any consideration of the consequences. They can't help themselves, so it is not worth reminding them of the need for restraint. The only advice one can give them is to compensate for the excess of energy expenditure with the equivalent in rest. As I said to a student chaplain of this Type, who had been a monk in the past, that with the demands of the job and his reactive tendency he was exhausted: 'You should reintroduce some measured doses of cloistered time into your life'.

The example of the Reactive Type demonstrates that one must make an effort to strike a balance by ceding to the demands of one's temperament and that the way of attaining that balance will be different in the Reactive Type in comparison to those who are naturally balanced (see Chap. IX).

2 / THE CONCENTRATED TYPE (Ill. 52)

There are those, on the contrary, whose reactive tendency is minimal. Their actions are not a response to the influences of their surroundings; they act completely independently of all external factors.

This gives them a morphological structure that, feature by feature, is the opposite of the Reactive Type. These belong to the Dilated type: a large body and face with a strong bone and muscle structure. But, as opposed to the Dilated Type that we are already familiar with, where the receptors are very open, this type has closed receptors. Face on, the mouth and nose are narrow and the eyes are close together, to the extent that the small face occupies a limited space within the large frame. In profile, the receptors are sunken into the face through a process of extreme frontal retraction which has the effect of straightening the lines. In addition, the receptors are not very mobile, giving the face an impassive expression, or a 'closed face', as I call it.

Psychologically, as I previously mentioned, the reactive tendency is reduced to a minimum which significantly affects their ability to adapt. In addition, they are very individualistic, which affects every action that they take by imposing their brand on everything around them.

Illustration 52. – I. THE CONCENTRATED TYPE

The retraction of the small face constricts the receptors, in contrast to the size of the frame, which corresponds psychologically to an internal concentration of energy. This gives the active and voluntary aptitudes control over intellectual and emotional receptivity. The resultant internal tension creates differing responses depending on the general structure of the face. In the first image, the general balance in the face gives the concentrated energy the freedom to behave reflectively, methodically, and with a steady output, which makes it a valuable asset. On the other hand, in the second image, a contraction creates tension in the fairly large receptors which worsens the blockage formed between the cerebral zone and the emotional zone. In this case, the concentration risks triggering brutal instinctive reactions. This is someone who is potentially aggressive and quick-tempered.

Body expression

This lack of sensitivity to outside influences determines attitudes and actions that are noted for their calm, their phlegm and their slow, measured activity. The Concentrated Type is stable, has a measured gait and is hardly ever influenced by any incidents that may occur around them. They don't tend to gesticulate but when they do their gestures are precise and correspond to the action they wish to take. They speak little and never gossip; they only say what needs to be said and they don't talk while working, wishing to concentrate on the matter at hand. As I have said, their face does not reveal their thoughts or feelings, which gives them a reputation for impassiveness that is not entirely justified.

Illustration 52. – II. THE CONCENTRATED TYPE

In the first image is someone who, due to his refined receptors, has no interest in material possessions. The intense passion indicated in the extremely tonic Retracted-Dented facial frame pushes him towards action and adventure. The woman in the other image is Jeanne Castille, an American teacher who dedicated her life to spreading the French language throughout Louisiana. Even though very sensitive, as indicated by the flaring nostrils, she nevertheless did not allow herself to be driven by emotion, only by reason (she says it herself) and her ambition to achieve her goal.

Instinct

In accordance with the dilated structure of the face, they have powerful instincts which are manifested through self-determination rather than influenced by outside factors.

Their sensuality is strong and their demands are based on quantity rather than quality. They do not succumb to sensual pleasure and are not often moved by their partner's aesthetic attributes. They are usually boorish, un-tempered by tenderness, and they tend not to consider satisfying the same needs of others that they search for themselves.

They also tend to be aggressive. This is the direct expression of their powerful vitality and their need for self-affirmation and domination. This may be expressed in violence due to the lack of emotional connection with others.

Due to the constriction in their communication zones, the Concentrated Type is comparable to a powerful river which, at some point, passes through a narrow channel of rock and forces the flow to rush through with unusual violence. In parallel, as their instinctive energy lacks free expression, it accumulates over time and builds tension so that when there is an opportunity of expression the reaction is violent. This violence is a mark of their sensuality and aggression, which are both expressed in the wish for the total and absolute defeat of their opponent. In cases where there is an abundance of this force, it can also translate into activity. The Concentrated Type is in fact notable for the potency of their actions and their need to complete a task, whatever it may be, without allowing obstacles to get in their way.

Emotional life

They have powerful feelings. They are passionate but it is a cold passion due to the extreme restraint that the closed receptors impose. As we have seen, they tend not to be at all influenced by outside factors. The environment that they are likely to consider pleasurable is reduced to a very narrow zone of expansion: their marriage partner and one or two friends. They are neither sociable nor friendly and make no efforts to please. They try to dominate and impose their own viewpoints in their relationships. They don't have a trace of the vanity of the Reactive Type as they don't care about other's opinions or look for praise or blame. They are proud, convinced that they are in the right and sure of themselves, only trusting their own thoughts and feelings.

They lack delicacy in their feelings and seduce or defeat by force of will.

We have seen by the structure of their receptors that they are sensitive but it is so severely restrained that it is not externally visible. This is what gives them the reputation for being phlegmatic and impassive. This certainly makes them the polar opposite of the Reactive Type's obvious sensitivity; they are able to keep their cool in all circumstances and they are the ones deployed to aid the wounded or bury the dead.

It should also be noted that their feelings aren't as dispersed as the Reactive Type. All of their emotions are concentrated on a specific passion which channels their entire personality onto a single path. For example, they don't mix business with pleasure, and when they have an important project to complete, they will self-impose a limit on their activities in order to be able to fulfil it with all the energy they have at their disposal.

I have said that their passion is cold. In reality, the concentration of feelings creates a powerful internal tension which remains contained and, remaining contained for so long, once it is given an outlet is very explosive. They are also vengeful, that type of premeditated vengeance that has been secretly planned and pursuit of the objective is relentless.

Intelligence

Between the two basic elements of intellectual process—receptivity and activity—it is evident that the second element takes priority in this case. The lack of receptivity is the Concentrated Type's Achilles' heel, the lack of ability to assimilate. They are narrow-minded, closed to the world and lack the flexibility to adapt according to circumstances. Throughout their studies, they have been shown to be less intelligent than the Reactive Type (all else being equal, if we can consider that the term 'equal' has validity here) as they are not very interested or open to learning and completely closed to a number of fields.

On the other hand, their best quality is their liveliness: they are very active, searching and creating experiences, work plans and projects. They don't have many ideas but, when they do, they like them to be precise and clear. They reason with logic and discipline.

This self-education leads them to very personal and rigid opinions which are not open to debate. They enjoy doctrine and their intelligence is most suitable for affirmation and construction rather than understanding what others may wish to communicate to them.

They lack imagination. They are active thinkers closely tied to logic and, above all, for their qualities of perseverance, they will see projects through to the end. They make great scientists.

Will

They desire action. They are tenacious, persevering and often obstinate. When they decide to do something, they will do it in spite of any obstacles that might appear. As opposed to the Reactive Type, they don't need to succeed in order to persevere. This desire for action leads them to dominate others and impose their own views on them.

They have excellent self-control. They know at exactly which point they should keep quiet and when to act. They dominate their passion. On the other hand, they are rigid and incapable of reconciling other points of view or circumstances.

They have the capacity for leadership and are often found in top positions. However, they lack the flexibility to be well-rounded bosses and good managers.

Professions

Professionally, their strength is their greatest asset.

In manual labour, they are valued for their strength, perseverance, steady pace and ability to see difficult tasks through to the end. You can find them in practically all professions that require the above qualities but that don't require improvisation and speed.

They are suitable for all sports that require strength and great concentration. Their lack of emotion is clearly an advantage in competitions as they can give their best performance without being influenced by their surroundings. They are more suitable for individual rather than team sports.

In commerce and industry, their advantage lies in the fact that they are good workers, consistent, dependable, reliable and unfazed by difficulties. However, they lack rapport with other people, including the public and their colleagues. As such, they are most likely found working as accountants, administrators or team leaders in businesses that are exclusively technical in nature.

They are suitable for careers such as first-aid workers and surgeons. However, they lack the personal touch indispensable for the majority of these kinds of careers. They are generally unsuitable for professions in the fields of psychology and teaching.

In the self-employed professions, they don't have the inquiring mind necessary to gaining the required knowledge. They make up for this deficiency by their dedication to work and their willingness to keep going to the end. They also don't have the speed of assimilation that the Reactive Type has, which gives the latter access to certain positions at a young age. They are slow and only reach their objectives through personal effort and experience gained over a long period of time. They are more comfortable in positions that require physical exertion rather than intellectual effort. They make better surgeons than doctors, or engineers on a construction site rather than in an office.

In politics, they don't make popular orators or diplomats. They have a great capacity for work and they make good assistants in government positions, dedicated economists and methodical accountants. It's rare that one has the stature to be a head of State.

CHAPTER VII
TYPES OF DOMINANT EXPANSION

In the first book, we saw that amongst the Mixed Types, with their combinations of dilation and retraction, there are those who are very clearly characterised by a pronounced expansion in one of the three zones of the face that contrast with the retraction of the other two. I call these *Types of dominant expansion*.

Popular opinion has always recognized the significance of each of the three zones. It is well known that lovers kiss on the mouth, brothers and sisters on the cheek and a schoolteacher will kiss his pupil on the forehead. Intuitively, we know that a large jaw is associated with a strong neck which is a sign of strong instincts, that a big nose with broad cheekbones is a sign of a passionate temperament and that a large forehead is a sign of great intelligence. Caricaturists take it a step further by accentuating the predominance even more by giving, for example, an exaggerated forehead to geniuses (see Ill. 3).

I described these predominant characteristics in the first book. In chapter I, I used caricatures as an exaggerated form of illustration and again in Chapter IV, this time in a less extreme fashion by more closely respecting a personality's balance.

This reference to common sense and to caricatures reminds us of the danger of defining a predominant zone exclusively by its size. It would be an error to conclude that there is a direct relationship between the size of the forehead and levels of intelligence. Morphopsychology teaches us that we must give priority to qualitative elements, especially the contrasts and harmony among the facial forms.

This consideration for the qualitative must be taken into account on various levels.

First and foremost, we must consider the differences in the facial shape (particularly its tonicity) and the receptors' level of vitality as these qualitative elements are decisive in establishing the size of the expansion zone.

Secondly, we must consider the degree of balance between the three zones. In certain cases, equilibrium is achieved through a hierarchy in which the predominant zone takes precedence over the other zones. Such is the case for Types with a dominant cerebral zone, whereby equilibrium is achieved when thought is supported by the emotions (when there is no conflict between the two) and the energy of the instinctive zone works with the other zones to provide a solid base for the generation of action and the achievement of objectives.

In other cases, equilibrium is lacking because the dominant zone overwhelms the other zones and has a kind of tyrannical hold over the personality. For example, if the cerebral zone is too dominant, thought lacks engagement with the emotional and instinctive zones, effectively operating in a void, creating abstractions, systems and ideologies. At its most extreme, it enters the world of fantasy, losing all contact with the real world (the 'dreamers').

In the same way, if the emotional zone predominates, the individual will always react on an emotional level, making it impossible to reason objectively with him about any issues that may arise.

Likewise, if the jaw area is extremely well developed, the individual is at the mercy of his instinctive impulses or has an overriding need for physical activity, or an extreme ambition that does not match his actual capabilities.

The psychological meaning of predominance

The concept of the expansion zone is very important and has multiple psychological meanings.

The dominant zone, defined by its size, is the zone that is the most open to the world and which reacts most actively to its influences. It is also the most interactive.

This abundance of interactions reflects the natural predisposition of the individual, where they find their joie de vivre, and it is the reason why they can consistently maintain the expansion over time.

The alternative, should expansion in the dominant zone be blocked for some reason, is that the individual feels profound fatigue, sadness and depression.

The predominant zone is the fastest to develop, beginning early in childhood and remaining the most active into old age.

It is here that we can have the greatest influence over children. Teachers should always take this into account in order to be able to help their students in the most effective way.

Most memories are stored in the dominant zone. The easy recovery of memories also enriches the personality.

The dominant zone dictates the choice of activities that the child enjoys and his choice of profession as an adult.

The abundance of interaction with the world, the powerful memory, great capacity for work and the profound satisfaction for his accomplishments mean that if the individual is creative, it is in the domain of the dominant zone that the creativity will come out.

For example, in the Type where the cerebral zone is dominant, this is someone interested in intellectual matters, for example, culture, art and literature. The person actively seeks out interaction with other intellectuals, past and present (1). It is there that he experiences the greatest pleasure and never tires of building on his knowledge (2). However, they can become depressed should circumstances dictate, for example, having to do exhausting manual labour (as a child, Dickens had to work fourteen hours a day putting tickets on boxes), or being imprisoned, (Dostoyevsky was in a penal colony, where he was denied all reading material) (3). Cerebral dominance manifests itself in childhood through the early development of the cranium and the forehead, and an expressive intensity in the eyes which reveals the awakening of intellectual activity. In old age, when all other forces are already in decline, the cerebral function maintains a large part of its previous abilities (4). It is by appealing to reason and imagination rather than feelings, and by satisfying curiosity and responding to his questions, that the teacher can influence the child's education (5). His memory records everything related to the intellectual domain: general ideas, concepts, literary or scientific material. The memory is, however, deficient in other areas, particularly in regards to facts and specific details about people or events (6). It is not necessary to force this individual to read or study as he is more than happy to do it, devoting a large part of his leisure time to it. At a later stage, his choice of profession will lie within the intellectual field (7). And finally, if he has creative talent, it is in this area that he will be inventive and carry out his life's work (8).

However, the retraction of the other two zones significantly reduces the ability for expansion in their respective fields. The dominant Cerebral Type reserves a very limited space in his life for feelings and passions and doesn't allow his emotions to influence his actions. In the same way, he doesn't have strong instinctive forces and he will happily adopt an ascetic life where his intellectual activities take priority. It is for the same reason that he does not indulge in physical activities, is not handy around the house and hardly ever takes part in sports.

Illustration 53. – DOMINANT EXPANSION—ARAPAHOE MOTHER AND BABY

As is typical in the Indian people, dominance in the emotional zone is noted by the width of the cheekbones, creating a hexagonal facial shape. In comparing the mother with the baby, it can be seen that the baby shows a surprisingly early development of the instinctive zone.

Illustration 54. – DOMINANT EXPANSION

Here are two portraits whereby the three zones are balanced, giving equal importance to the instinctive, affective and cerebral life. On the other hand, the three photos of children demonstrate, from left to right, a dominant instinctive zone, a dominant emotional zone and a dominant cerebral zone.

The role of the zones in retraction

The morphopsychologist must never forget that *the organism is a whole*, reflected in the face whereby the parts cannot be disassociated from one another and analysed in isolation. The flow of vital energy runs equally everywhere and, from one moment to the next, is carried towards the outside world (zones in expansion) or towards the inner world (zones in retraction).

The zone in expansion expresses itself first. It is more open and quantitatively more important to the extent that we find ourselves tending to focus on it exclusively. But that is a mistake as expression in the zones of retraction—while being more reserved, more discreet and slower —is still important from two perspectives.

Firstly, the zones in retraction are repressed with the frequent result that they are expressed indirectly through the zone in expansion. The energy of the repressed tendencies, unable to express themselves directly, therefore remains intact. An emotional upset, for example, could be transferred to the cerebral zone in the form of a dream or some imaginative creation or push the individual towards physical action or adventure as a means of diverting the repressed energy.

Secondly, the zones in retraction are more sensitive than the zones in expansion and suffer more from the harmful effects of the environment. They are demonstrably more vulnerable. Even when the harmful event directly affects the zone in expansion, it is impervious, while, in the meantime, the zone in retraction suffers. So, someone with a dominant cerebral zone who is overtaxed with intellectual work will not suffer from a migraine or a psychological weakness but may be affected by digestive problems or muscle pain. Conversely, someone with a dominant instinctive zone who over-indulges may not suffer from indigestion but instead from a migraine or an asthmatic episode. The conclusion is that one must not apply the remedy to the organ that is suffering but to the organ which is the origin of the suffering.

We can see then that the apparently simple distinction between the three zones and the notion of dominant expansion poses a number of delicate problems for the morphopsychologist. He must analyse the facial shape and facial expression of each zone by clearly distinguishing: the round facial shape and atonic expression of passive expansion; the round facial shape with planes and the tonic facial expression of active expansion; and the angled shape or retracted–dented shape of controlled expansion. The psychological meaning of the zone in expansion is different in each case and we will see the absolute clarity that these distinctions bring particularly to the study of foreheads.

1 / TYPES OF INSTINCTIVE EXPANSION (Ill. 55 and 56)

This is characterised by expansion in the jaw area which corresponds to the instinctive–active life.

Morphologically, the head and face form an inverted, truncated cone (or, in profile, a trapezoid). Measuring the size by diameter and volume, as in anthropometry, is of no use to us in this case as what counts here is essentially the proportions of the jaw zone in relation to the two other zones which are in relative retraction, as well as the degree of difference in the shapes.

We should distinguish between:

- *Passive expansion*: a round facial shape with soft lines and no clear jawline, pale skin and a soft mouth with full lips which are always slightly open (Ill 55. Fig 1).

- *Active expansion*: a round, firm facial shape, warm skin tones (pink cheeks, red lips) and a strong tonic expression (firm mouth) (Ill 55. Fig 2).

- *Controlled expansion*: a curved or retracted-dented facial shape and a very firm mouth (Ill 55. Fig 4).

Psychologically, the predominance of the instinctive life consequently ensures a firm footing in material reality. The instinct will always be stronger than emotions or reason.

In the *passive form*, the *instinct for nutrition* dominates, engendered by a strong need for nourishment through gluttony and sometimes overindulgence of alcohol. This also includes the sexual instinct in the form of both passive and base pleasures of the flesh.

In the *active form*, these same instincts represent a need for activity. For example, the individual in Fig. 1 has general passivity as a dominant factor but, given his firm mouth, he will certainly be prone to gluttony, as a gourmet who prefers high quality food. The great musician Rossini, whose portrait is shown here, was a connoisseur and it was said that he would prefer a good meal to listening to a symphony (Ill. 56 – II).

Illustration 55. – INSTINCTIVE EXPANSION

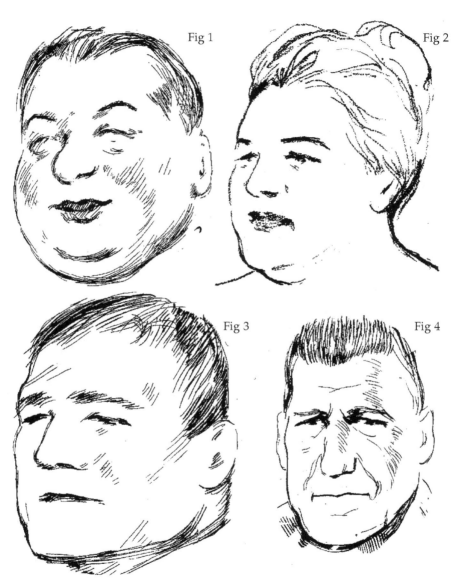

Fig 1

Fig 2

Fig 3

Fig 4

Instinctive expansion has a different meaning depending on the facial shape. The man in the first portrait has a facial shape that lacks tone. The level of tone is somewhat better in the woman. The retraction of the forehead in the portraits of the two men underneath suggest that their instinctive forces are under control and could be put to good use.

What appears here, derived from the instinct for nutrition, is the *instinct for acquisition*. This makes the pursuit of material goods a permanent occupation and determines the choice of field of business. The *instinct for activity*, working with the hands, is also present and, taking into account that not all of the vital energy is dedicated to pleasure, some remains available for activity.

One can see the need for activity best achieved in the Controlled Expansion Type. Whereas the vital energy is dissipated externally in the two prior types of instinctive expansion as a response to outside stimulants, in the case of the controlled expansion it is more focused and can be used for concrete action.

As people like what is similar to them, the Instinctive Expansion Type, solidly supported by the large base of their face, show a preference for people of weight, those that guarantee them a solid material situation, substantial homes, large furniture, comfortable armchairs and good quality clothing. They are not very attuned to the aesthetic so, for them, a beautiful woman is a woman of a solid stature with a good covering of flesh. Their self-esteem depends upon the strength of their action, their assets and their material success.

Their emotional life takes a back seat as the retraction of the middle zone limits the field of their social relationships. They are not sociable but their family is important to them as they see it as a type of possession. Things and people are only interesting in so far as they are useful. Tenderness and feelings are accorded very little space in their life.

The field of expansion in the cerebral zone is reduced, indicated in the narrowness of a low forehead, suggesting that their intellect is also subservient. Instincts govern their life, never thought. They are closed-minded and learn only the minimum number of ideas that they consider of practical use. This means that they aren't good students and would prefer to learn a manual skill. They therefore have a limited number of ideas, which are always the same standard ideas, and they are at their most efficient when doggedly pursuing the realisation of these ideas. They lack imagination and if they invent something then it will be connected to manual work, such as creating a new instrument or a new work technique.

One should be careful, nevertheless, of what I have just said in relation to their equilibrium. In some, the structure of the forehead is very strongly retracted and accompanied by deep-set eyes. This indicates an acute awareness that, even though they are unable to counterbalance their instinctive impulses, they can suppress and block them. This occurs mainly in childhood where the subject has been affected by strong constraints in their education which have had the effect of restraining the development of the powerful instincts. This creates a conflict between these two contradictory forces: the expansion of the instinctive and the retraction of suppression. Sometimes the instinctive triumphs and dominates and, at other times, the conscience controls it; however, due to its relative weakness, it can only achieve control through a brutal blocking action which inhibits all impulses. This conflict makes the individual neurotic and the morphopsychologist may be surprised to note that the subject's nervous and fastidious behaviour doesn't correspond with what he thought he would have believed able to deduce based on his analysis of the predominance of the instinctive zone.

This unusual situation is an example of the type of error to which our science is susceptible; however, it is an instructive error. Faced with it, you can be sure that the subject's actions won't conform to their natural tendencies. These have been inhibited by neuroses. One day the subject may be able to free himself of these neuroses and show his true character, that which the morphopsychologist deciphered from the face's traits.

Professions

Those with an expansion in the instinctive zone are particularly suited for handling materials as labourers. They are handymen and builders who work at a slow pace without allowing any distractions to interrupt them.

They are not city people, preferring to be in the countryside. They don't need the company of other humans, preferring that of nature, the countryside, the forest, the sea and the company of animals. For this reason they are often found amongst farmers, foresters, livestock farmers and seamen.

They are valued in commerce and industry for their common sense and the ability to see a task through to its conclusion. They are more suitable for working with large objects rather than delicate things which tells us which kind of manufacturing and sales industries are most suited to them. They are most apt to work with mass consumer products: for example, in flour mills, as butchers or bakers, or selling livestock or large machinery.

Illustration 56. – I. INSTINCTIVE EXPANSION IN THE YOUNG

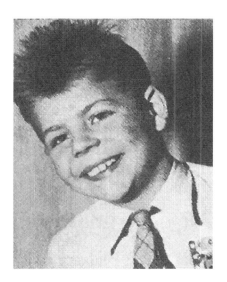

An expansion in the instinctive area with tonicity in youth indicates a good aptitude for manual work. This is the case of these three boys who are more suitable for practical work than intellectual studies. The boy on the top left won a prize for an original meccano set model.

Illustration 56. – II. THE GREAT MUSICIAN ROSSINI

This face is both strong and harmonious: the three zones are balanced. However, the jaw dominates, is tonic and in expansion, from which we can deduce that he was both a gourmand and a gourmet.

They are not generally found in social work as they are not emotionally open and lack the social skills that are indispensable in these fields.

Their minds are too closed to be successful in the self-employed professions. In education, they are only suited to be technical assistants.

Their physical strength makes them suitable for individual sports such as boxing, shot put and weight lifting.

2 / TYPES OF AFFECTIVE EXPANSION (Ill. 57-58-59)

This type is characterised by a predominance in the nasomalar region which corresponds to the affective life.

Morphologically, looking face on, the face is broadest at the level of the cheekbones, creating a hexagonal facial shape. From the profile, we can see that the nose is large and juts forward to a significant degree and, starting at the point of the nose, all lines angle backwards: the forehead angles back as does that of the chin, depending on the subject. The face may be short or long depending on the level of tonicity. We will see that there are strong parallels between this morphology and that of the Lateral Retracted Type.

We should distinguish between:

- *passive expansion*, which is notable by a plump, soft nose, slightly turned up like a child's and with heavy and not very mobile nostrils (Ill. 57 - I);

- *active expansion*, which is characterised by a rounded facial shape with planes and a straight nose with narrow nostrils that flare (Ill. 57 – 2); and

- *controlled expansion*, which is characterised by a curved or indented facial shape which makes the cheekbones stand out (more in the second case than the first), with an aquiline or hooked nose and nostrils that are sometimes open and sometimes closed (Ill. 58).

Illustration 57. – I. AFFECTIVE EXPANSION

We have here a comparison between two types of affective expansion. In the first picture is a woman whose face clearly lacks tone in all three zones, the nose is projected forward, pulling the upper lip with it. She has a plump nose with a childlike, concave shape, framed by soft cheeks. The second is of a man with a very tonic face particularly marked by the strong projection of the cheekbones and a nose that, although small, has nostrils that vibrate, which is a sign of the expression of his passionate character.

Psychologically, they place a great deal of importance on emotions in their daily life. They constantly need emotional connections with others and through social contact. The emphasis is on their feelings rather than logic. I should add that memories with an emotional aspect predominate over other types of memories. The author Marcel Proust is a clear example (Ill. 59).

Illustration 57. – II. TYPES OF AFFECTIVE EXPANSION

Expansion in the emotional zone is very frequent in the native Indian and oriental races. Here are two examples. The Indian chief Sitting Bull has a particularly pronounced affective zone. The young Vietnamese girl's Venusian1 nose is framed by very broad and tonic cheeks.

In those where *passiveness* dominates, their emotional life is nourished through tenderness and the need to be loved and to receive love from others (typical childlike behaviour).

From a very early age, those where *activeness* dominates are extremely sensitive and therefore experience every impression vividly. They react immediately to anything that has an emotional resonance, sympathising with the joys and pain of others. They are passionate and impulsive,

---

1: See Book 3, Chapter IV for an explanation of the planetary types.

dynamic and enthusiastic; they get carried away but they tire just as quickly.

In those with *controlled* expansion, this same emotional dynamism is apparent but only in their preferred surroundings; it remains under control in other situations and is often hidden behind a cool exterior. The feelings and passions of the more concentrated type are more constant.

The other two stages—cerebral and instinctive, being in retraction—have a significantly less important role. The instinctive is, in part, repressed: in love, for example, the Affective Type has less of a need to satisfy instinctive needs than emotional attachments.

As far as intelligence is concerned, it can make the affective expansion dynamic but logical thought never reigns; feelings always lead. For example, conduct may be guided by generous ideas but may contradict hard logic. (I also call these 'Social Creators'. Ill. 58)

Illustration 58. – I. EXAMPLES OF THE AFFECTIVE EXPANSION TYPE

In a study I conducted with Marielle Clavel, dedicated to Social Creators, I showed that the vocation of the majority of the founders of developmental social works has been in part determined by their strong affective expansion. Amongst others are Dr. Schweitzer and Mother Theresa, each one remarkable for the size of their affective zone: their broad cheekbones and large and fleshy nose with nostrils that vibrate—a sign of the expression of their passionate character.

Illustration 58. – II. ARTHUR RUBINSTEIN

Affective predominance is very pronounced in the great pianist Rubinstein. The general style is that of a Lateral Dilated–Retracted Type. This has affected not only the private life of this concert pianist but also his choice of music.

Professions

Those with a dominant affective zone look for jobs that involve working with other people and, depending on the degree of retraction, human interaction more or less within their comfort zone. They are not solitary people and prefer to work in a team. However, should circumstances mean that they have to work alone, they will look to animals for company. They also enjoy working in the countryside, in crop and livestock farming.

They are attracted to social careers as nurses, first-aiders, social workers, educators or group facilitators.

They fit in more easily, for the same reasons, in commerce rather than industry.

In the self-employed professions, they prefer to choose work that requires human interaction: as general medical practitioners rather than laboratory technicians, engineers on a building site rather than in an office or trial lawyers rather than legal advisors.

No matter their talents, in art they are attracted to emotionally expressive styles (see the case of Rubinstein, the great pianist, Ill. 58).

While creative, they don't operate in the field of ideas, systems or art forms. They create specifically in the area of human problems, desiring to find new practical solutions for the good of mankind. They don't write; they live. And if they do write, it is only afterwards, to relate what has been accomplished and to garner support.

Illustration 59. – THE AFFECTIVE EXPANSION OF MARCEL PROUST

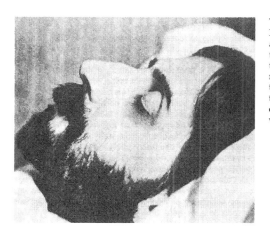

The usual portraits of the great writer Marcel Proust barely reveal the dominant affective zone. It has taken this profile after death to demonstrate how important this dominant zone was, notable by the majestic nose and the very deep-set eyes, the depth of the contours surprising on this slender face. This explains how his emotional life played a big role in Proust's work (photo Helleu, BN).

3 / TYPES OF CEREBRAL EXPANSION (Ill. 60 and 61)

The Cerebral Expansion Type is characterised by a predominance in the cerebral zone and intellectual life. This predominance is exclusive to the human species, the development of the cerebral apparatus being one of the main distinctions between man and those animals that are genetically closest to him. This is already visible in the infant when compared to an animal's young. But when we compare one person with another, it is clear that the cerebral zone is not developed in the same way for everyone, which justifies the need for the description of a Cerebral Expansion Type. The existence of this type has been known for a long time and has often led to applying a value of intellectual aptitude according to the size of the forehead and cranium through the type of measurement that anthropologists make.[2] But if there is a statistically significant proportion of types of cerebral expansion in thinkers, particularly great creators, we risk making a serious error in judgement by wishing to draw general conclusions and applying them to one individual in particular.

I have demonstrated that, in order to make a fair analysis, it is necessary to substitute a quantitative statistical evaluation for a qualitative analysis based on two essential elements: the differentiation of the facial shape and the harmony of the proportions. This is my formula: *a large forehead is only a sign of great intelligence if it is distinctive and its proportions are harmonious.* I will explain what I mean by that in more detail.

Morphologically, the Cerebral Expansion Type is characterised by a predominance in the upper zone: the cranium and the ocular receptor (Ill. 60).

- *Passive expansion* makes the forehead uniformly rounded with bulbous eyes on the surface of the face, accompanied by an expression which lacks tone (Ill. 60, Fig 1).

- *Active expansion* also makes the forehead rounded but with planes which make the facial shape firmer and reduce its size a little. (They are usually smaller than that of passive expansion.) The eyes are bulbous, too, but the expression is more lively and intense (Ill. 60, Fig 2).

- *Controlled expansion* is different in that there is a clear demarcation between the three zones which we have already studied in the section on frontal retraction. It is important to highlight that the intellect is greater where there is controlled expansion, where thought is only organised when managed at this level (Ill. 60, Fig 3).

Psychologically, they are characterised by the importance that they give to their inner thoughts; it is the intellect that governs, not instincts or feelings.

2: The anthropologist Broca compared a group of manual labourers with a group of intellectuals and showed that, statistically, the perimeter of the brain of the former group was smaller than that of the latter.

Illustration 60. – CEREBRAL EXPANSION

Fig 1

Fig 2

Fig 3

Differentiation and harmony in the forehead are essential to understanding the intellect. Above, we can see the difference between a forehead that lacks tone on the left and the strong forehead on the right. Below, we can see the forehead of the illustrious savant Pasteur which is very straight due to frontal retraction.

When *passivity* dominates, the mind effortlessly assimilates, without discernment, all impressions that it receives. For example, one reads profusely but without choosing the subject matter. The memory is extensive and retains everything; the individual is very learned but lacks energy; recalling memories is not easy; he is never critical and does not make any selective analysis or his thoughts are imprecise. This type of thinking is not accompanied by a clear mind but by a vague perception, as in a dream. This state dominates within a young child prior to rational thought but there remains a certain capacity to understand the reality of things through intuition and in the form of images. When this state continues into adulthood, this plasticity is favourable under certain conditions as it can promote the unconscious work of the mind which is sometimes the origin of particular artistic talents, especially in music and mathematics.

When *activity* dominates, receptivity is counterbalanced by a good adaptation to the world of concrete reality but without any particular originality, the subject being a direct reflection of his surroundings. Those with active expansion excel in practical fields such as commerce, industry and where it is necessary to use already acquired concepts and transmit them through education.

When *controlled* expansion dominates, as we have seen, a gateway is opened in how the intelligence accesses the mind: reflection, calculation, organisation, anticipation, imagination and construction. What stands out in these Types is *the triple combination of possibilities*. The lower section has a projected brow bone and temples that are slightly retracted, which corresponds to a good connection with material values and the ability for realisation. The middle section is either flat or sunken, corresponding to the power of reflection, an understanding of the elements of any given problem. The upper section indicates the power of the imagination. I should underline the importance of the imaginative zone. It represents to some extent the forehead of the child that remains in the adult (which, as we know, has an almost uniform roundness). The mature adult therefore retains the child's abilities: the primary ability to think in images and cosmic communication via the subconscious, which means that, when this section is very well developed, it indicates the prevalence of a childlike mind which the subject will always refer back to. Many creative people believe that their creative talent, whether artistic or literary, depends in a large part on the return to the primary sources of life.

The other two zones of the Cerebral Expansion Type are in relative retraction. Emotions do not intervene much in daily life and the subject is moved through reasoning or imagination but not through feelings, and he cannot be influenced through emotion. The instincts also take on a secondary role and are never acted on. For example, the union of the sexes is not principally determined in this case by pure sexual attraction, nor by emotions: it is logic, a calculated interest, that plays the definitive role or it is through imagination in the form of a fanciful daydream.

It is vital at this point that the morphopsychologist brings in the *qualitative notion of harmony* that I mentioned earlier.

First and foremost is the harmony in the forehead itself. Firstly, we must analyse the balance between the three zones of controlled expansion, a balance which, if achieved, gives the intellect qualities of being both concrete and abstract, logical and intuitive, and spontaneous as well as reflective. Second is the angle of the forehead, as harmony comes from a medium degree of slope, at an equal distance between extreme lateral retraction—reflecting impulsiveness and spontaneity—and frontal retraction, with its inhibiting effect. Thirdly, it is in the balance between the structure of the forehead and that of the ocular receptor which is ideally balanced between the receptivity of impressions and their storage.

On the other side of the coin, where there is disharmony, we cannot conclude that the size of the forehead relates to the size of the intellect. So, firstly, disharmony is produced when the development of the three zones—observation, reflection and imagination—is exceedingly unequal; secondly, when the forehead is either too inclined or too vertical and; thirdly, when there is a contradiction between the eyes and the forehead. A large forehead equipped with a very large imaginative zone and deep-set eyes indicates a richness of thought but self-absorption, the inability to enrich one's self by assimilating the impressions received from the outside world. He is an ideologist, fanatic of doctrines and therefore unable to produce great works. On the other hand, someone with a small forehead with big eyes that are open to the exterior world may lack imagination and creative abilities but is nevertheless receptive to ideas and is very productive. The disharmony is apparent when a small forehead is accompanied by very deep-set eyes, indicating that there is a lack of input from the exterior and few reserves, leading to a poverty of ideas (Ill. 61-I).

We will now address the harmony between the cerebral zone and the rest of the face. When the retraction of the two lower zones is pronounced or atonic, thought appears to be freed from the constraints of emotions or instincts and therefore develops independently. However, this apparent advantage brings with it the serious disadvantage of being deprived of the support of an instinctive-affective life. Thought no longer has its roots in profound vitality and, without that essential nourishment, it tends to desiccate, like a plant deprived of sap, as we have already seen in the Atonic Retracted Types.

When, on the other hand, the two lower zones, albeit subordinate to the cerebral zone, are sufficiently developed for there to be a balance between thought, emotion and instinct, the imagination is enlivened by this general input and is therefore much richer.

Illustration 61. – I. THE FOREHEAD AND THE EYES

 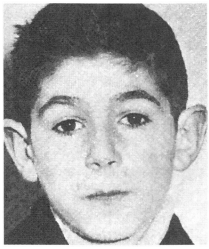

One must take the greatest care in establishing the relationship between the forehead and its sensory receptor, the eyes. Here are two opposing cases. The first has a strong cerebral expansion with a retraction which straightens the forehead and which is markedly different in three zones. However, the deep-set eyes indicate a lack of openness to the world where thought is self-absorbed, as in a fanatic, a dogmatist or even a prisoner deranged by his own ghosts. In the other portrait, we see a type of cerebral retraction in the small forehead which is locked in-between narrow perimeters. However, the eyes are open to the impressions of the outside world which give the subject a lively, up-to-date and pragmatic thought process which may be more efficient in daily life than in the previous case.

When we study the morphology of great men, we should not limit ourselves, as we tended to do in the past, to the study of the forehead as the only noble part of the face: we must consider the other parts, as well. For example, in the following two portraits, the morphology of the forehead is very similar, indicating great intellectual abilities. However, in one, the rest of the face has a pronounced retraction while the other is dilated in the style of someone who has both feet on the ground. The first is a dilettante, curious about everything, cultured but who never goes beyond the superficial in whatever he is interested in. He is effectively a 'butterfly'. The other, however, may be a creator whose imagination is nourished by his entire being which enriches both his creations as well as the ability for realisation (Ill. 61-II).

Illustration 61. – II.

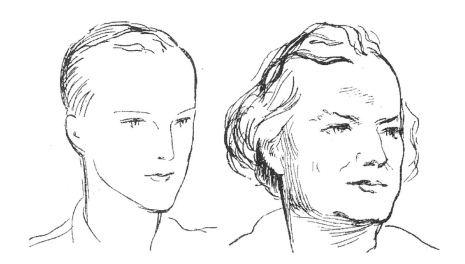

4 / TYPES OF DOUBLE EXPANSION

The equilibrium of the Dominant Expansion Type is often complicated by the strong dominance of one function over others, making it impossible to describe without over-simplifying. However, when there are two zones in expansion and one in retraction, as in the Double Expansion Type, we are closer to what occurs in real life.

We must address how the contrast between two zones in expansion and one in retraction might work in harmony.

However, another problem arises when equilibrium is established between two expansion zones. Will they join forces and work together? Or will they independently compete for dominance, so that one either becomes permanently dominant or they alternate depending on the situation?

Double Expansion Types are very complex and the morphopsychologist must analyse each case by evaluating the morphology of each of the individual parts of the face and then provide a synthesis integrating all of the tendencies present.

I will give examples in this chapter and the more we address the complexity of the morphopsychological Types, the closer our description will come to reality as we recognise the different types that cross our paths on a daily basis.

A / THE INSTINCTIVE–AFFECTIVE TYPE (Ill. 62-65)

Co-dominance of the instinctive and affective zones is a very common occurrence, as much in man as in the mammals that man resembles.

Morphologically, this predominance is indicated by the strong development of the two inferior zones and is clearly seen in profile, which juts out like a 'muzzle' as we see in many animals. Here, as in all descriptions, we must add the level of tonicity, the degree of refinement in the different elements, the general harmony of the face and finally, the analysis of the forehead which is important despite being the least developed zone.

Psychologically, the instinctive–affective life governs behaviour, with thought relegated to a secondary role.

Where the predominance is extreme, as in Ill. 62-I, the face is large and the neck thick, contrasting with the very small cranium and forehead. From this, we can conclude an animal-like mentality with a dominance in the affective life that lacks any counterbalance whatsoever. This indicates that the subject surrenders to his feelings, desires and passionate impulses without paying heed to reasoned thought. In other instances, ideas have a role to play, but a subordinate one, and are always subject to the dominant instinctive and affective interests. Clearly, there exist many different combinations and, where there is stronger development in the cerebral stage, greater harmony exists between the different personality strengths; however, even if the intellect is well developed, as in the case of Ill. 62-II, and has a certain level of independence, we must always take into account that an instinctive–affective predominance imposes concrete reality on thought and does not emanate from abstract ideas.

Illustration 62. – I. INSTINCTIVE–AFFECTIVE EXPANSION

Here are two extreme cases where predominance in the inferior zones is overwhelming, to the detriment of the cerebral zone which is very retracted. There is more to study in these two subjects whose thought processes are relegated to uncomplicated ideas which are always connected to practical applications.

As I have already mentioned in regards to the Instinctive Expansion Type, the cerebral zone exercises an element of control over the other functions. If he is a Dilated Type, particularly if the eyes are bulbous and lack tone, this control function is barely active. However, if he is a Retracted Type and the eyes are deep-set, awareness of his hypersensitivity tends to inhibit his impulses. There are even cases where the conflict between this inhibition and emotional impulses create deep conflicts in the personality.

This is where we observe a neurosis of recurrent moral anguish in the Instinctive–Affective Expansion Type, with the result that their actions are contrary to what is to be expected.[3]

Here, as elsewhere, harmony comes from the homogeneity of the structure of the different zones. For example, there can be a very tonic-shaped jawline with pronounced angles with, at the same time, a lack of tone in the affective zone, for example the concave nose of a passive type. This lack of harmony creates a conflict between the energetic, dominating and independent attitude of the instinctive with the dependence of the affective zone. This morphological style explains the ambition to achieve, while having to contend with the tender and passive elements in their personality (see Ill. 81, a portrait of Lily Palmer).

Illustration 62. – II. INSTINCTIVE–AFFECTIVE EXPANSION

Here are two people whose instinctive-affective predominance does not exclude the possibility for concrete and pragmatic thinking which, supported by the solid base, can make them very efficient in the commercial or industrial domains.

3: I studied Blaise Pascal and found his case to be all the more remarkable as he was an extraordinary inventor (*Caractérologie et morphopsychologie*, Chap. IX, 1 vol, Ed. PUF). In Ill. 64, in the portrait of Pascal you will find an important example of the instinctive–affective type.

Illustration 63. – I. EXAMPLES OF THE INSTINCTIVE–AFFECTIVE TYPE

The same strength of the instinctive–affective type is found here in these two characters. The forehead is small, which suggests very clear ideas, but restricted to practical applications. The first is Napoleon Bullukian, an Armenian and very able construction worker who created an industrial empire. The second is Raymond Berthault, a large-scale businessman who created a distribution chain which became very successful due to its owner's dynamism.

Illustration 63. – II. EXAMPLES OF THE INSTINCTIVE–AFFECTIVE TYPE

In a different way, these two women provide us with examples of a strong, harmonious instinctive–affective expansion, with a very present and active mind. The first portrait is of Melina Mercouri who played an important role in Greek politics within the popular party. The second is the wife of Edison, the great American inventor.

Illustration 64. THE INSTINCTIVE–AFFECTIVE EXPANSION OF PASCAL

It might seem surprising to include Pascal's face amongst other examples of the instinctive–affective expansion type but, without a doubt, he would associate himself with the portraits in Ill. 63. However, I have chosen to separate it. As I demonstrated in a separate morphopsychological study dedicated especially to this great genius, his originality comes from this predominance and not, as one might have imagined, from a predominant cerebral zone. I demonstrated that this explains the majority of Pascal's character traits and the unusual character of his work, which is as much literary as it is scientific. One can see that his forehead is not particularly large; it is harmoniously differentiated which, as we know, has significant intellectual qualities (see the article in the *Revue de Morphopsychologie* from 1983, no. 3, 'Génie et Névrose. L'extraordinaire destin de Pascal').

Illustration 65. THE INSTINCTIVE–AFFECTIVE EXPANSION OF HELEN KELLER

Here is a photo of the American celebrity, Helen Keller, who was born both deaf and blind who, through fierce determination, was able to overcome her disabilities and become a writer and very talented conference speaker. Before seeing her portrait, I imagined that the privation of the two most importance senses, hearing and sight, could only result in a very pronounced retraction, but when I saw her face I could see the surprising expansion in the instinctive and affective zones where there is a great openness to contact with the world, taste and smell. I understood my mistake: that if it had been possible to educate Helen Keller through her sense of contact and touch, which was what remained—and despite her lack of sight and hearing, was very open to the world around her—had all her senses been affected, it would have been impossible to educate her.

B / THE AFFECTIVE–CEREBRAL TYPE Ill. 66)

The double predominance of the middle and upper zones is also a very common combination. Dr. Jung was wrong in stating that that the function of thought, combined with that of sentiment, was incompatible and therefore not viable.

Morphologically, both the cerebral and affective zones are very well developed while the jaw zone is comparatively reduced. The face is therefore broad in the upper area, gradually narrowing towards the lower part.

Psychologically, we cannot give a definitive description of the personality of these subjects as it depends entirely on the equilibrium between the three zones and the forehead.

In extreme cases where the jaw area is particularly deficient, all expression of instinct is inhibited and behaviour is timid, lacking courage and self-confidence. There is also a sense of detachment from essential needs and a disregard for the material and practical which they consider vulgar. Whatever the size of the intellect and capacity for emotion, neither are rooted in concrete reality and tend to function in a vacuum, in some way detached, while the lower zone does not allow intellectual thought or emotions to surface.

Where there is a better equilibrium, separation from the instinctive life favours the sublimation of thoughts and feelings, providing access to creative opportunities. This is the case in many great men.

The problem, in this case, is to appreciate what the resulting function of this double predominance will be: if there will be collaboration between thought and feeling in joint activities or if one becomes dominant over the other, or even if they alternate their domination. These are specific cases where, in order to pass judgement, it is necessary to synthesise all of the facial traits, understand the global expansion (breadth and tonicity), the equilibrium and the homogeneity or heterogeneity of the facial structure. Here are some portraits with explanatory comments to illustrate what I have just said.

Illustration 66. – I. CEREBRAL–AFFECTIVE EXPANSION

Contrary to what Jung maintained, this expansion is very common. Here are some examples. In the young girl, although her nose is quite small, the jutting forward of the cheeks indicates an expansion of this zone while the forehead is high and wide and the eyes, positioned somewhat deeply, are large. The other portrait shows the author Roman Rolland (drawn by Dauce from a photo). The double expansion is very pronounced while the instinctive zone is smaller, which tells us that he is not a man of action but has the temperament of a passionate thinker, as his words demonstrate.

Illustration 66. – II. CEREBRAL–AFFECTIVE EXPANSION

Here are two illustrious characters, Saint Vincent de Paul and Anderson, who have a strong cerebral–affective expansion in common but within different morphological styles, which explains the difference in their destinies. Vincent de Paul was a 'social creator', a man with a large, generous heart and the creator of 'Oeuvre des Enfants Trouvés' and a fellowship dedicated to looking after the sick. But he was also a man of great intellect, the founder of a monastery whose organizational skills were critical to realizing his good works. His face is short with firm contours and his eyes are penetrating, all signs of tonicity and action.

Anderson, the Danish writer, is almost completely the opposite. The length of his face indicates a lack of tone and the tendency is towards dreaming rather than action, towards imaginative fantasies. This lack of tone can be seen especially in the large, imaginative forehead and the dreamy look in the eyes.

C / THE INSTINCTIVE–CEREBRAL TYPE Ill. 67)

More unusual is a double expansion which allies the instinctive and cerebral zones, as these zones are physically separated one from the other. In order to work together, they must pass through the intermediate affective zone.

Morphologically, the two zones in expansion are separated by the affective zone in the middle which is in retraction. Face on, this often gives the facial shape the form of a mandolin due to the narrowness of the cheekbones or the retraction appears in the length with a shortening of the nose. In profile, there is typically a concave area in the middle of the face with the nose going inwards while the forehead and the chin jutting forward.

Psychologically, we can deduce that the vital expansion comes from two different domains: that of the instinctive life and that of the intellect. Feelings, on the other hand, have a very small role to play or at least a very limited influence; they do not impact their social life but they do limit emotional relations with their closest friends and family and can even, at the extreme, become completely egotistical and totally self-absorbed.

Illustration 67. – I. CEREBRAL–INSTINCTIVE EXPANSION

When the affective zone is reduced, it is a sign that either thought or action dominates conduct and not feelings. This little girl may appear affectionate due to the dilation in her face but the small nose indicates a very personal and selective sensitivity. In the same way, we can say that this head of industry's actions are not dictated by his feelings; he will conduct business based on logic or material interests.

It is possible for the instinctive and cerebral domains to remain separate. On the one hand, the instinctive life remains unsocialised and expresses itself through pure instinct. On the other hand, there is independence of thought whereby the form of thought depends upon the structure of the forehead.

In other cases, an accord is made between the two: either the instinctive life dominates and imposes on the intelligence or the mind dominates and uses the majority of the instinctive energy to act upon its plans. This last alternative is often found amongst creative people.

The positive aspect of this facial structure manifests itself in certain professions where the intervention of the affective zone may impede the action to be taken and so benefits from the reduction in this area. In superiors and heads of state, one might consider their attitude as devoid of sentiment and cynical but it is due to the need to prevail over an idea or objective at any cost (Bismark Ill. 67-II).

Illustration 67. – II. EXAMPLES OF CEREBRAL–INSTINCTIVE
EXPANSION

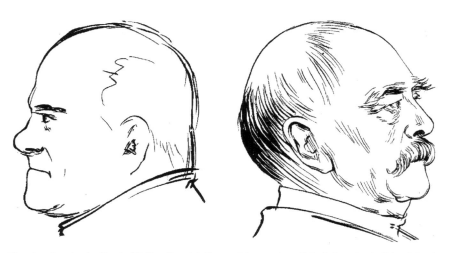

Here is a drawing by Pazzi of Father Grandet, the avaricious and egotistical character in Balzac's book. The other drawing is of the German statesman Bismarck. Dominance of the cerebral–instinctive zones is frequently found amongst statesmen, which is explained in the text. (The drawing is based on a painting by Lenbach.)

D / THE LATERAL–NASAL RETRACTION TYPE (Ill. 68-70)

We have just seen that certain morphopsychological types have a retracted affective zone which inhibits feelings and has therefore a modest role in behaviour. I have, however, discovered that this type of retraction often appears in a more complex model: it is at first disconcerting when we see morphopsychological traits of expansion combined with retraction. What is particularly common is an affective zone which has a strong frontal retraction that is drawn back to the facial bones on each side of the nose, flattening the cheek and making it slightly concave at this level. In contrast, the cheekbones are broad, therefore in expansion, and the nose is quite big, projecting out on the face. Morphopsychological analysis tells us that this paradoxical structure means the affective life conflicts with itself. The width of the cheekbones and the size of the nose indicate a large affective expansion while retraction of the cheeks reveals the demands imposed by his preferred surroundings. One must then conclude that, unless in one's preferred surroundings, the affective expansion is generally suppressed and introverted.

Illustration 68. – I. INHIBITED LATERAL–NASAL RETRACTION

In order to understand the psychological meaning of a lateral–nasal retraction, it is vital that it is not analysed in isolation but as part of the facial structure as a whole. Affective suppression differs according to what is made possible in the other zones. When a lack of tone impedes the active exteriorisation of a tendency, the retraction has an inhibiting influence, creating melancholy and paralysis which often results in anxiety.

This morphology can have a number of variations. First of all, how far the cheekbones stand out indicates the intensity of his subconscious emotional needs. Secondly, the lateral–nasal retraction may be more or less pronounced, demonstrating the degree of suppression. And thirdly, the structure of the nose counts, too: a fleshy nose indicates tenderness; a fleshless nose reveals a dry personality; a short nose is the sign of a lively temperament; and a long nose is a sign of passiveness.

It is crucial that we analyse the affective zone in relation to the two other zones. It should be noted that the emotional force that is repressed by the retraction accumulates internally under a growing tension. By virtue of its dynamism, the repressed emotional forces need to be released. This release can sometimes be achieved in the affective life itself, within an individual's preferred surrounding, where the subject can either reach fulfilment or find release through a sudden eruption of all repressed feelings. In this last case, the subject loses control and gives free rein to his anger.

Illustration 68. – II. INTERNALISING LATERAL–NASAL RETRACTION

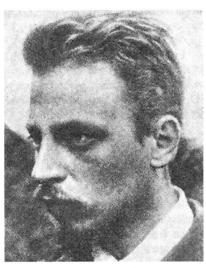 

In certain exceptional people, the suppression is internalised and nourishes the inner life. We can see it in the photo of the Swiss poet Rainer Maria Rilke. Next to him is a drawing of the German poet Uhland where the particularly pronounced expansion in the cerebral zone has a dynamising effect, partly compensating for the lack of tone in the chin and explaining the transfer of the affective life towards the mind. Here, however, we are at the limits of disequilibrium.

But fulfilment can also be attained by diverting into other easier routes provided by the two other zones. If expansion is greatest in the instinctive–active zone, the repressed emotions are transmuted into action. If it is, on the other hand, in the cerebral zone, then they will fuel dreams or other mental creativity.

The complexity of these situations is often disconcerting for the observer. Being able to analyse this complexity is precisely one of the main advantages of the morphopsychological method. In brief, I would say that a lateral–nasal retraction sometimes has an *inhibiting* effect, sometimes a *dynamic* effect and is sometimes *productive*.

Inhibiting retraction (Ill. 68) – When a number of signs of atony—for example, a long and soft nose, a weak jaw and expansion in the imaginative part of the cerebral zone—a lateral–nasal retraction has a paralysing effect. If this retraction is not very strong, it translates simply into shyness and indecision. When it is very pronounced, however, it can indicate an inability to adapt to society and an inability to act so that the subject retreats into his mind or some kind of neurotic debility persists.

Dynamising retraction (Ill. 69) – When the facial structure is tonic, the retraction has a dynamic effect and the suppressed emotional life is expressed in physical or cerebral activity. As we have seen in the Lateral Retracted Type, but even more intensely here, emotional disappointments cause intense suffering and the result is often that the subject will take refuge in adventure.

Productive retraction (Ill. 70) – When the cerebral and instinctive zones are tonic, when there is a concentration of the emotions, when internal tension creates dynamic impulses and when the vital force flows into the domains of thought and action, all converge to enrich the personality and to produce individuals of merit. This structure is found in a great number of creators. Here are a few random examples. When we want to analyse such extreme diversity using the morphopsychological method, we must never lose sight of the fact that an affective retraction, which indicates introversion, is only one part of a whole of which each element must be studied. And if this structure were different, the psychological meaning of a lateral–nasal retraction would be different.

Illustration 69. DYNAMIC LATERAL–NASAL RETRACTION

When tonicity dominates in the face, the suppressed emotions are released into action: the more intense and concentrated the suppression, the more intense the release. This dynamisation makes for determined and influential leaders. The second drawing is of von Moltke, a Prussian General in the War of 1870. Number 3 is the French General Foch, victor of the 1914–1918 war. And number 4 shows Abd El-Kader, an Arabian leader known for his courage and noble heart.

Illustration 70. – I. PRODUCTIVE LATERAL–NASAL RETRACTION

When there is both internalisation and dynamism, a lateral-nasal retraction has a productive effect on the personality. The effect is obviously different depending on the intensity of the retraction. On the left is the poet laureate Lamartine whose retraction is not prominent and so doesn't affect the face's harmony. The expansion in the cerebral zone dominates. This retraction explains why Lamartine was a poet in his private life, which was nevertheless compatible with his need to be in the public eye in politics. The retraction is much more pronounced in Albert Roussel, the great French composer, where the vital force was drawn to his huge forehead. Early on, he found himself in the wrong career as a marine officer but it wasn't long before he found his place as one of the great musicians of his time.

Illustration 70. – II. PRODUCTIVE LATERAL–NASAL RETRACTION

As we have already seen, lateral–nasal retraction is often found in great men where the concentration of affective forces favours a strong expansion in the cerebral zone, nourishing a rich intellectual life. The first drawing is Guizot, a very influential minister during the Reformation. He was both a statesman and a talented writer. The second drawing is of the great German composer, Richard Wagner. His face is notable by its powerful vitality. He was an accomplished man who was nevertheless introverted due to a lateral–nasal retraction.

CHAPTER VIII

THE COMBINATION OF VITAL FORCES

In comparing the Dilated with the Retracted Type at the beginning of this book, I stated that this schematic comparison is primarily of educational interest. The keen morphopsychologist must go beyond the schematic to access the concept that is closer to the psychological reality of Mixed Types, which are combinations of dilation and retraction.

We first encountered Mixed Types when I explained how levels of tonicity create different effects, then the importance of the dynamic character of retraction and the necessary complexity that this brings to the study of faces and, finally, in demonstrating the importance of double expansion in the Dominant Expansion Type.

We must explore this area of combinations further and liberate ourselves from our tendency to make schematic comparisons. Our mission must be to bring together the innumerable, diverse human Types that we come across in our lives.

Step by step, I will demonstrate the frequency of dual combinations which are relatively simple to analyse. Then we will study triple and quadruple combinations through a painstaking explanation in accordance with the laws of morphopsychology which will help us to find real examples amongst those in our family environment or in interesting, original personalities.

We will go through the fundaments of the science, which is deliberately schematic, and through a progressive process we will reach a human reality that is less schematic but more real. In other words, we have moved from science to art but without ever losing the sight of the fundamentals of morphopsychology. In the same way, my work, designed to be scientific, also fulfils my objective of creating a practical teaching method which, to interpret faces, must be followed.

1 / THE DILATED–LATERAL RETRACTED TYPE (Ill. 71 and 72)

When lateral retraction appears in a Dilated Type, it brings an additional element of passionate dynamism. In addition, the dilation tempers the impulsive energy of the Lateral Retracted Type. In passing, we should note that this combination often appears in the Tonic Dilated Type that I described previously.

Morphologically, the facial frame is broad with fleshy skin, which is a sign of a Dilated Type. However, some lengthening of the face and the addition of planes are typical of the Lateral Retracted Type. Above all, in profile we can see that the two lower zones are projected forwards in a kind of 'muzzle'. The nose particularly juts out beyond other parts of the face and, as the ridge of the brow bone forms part of the respiratory zone, it also projects forwards to the extent that the upper part of the forehead is clearly inclined backwards.

Psychologically, they are well adapted to a social life, naturally considerate and optimistic, with an appreciation for the material things in life. They are also blessed with concrete and practical abilities such as a talent for business. The Dilated Type fits into this description but the Dilated–Retracted Type is more active, approaching everything with a greater enterprising spirit and passion for adventure.

The combination of these two extrovert types accentuates each one's tendency to focus on life in the outside world and to avoid suffering in their inner life. This combination makes them very sociable, with a need for a wide range of affective relationship. They are generous and prefer practical, down-to-earth work that is based in the present moment and they have a rich, instinctive life as much sexual as combative.

Illustration 71. – I. THE DILATED–LATERAL RETRACTED TYPE

This is a very common combination. The lateral retraction has a dynamising effect on the Dilated Type and can be seen in profile where the lines are angled back and the facial shape becomes more tonic. In the images above, from top to bottom, we see various degrees of progression adding an element of retraction to the forehead, which confers its own qualities. This is very clear in the photo of the American novelist, Pearl Buck, where productivity (dilation) is accompanied by deep reflection (retraction).

Illustration 71. – II. AN EXAMPLE OF THE DILATED–LATERAL RETRACTED TYPE: THE VAUDEVILLIST LABICHE

This harmonious combination of dilation (width of the facial frame and fleshiness) and lateral retraction (angled forehead and nose, very accentuated brow bone), discreetly balanced with a touch of frontal retraction (firm mouth and deep-set eyes) tells us a lot about the theatrical talent of this vaudevillist, whose plays, based on the social reality of his time, are full of action (Photo by Nadar).

They have a great *will to take action* and can exert great effort; however, action cannot be sustained over time.

Their *self-control* depends a great deal on the conditions of the surrounding environment. If it is an environment that allows dilation to predominate, it gives the person gravity and sufficient self-control to manage his impulses. But, if lateral retraction dominates, he will give in to his impulses which disturb his equilibrium and lead the subject to take risks without always taking the consequences into account. This may depend on age: it is habitual for the impulsive character of lateral retraction to predominate in youth while dilation at a mature age makes the character more prudent and calmer.

People with this combination can be found in the same *professions* as the typical Dilated Type. This combination is similar to the Tonic Dilated Type but with a greater interest in human factors. (For that reason, it is closely related to the Affective Expansion Type which I will describe later on.) When lateral retraction dominates in this combination, there is an added impulse factor, creating a desire for activity, adventure and risk, which makes them good coaches and leaders. It is for this reason that, as with the Tonic Dilated Type, they are popular orators: their dominant dilation means that they understand the concerns of the population, particularly those in relation to immediate material needs; meanwhile, their dominant lateral retraction makes them forward looking and progressive. As a result, they figure amongst revolutionaries. They are not the type that base revolution on an ideology but, rather, they are those who simply desire a change in the status quo and greater freedom. There were men of this type during the French Revolution, Mirabeau for example, whose strong component of dilation made him opportunistic and moderate.

One of the most important examples is Beaumarchais (Ill. 72 Fig. 2). Born of the masses but ambitious for material goods and honours, he indeed managed to obtain riches and was awarded titles. As a Dilated Type, he had common sense, was well adapted to social life, had a talent for business, was cheerful and optimistic, had a sensual interest in women and was quite generous. The element of lateral retraction gave him audacity, an adventurous spirit, the temperament of a rebel and a taste for risk to the point of recklessness, proof being that his writings were judged seditious for which he was sent to the Bastille.

In a completely different area, the Salvadorian Bishop Romero is also a good example of this morphological type. He became a preacher and defender of the people oppressed by the reigning oligarchy. Heedless of the risk he was taking in attacking it, he was assassinated by paid assassins.

Bishop Romero's case introduces us to the group that I call 'social creators', those men and women who rebel against social conformity, who fight for greater human justice and who find new ways to promote a better social order. However, for their action to be consistent over time, they often need the support of frontal retraction which the simple combination that we have studied here does not have (Ill. 87).

Illustration 72. EXAMPLES OF THE DILATED–LATERAL RETRACTED TYPE

Very diverse talents can be found within this combination, each characterised by their tendency towards extroversion and their dynamism. They are politicians and popular orators speaking with passion and impetuosity, such as Gambetta.

Beaumarchais is an excellent example of this type: an adventurer and playwright whose life was full of romantic interludes.

2 / THE DILATED–FRONTAL RETRACTED TYPE (Ill. 73)

The originality of this combination of dilation and frontal retraction resides in the element of introversion which counterbalances the exclusive extroversion of the Dilated Type, creating a better equilibrium and giving more strength to the 'self'.

Morphologically, the shape of the frame is that of the Dilated Type but is less rounded and more that of the curved facial shape. The contours of the profile show a straightening of the lines. The receptors show the first degree of retraction which I call 'sheltered receptors': the mouth has full lips but which are firmly pressed against each other; the nostrils are sheltered behind the lobule of the nose which gives it the beginning of an aquiline curve; and the eyes are set a little into the orbit. It is particularly important to point out the change in the shape of the forehead where the uniform roundness of dilation is substituted by a shape that is differentiated in three superimposed zones: the brow bone, the middle flat section of reflection and the upper zone which is the rounded area of the imagination, and of medium size.

The morphopsychologist should take care in evaluating the respective proportions of dilation and frontal retraction as they vary from one person to another and each one's psychology depends on it. The two components of the combination often don't begin to operate at the same time. General dilation, which is a factor in vital expansion, is present during growth, while frontal retraction comes with maturity. For example, a subject of this type will show a great openness of heart and mind early in his life. He loves being in the company of others and has many friends, he has an intellectual interest in a variety of subjects and he will work in different fields. As he becomes older, he will become more selective, as much in his affective life as in intellectual and professional choices.

In most cases, the two tendencies are evenly distributed across the face; however, on occasion, each one affects a different zone. One of the most remarkable examples is that of the author, Balzac, who, at first sight, appears to be a classic Dilated Type due to his physical corpulence and his broad and rounded face. However, on closer inspection, his face appears to be composed of two different superimposed parts, the two lower zones belonging to the Dilated Type while the upper zone is typical of frontal retraction due to the very differentiated forehead and deep-set eyes. You can see this in the photo which I have divided in two (Ill. 73-II).

Psychologically, the aptitudes of the Dilated Type are combined with those of frontal retraction— reflection, reserve and self-control—which correct the excess of extroversion by contributing elements of introversion and individuality.

They are flexible which makes adaptation quite easy but, as opposed to the Dilated Type who can adapt anywhere, this type wishes to tailor-make an environment for themselves. Within their preferred surroundings they are exactly like the Dilated Type in both character and aptitudes. However, outside of this environment, their feelings and outlook are more individualistic and they maintain a certain distance from others and things.

Illustration 73. – I. EXAMPLES OF THE DILATED–FRONTAL RETRACTED TYPE

1

2

3

This combination is also very typical and is identified by a straightening of the profile and sheltered receptors. It is a combination of extroversion and introversion whose significance varies according to the quantity of each component part. In Thiers (Fig. 3), the internalising retraction is very pronounced, giving him the great organisational abilities of a statesman.

236

Illustration 73. – II. BALZAC

Sometimes, instead of a homogenous association, the dilation and frontal retraction juxtapose in some way or another. In the singular case of Balzac, the structure of the cerebral zone has a strong retraction superimposed on a typical Dilated Type. This is clearly seen by dividing the photo.

Expansion in the affective zone means they are less spontaneous than the Dilated and Lateral Retracted Types. For example, they are generous but only after pausing to make a considered decision. However, they will always keep their promises.

Just like the Dilated Type, they are sociable, friendly and like to have good relationships but they don't allow themselves to be manipulated and quite often try to impose their authority over others in friendships.

They are not simply men living in the 'here and now'; they use past experience to help them deal with the future and to ensure that their actions are well planned. This makes them more consistent in how they manage their feelings and objectives.

The quick, spontaneous intelligence of the Dilated Type is combined with new possibilities, notably the capacity for reflection and methodical analysis of situations which produce a better organised thought process.

They combine the Dilated Type's flair and situational awareness with logical reasoning. They are interested in facts, people and material things but they can also expand on general ideas and therefore approach problems in a scientific manner. Their imagination is always rooted in reality, aspiring to find original solutions that are grounded in reality.

At a higher level, the German author Goethe is a good example of this combination (although even more complex due to his cerebral expansion). Despite great originality of thought, Goethe's dominant dilation meant that he was conservative and hostile to change and, in relation to his literary works, he behaved like a prudent administrator. One of his biographers, Stefan Zweig, described this development as a sort of alluvial, formed over time which we can say is characteristic of this combination, echoed in this text: '*The powerful and concrete instinct for conservation of his self leaves only a limited space for change for the benefit of stability. Intelligent and in favour of the established order, Goethe only accepted what he believed was favourable for himself. He wants to increase his possessions but he never allows himself to get lost in the depths of things to the point of being transformed by them*'.[1] (See Goethe's portrait, Ill. 30.)

Will

The combination of introversion and extroversion makes this type both firm yet flexible in their will to take action, resulting in perseverance without pointless obstinance. In their actions, they are respectful of customs and traditions and the life rules that they follow take circumstances into account.

Their *self-control* is better than that of the Dilated Type as their internal self maintains good control over instincts, feelings and thought. In the area of morality, they align their principles with the prevailing customs.

Professions

In order to analyse their professional aptitudes, we must carefully consider the equilibrium between the elements of the combination. If there is a good equilibrium, the abilities of both the Dilated and Frontal Retracted

---

1: Unpublished translation.

Type reinforce each other. The skills that we have already learned that are typical of the Dilated Type are combined with those of reflection, organisation and an understanding of concepts as a whole, which makes subjects of this type more efficient in all domains and suitable for managerial and senior positions. Their value lies in being able to combine practical abilities with general concepts.

In manual labour, they demonstrate practical skills and an understanding of method. However, they can achieve higher-level jobs where thought directs manual labour and engenders innovation.

In industry and commerce, they tend not to be found in manufacturing or the business of raw materials but more in that of pre-manufactured goods, like the Frontal Retracted Type already mentioned.

They often work in self-employed professions including medicine, law, psychology and sociology where they tend to rank amongst the best.

They are successful scientists thanks to their organisational sense, clarity of thought which they apply to everything they do and their capacity to take prior experience into account. They are also very good at transmitting the knowledge they have acquired and therefore make good professors.

They may have artistic talent but do not produce great works as they lack the internal complexity and inner turmoil which is the driving force of creativity.

They make very good superiors. While the Dilated Type are good, cordial and humane supervisors to their subordinates and a combination with the Lateral Retracted Type gives them abilities as coaches, the Dilated–Frontal Retracted Type rise even higher in the professional hierarchy due to their natural authority and ability to manage problems.

3 / THE DILATED–INDENTED RETRACTED TYPE (Ill. 74)

When a Dilated facial shape is full of reliefs and dents instead of being round and full, the resultant characters are noted for their originality, whether good or bad. As in the combination with frontal retraction, the exclusive extroversion of the Dilated is compensated for with the addition of an element of introversion, resulting in a strong sense of self. However, in this case, the passage from the external life to the inner life is bumpy and is at the origin of an intense dynamism combined with difficulty in maintaining equilibrium.

The problem here lies in harmony, more so than in the other combinations. When there is an even distribution of the reliefs and dents in every zone in the face, achievements are an even mix of both the external and inner life. When there is the opposite, disharmony, the personality is often divided against itself: either he passionately launches himself into projects or he pulls himself back, concerned with ensuring that the action is in accordance with the profound demands of the self. Either of these approaches can easily be taken to excess. Understanding the resulting equilibrium requires a case-by-case analysis. The vital energy that accompanies dilation ensures stability and efficiency in their actions.

Morphologically, within the Dilated Type's broad face and solid bone structure there is a tortured facial shape, with dents (in the temples, cheeks, in the centre of the forehead) and reliefs (in the upper part of the forehead, upper cheeks, the angles of the jawline). The receptors are widely distributed across the face (dilation) and clearly sheltered in profile (retraction). The facial expression is passionate, animated by an inner flame which is expressed with a certain ferocity.

Psychologically, the strength of their vitality drives their passions which are nevertheless only ever expressed within their, truthfully quite large, preferred surroundings due to their dilation. They don't really feel alive except in an environment fuelled with passion. They experience both love and hate powerfully and feel it in the depths of their being, able to restrain and intensify their feelings. They can be vengeful but their passion is usually tempered by their dilation which brings a measure of control, tenderness and tolerance.

They are sensitive to the social climate around them and are concerned about what others think of them, but they can focus on their inner being and proudly stand by their convictions. They have a great deal of natural authority and like to be in charge. Nevertheless, they often experience internal conflict, resulting in periods of elation or depression.

Illustration 74. – I. THE DILATED–INDENTED RETRACTED TYPE

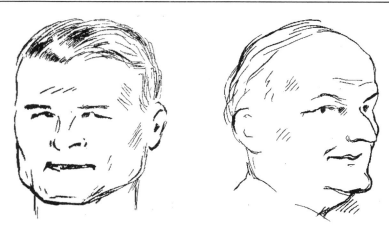

The indented-retracted shape is superimposed upon a Dilated frame, adding a tortuous surface to the strength of the frame which, psychologically, results in a personality that is both strongly extroverted and introverted. This gives the person an unusual dynamism. However, the psychological significance varies according to the types of combination. In comparing these two portraits, you can see that the solidity of the basic structure, sculpted by reliefs and depressions with broad and tonic curves, gives the subject in the first portrait a passionate dynamism for achieving objectives. This quality doesn't exist to the same degree in the second portrait where the facial shape has more curves and is more fragile, giving some predominance to internalisation. We will see on the following page that this structure is quite common amongst creators in all kinds of domains, for example, musical creation (Beethoven) or the abilities of great statesmen (Ghandi and Gladstone).

They have an acute intellect that is driven by passion. No matter the creation, what is important is the passionate desire to create it. Their character is their greatest asset due to their intense will to take action and their strong personality. However, their ability to achieve things of value can only be determined following a careful evaluation of their morphological structure. This depends, in part, on the equilibrium that is achieved between the powerful, antagonizing forces of extroversion and introversion. In addition, their ability depends on the structure of the forehead. When the forehead is large and harmoniously distributed throughout each of its zones, they can achieve important works.

Professions

They have aptitudes in all of the professions of the Dilated Type, particularly in business, but with less thirst for the accumulation of material goods and more for the attainment of power. Their passionate temperament can create difficulties in social relationships and team work. If they are not particularly talented then they will have fewer professional opportunities, but if they have talent then they will find their place in leadership positions.

Illustration 74. – II. EXAMPLES OF THE DILATED–INDENTED RETRACTED TYPE

Here are three great passionate characters: the great musician, Beethoven; the English states-man, Gladstone, who left his mark on the politics of his country; and Gandhi, the leader of Hindu independence. He was remarkable for his passion and the unceasing energy he displayed in his pursuit of freedom.

In their chosen profession, they act like the Dilated Type with all the intellectual and affective abilities that this implies; however, they are susceptible to anything that brings out their dominant passion and, if it conflicts with their personal convictions, they can either explode or shut down as they retreat into themselves.

Their professional aptitudes are therefore influenced by their internal equilibrium. This equilibrium, which we have already seen in the Indented–Retracted Type, hinges on whether they have been able to find harmony. More so than in other types, their effectiveness in their chosen profession depends on whether they can realise their dominant passion in their work.

4 / THE LATERAL RETRACTED–FRONTAL RETRACTED TYPE (Ill. 75 and 76)

I have already demonstrated the key differences, both morphologically and psychologically, between the Lateral Retracted Type and the Frontal Retracted Type and that they can almost be considered opposites. However, this differentiation, although necessary as an initial framework, then must be adjusted, since we have observed in the combinations of these two types that they associate the dynamism of lateral retraction with the self-control of frontal retraction.

Morphologically, it is important to establish the role of each of the components in the overall morphology. Sometimes lateral retraction predominates and so we must be aware of the subtle signs of frontal retraction: a slight difference in the form of the forehead or a light sheltering of the receptors (Ill. 75-I).

Conversely, frontal retraction may dominate and lateral retraction may only be visible as a slight angle in the forehead, a nose that is slightly pointed forward or a more open sensory receptor (Ill. 75-II).

At other times, there is a balance between the two which is generally a sign of strength. It can be seen in each zone: in the upper zone, the forehead is moderately inclined, neither particularly angled nor very vertical; the eyes are lightly sheltered; the middle stage shows an aquiline nose which in its shape reveals a double movement that, taken from the root, makes it first of all point forward and then curve back on itself; and, in the lower zone, the jaw juts forward slightly (Ill. 75-II).

As I have previously mentioned, it is important to identify the angle of the forehead from a pronounced angle of 45° which is lateral retraction and is a sign of impulsivity, to a completely vertical forehead which is a predominant frontal retraction and is a sign of inhibition.

Psychologically, we must understand if a balance is established between these two opposing tendencies as the efficiency of the subject depends upon it. Lateral retraction is the engine; frontal retraction is the brake. A machine doesn't work well unless the brakes are strong enough to manage the engine. In parallel, the actions of the human organism must be able to regulate the effort required by the situation, whether it is moving forward or holding back.

This combination is found where it is necessary to combine dynamism with self-control, allowing the living being to use their energy to achieve maximum efficiency.

Greater efficiency and manual skills are achieved in manual activities in many professions through this combination. It is also frequent in sportsmen as it gives them both strength and speed of execution as well as the confidence and precision achieved through focus in the moment of action.

We must consider the risk factor. The adage 'Victory favours the brave' may be true but some risks may be so audacious as to, due to impulsiveness, lead to failure by not taking all circumstances into account. In addition, in any joint enterprise business partners also must be taken into account. In an independent business, the dominant lateral retraction has the freedom to attain the highest degree of success but, in a team, it is necessary to consider the partners' interests. For example, a competitive skier can give it his all in order to win, even risking his life; however, if he is a ski monitor or mountain guide, then he has to moderate his enthusiasm and calculate his actions to avoid putting the other skiers that he is responsible for in danger (Ill. 75-II).

Illustration 75. – I. LATERAL RETRACTED–FRONTAL RETRACTED TYPE

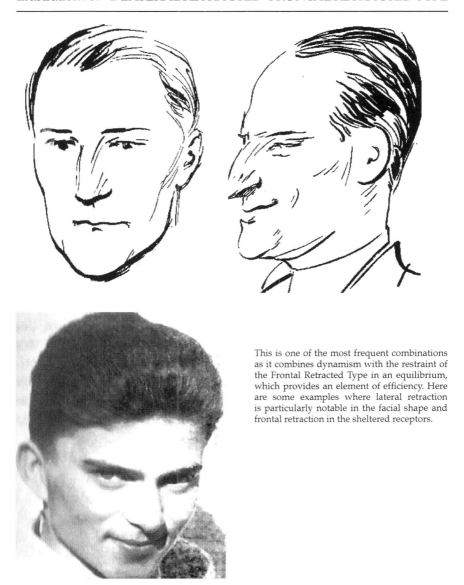

This is one of the most frequent combinations as it combines dynamism with the restraint of the Frontal Retracted Type in an equilibrium, which provides an element of efficiency. Here are some examples where lateral retraction is particularly notable in the facial shape and frontal retraction in the sheltered receptors.

This applies to all occupations. The combination is often found in professional businesses which involve movement, adventure and risk; however, with the control provided by frontal retraction they will be more successful. For example, if a Lateral Retracted Type decides to launch himself into a voyage of exploration, his ally, frontal retraction, will manage the preparations for the trip—the time of year, the best itinerary—and refer to past experiences to minimise the possibilities of failure.

Illustration 75. – II. EXAMPLES OF THE LATERAL RETRACTED–FRONTAL RETRACTED TYPE

This combination is particularly present in sportsmen and adventurers. On the top left is the famous Swiss mountain guide, Nieberl, and next to him is a portrait (drawn by Dauce) of Nansen, the great Norwegian explorer. Below is the great pianist and composer Liszt, who was, in his own way, a pioneer in music.

It is obvious that everything depends on the proportions of the two tendencies and the morphopsychologist must be aware of this in his analysis. The more lateral retraction dominates, the greater the aptitude for action and movement. And if frontal retraction dominates, the subject is better adapted to professions that require reflection, calculation and long-term planning.

5 / THE LATERAL RETRACTED–INDENTED RETRACTED TYPE (Ill. 76 and 77)

Morphologically, they are similar to the Lateral Retracted Type by the lengthening of their face, the angled lines of the profile and their open receptors. The main difference is that the flat, curved lines of the contours of the Lateral Retracted Type's face are replaced by a more irregular outline with dents and reliefs. Their face is extremely expressive, their nostrils quivering and their eyes shining.

Psychologically, they are similar to the Lateral Retracted–Frontal Retracted combination but their personality is more complex, which is a result of the antagonism between their passionate impulses and the tendency to internalise.

They are intense: fiery. Their gestures are impetuous, their passions are fierce, they are enthusiastic and quick to anger. They also follow their primary instincts. Drawn to excess, they are extreme in whatever they do, both good and bad, hating what they call the tepid average man. There are those who are naturally loyal and generous and able to put all their energy into a good cause, and those whose nature is troubled and they rebel against everything. They are renegades. In both cases, they are hot-headed and finding a balance is difficult, which causes problems professionally. It is clear that they need to be in an energetic work environment where they can find satisfaction, preferably one where there is constant change, travel and adventure. After trying and failing in a variety of professions due to their impulsivity, they often join the army as they think that it will give them the adventurous life and the discipline that they need to control their own lack of discipline. They need to be in a structured environment, being incapable themselves of following certain rules of conduct which would make them more efficient.

Illustration 76. – THE LATERAL RETRACTED–INDENTED RETRACTED TYPE

1

2

3

When the Indented retracted facial shape is combined with a lateral retracted structure, passionate impulses reach their maximum. However, the conflict between these two tendencies engenders an internal tension that exposes the subject to sudden explosions. In no. 3, the polar explorer, Paul-Émile Victor, combined his spirit of adventure with his abilities for reflection and organisation.

6 / THE FRONTAL RETRACTED–INDENTED RETRACTED TYPE (Ill. 77)

Within the Indented Retracted Type, there are a number of intermediary points of combination with dilation, lateral retraction and frontal retraction. The same rules that previously explained the means of distinguishing between the Lateral Retracted Type and the Frontal Retracted Type apply here. The only commonality amongst these combinations is the indented retracted shape.

Morphologically, this combination has a narrower facial shape than the Dilated–Indented Retracted Type. The profile is straighter than the Lateral Retracted Type and the receptors are protected. The facial expression is intense but is more contained, sometimes, at first sight, appearing cold.

Psychologically, they have the same intensity, the same passionate impulses, the same zealous predisposition, but they can restrain them when necessary and keep them in check. They have more depth than the Lateral Retracted Type. Their affections and aversion to others are no less powerful but are more concentrated and, for that reason, more constant. The same opposition can be found in their inner life. The Lateral Retracted are passionate about everything: when something piques their intellect, it kindles their imagination and their ample initiative takes over. However, the passion itself often burns out and they lose interest in the thing without giving themselves the chance to follow it through to a natural conclusion. Conversely, the Frontal Retracted Type is reflective and thorough. The fire burns as brightly as the others but it is better regulated. The imagination is just as active but more ordered.

They like to take action, which makes them consistent and persistent. They also have good self-control, knowing how to handle themselves. As a result, they have the authority required to make good bosses.

Professionally, they are very practical with capacities both for reflection and strategizing and they are serious about their work. These factors combined make them very efficient. However, the frontal retraction must not be too pronounced. For example, a forehead that is too vertical, with a horizontal brake line across the forehead, creates a blockage and threatens to bring the machine to a halt, thus impeding further activity.

Illustration 77. – FRONTAL RETRACTED–INDENTED RETRACTED TYPE

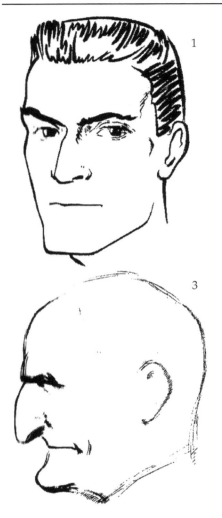

When the indented-retracted structure is combined with frontal retraction, there is a dynamising effect on their abilities, whether potentiating the impulsive force or the intensity of reflection and internal strength, as in the case of the 'brake line' (no. 2). In the most extreme form, the concentration of passion is at its highest and the subject may be an aggressive character, a 'renegade' (no. 3).

7 / THE REACTIVE–FRONTAL RETRACTED TYPE (Ill. 78)

In Chapter VI, I explained that the exclusive reactive tendency can be dangerous due to the fact that all available strength is quickly drained. A compensatory factor has to come into play in order to reach a better equilibrium. This compensatory factor is often achieved through frontal retraction localised in one of the three zones. This introduces a sensitivity towards introversion which alerts the subject to the imminent exhaustion of his vital energy, creating a safeguard.

Illustration 78. – REACTIVE–FRONTAL RETRACTED TYPE

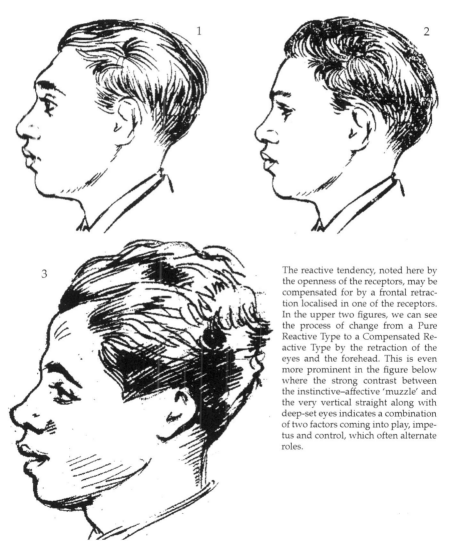

The reactive tendency, noted here by the openness of the receptors, may be compensated for by a frontal retraction localised in one of the receptors. In the upper two figures, we can see the process of change from a Pure Reactive Type to a Compensated Reactive Type by the retraction of the eyes and the forehead. This is even more prominent in the figure below where the strong contrast between the instinctive–affective 'muzzle' and the very vertical straight along with deep-set eyes indicates a combination of two factors coming into play, impetus and control, which often alternate roles.

Morphologically, this is usually achieved through the partial closure of one of the receptors: the mouth (pinched lips), the nose (the nostrils closing in on the central partition) or the eyes (deep-set). The eye receptor is particularly important as it is directly connected to self-awareness and therefore exercises control over impulses.

Fatigue, and the sensation of fatigue, which is not the same as exhaustion as one often assumes, is very important as it acts as a warning that exhaustion is imminent if remedial action is not taken. I call this the 'back-up plan' as fatigue protects the subject from the dangers of exhaustion. This is a very simple reaction; however, the Reactive Type suffers from an unusual condition known as asthenia which is an intense and persistent fatigue. It manifests itself in the morning by a particularly strong sense of weariness, headache, stiffness and a feeling of powerlessness to act. This indicates that the previous night's rest was not sufficient to replenish the energy spent the day before. However, those suffering from asthenia often re-energise during the day and into the evening. As a result, Reactive Types suffer from highs and lows in their energy levels.

Compensation through a localised frontal retraction is not enough to create the harmony of the balanced Frontal Retracted Type. An alternation of roles often appears, not on a daily basis as in the above case, but over quite long periods of time. It is through these combinations and their alternations that lead us to the concept of 'conversion', a surprising and sudden lifestyle change. It is not important whether or not we attach a religious connotation to the word; the fact is that the most striking examples can be observed in the religious professions. When the morphopsychologist studies the faces of men and women with religious vocations, he is astounded by how frequently he comes across the Reactive Type. Their evolution is no less surprising as often—after a normal, free childhood where impulses have free rein—there is a sudden and complete turnaround, entering cloisters and turning a life of dissipation of vital energy into the completely different life of contemplation, which is effectively a concentration of strength. François d'Assise, P. de Foucauld and Eve Lavallière are examples, amongst others. They had the Compensated Reactive Type facial structure with a retraction of the forehead, allowing us to understand their abrupt change as they become aware of the dangers of their reactive tendency. Here is where the compensatory force comes into full effect. Even conceding the spiritual influences of the religious, it doesn't take away from the fact that a change in character through conversion is consistent with the biological mechanism of an internalising retraction. It is interesting that Reactive Types with religious vocations instinctively choose a religious order that doesn't require completely breaking contact with the world as it is a means of maintaining their equilibrium. It also serves to satisfy the two tendencies that they are torn between: the tendency for expansion which is quenched by worldly life, and the conservative tendency in which taking refuge in cloisters benefits their inner life. We have already seen the example of a student chaplain, content working in his ministry because of his largely uncompensated reactive tendency, but who paid for it with asthenia, which is what brought him to consult me. His entire life had been affected by these changes: the very mundane life of a rich, young man followed by the sudden contrast of the cloistered life with its strict rules, which are very difficult for a Reactive Type to cope with. As a result, he fell ill. Working as the student chaplain suited him better but that came with the risk of mental exhaustion. In order to achieve a better equilibrium, I suggested that he reintroduce some time in cloisters in addition to his daily life as a chaplain. And this advice, duly followed, helped him re-establish his equilibrium.

Illustration 79. – ALFRED DE MUSSET

The slenderness of Alfred de Musset's lateral retracted face makes the poet fall under the Reactive Type. He was a dandy with a lively spirit and an attraction to the erotic. However, a frontal retraction in the middle zone provided a compensatory factor, giving him an element of introversion from which he was able to write *Les Nuits*.

There are also examples outside of the religious professions. Many talented people that belong to the Compensated Reactive Type have experienced similar changes that have affected their entire lives. For example, the poet Alfred de Musset shows these characteristics: a mostly slender face with open receptors; an angled forehead; and signs of frontal retraction in the form of a lateral–nasal retraction which made his eyes slightly set back (Ill. 79). As a young Reactive Type, he lacked self-control and was somewhat of a dandy–a spirited, superficial character–at the time of writing his first poems. Though he wrote, *'Man is an apprentice, pain is his master, and no one can know themselves without having first suffered'*,[2] bitter experiences made him turn into himself, thanks to his lateral–nasal retraction, and it is then that he wrote *Les Nuits*, poems with so much more depth than his first poems.

In conclusion, the psychology of the combined Reactive Type is double-edged as they are similar to the frontal Retracted Type but with less equilibrium due to the contrasts in their facial structure. The difficulty for the morphopsychologist is to understand to what extent they are able to make an efficient use of the alternation between their opposing tendencies. In doing so, both external influences and periods of reflection on their inner life give their feelings, thoughts and actions an added dimension and thereby enrich them. If they can attain this, they will often be able to produce good works, particularly in the fields of art and literature.

This alternation between extroversion and introversion makes them particularly sensitive to the human condition and facilitates a connection with the philosophical, social and psychological sciences.

8 / DILATED–LATERAL RETRACTED–FRONTAL RETRACTED TYPE

The more faces the morphopsychologist studies, the more complicated his work becomes. It is worth mentioning that when we look closer at many of the dual-combination characters that we have analysed here, we can see that they complete this morphological dualism with secondary traits from other types, creating combinations of three or four elements. Within the limits of this book, it is clear that we cannot study all of the almost infinite varieties.

2: Unpublished translation.

An example is the very common triple combination of Dilated, Lateral Retracted and Frontal Retracted traits:

Dilation in the overall shape of the frame, a fleshy facial shape and fairly open receptors;

Lateral Retraction in the tonicity, degree of affective expansion and sloping lines in profile; and

Frontal Retraction in the partial straightening up of the lines where the angle is in between the more pronounced angles of lateral retraction and the total straightening up of frontal retraction. In addition, frontal retraction exists in the sheltered receptors and differentiated facial shape. For example, the forehead is testament to these three components: dilation is represented in its roundness; lateral retraction in the flatness in the lower zone (at the front and in the temples), sloping backwards; and frontal retraction in that the angle is not acute and above all the line of the profile is differentiated in three superimposed zones.

Psychologically, the adaptability of the Dilated Type combines with the dynamism and enthusiasm of the Lateral Retracted Type, along with the Frontal Retracted Type's qualities of choice, reflection and self-control, with a few variations according to the predominance of one or another element.

Instincts are expressed with the great force of expansion but nevertheless restrained, which allows an element of sublimation and partial use of the vital energy for the purpose of achieving objectives.

The affective life is characterised by extroversion due to the dominance of dilation and lateral retraction, but frontal retraction limits this sense of freedom to the preferred surroundings. In addition, the inner life is nourished by what is extracted from the external life.

Intelligence is allied with the practical ability of the Dilated Type, the spontaneous vivacity of the Lateral–Retracted and the capacity for reflection and abstraction of the Frontal–Retracted.

The will to take action is balanced, due to restraint and self-control that never reaches the extreme of paralysis.

Professionally, this combination of the three most efficient components opens the door to success in a great deal of professions: those of the Dilated Type, Lateral Retracted Type and Frontal Retracted Type. This mixed type's professional path must, of course, be inspired by the particular demands of his chosen profession.

However, it is also determined by the morphological dominance. We have to take into account that, in most cases, the combination of the three components is not enough to identify professional abilities as this is nearly always complemented by a zone in expansion: cerebral, affective or active–instinctive. The following portraits offer some very clear examples, for example, the contrast between the two doctors, Dr. Chassaignac and Claude Bernard, with the emphasis on the practical and technical of the first due to his dominant instinctive zone, and the ability for intellectual creativity of the second due to the strong dominance in the cerebral zone (Ill. 88).

9 / COMBINATIONS OF TONICITY AND ATONY (ILL. 80)

It might, at first, appear to be contradictory to associate tonicity with atony as our spirit, with its tendency to systematically create contrast, dictates that these two structures exclude each other. However, over the course of this book we have seen that this phenomenon frequently appears in nature in complex structures.

Up until now, we have examined extreme cases of tonicity and atony. Strong tonicity is a sign of an active dominance; it belongs to subjects who are not very receptive, are not easily influenced and who wish to dominate other people and things, manipulating them for their own purposes even to the point of aggression. The opposite, atony, is a sign of passivity, receptivity, a lack of confidence, decisiveness and the ability to achieve objectives. Each of these extremes has its own value and that which is considered a strength, in one, is a weakness in the other. Each individual applies their own value to these two elements according to their own personal criteria. In modern Western civilisation, we tend to value tonicity and to condemn atony, as activity, efficiency and earning a salary are the most important values and idleness is considered 'the mother of all vices'.

Illustration 80. – COMBINATIONS OF ATONY

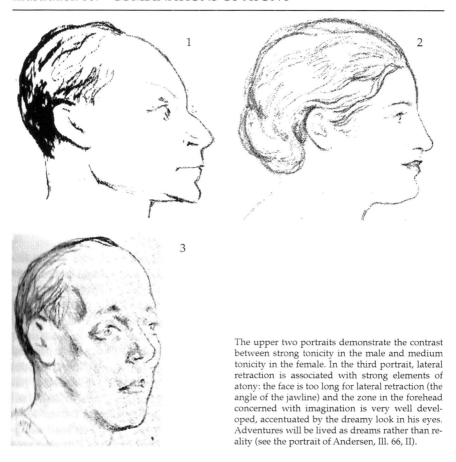

The upper two portraits demonstrate the contrast between strong tonicity in the male and medium tonicity in the female. In the third portrait, lateral retraction is associated with strong elements of atony: the face is too long for lateral retraction (the angle of the jawline) and the zone in the forehead concerned with imagination is very well developed, accentuated by the dreamy look in his eyes. Adventures will be lived as dreams rather than reality (see the portrait of Andersen, Ill. 66, II).

Morphopsychology itself teaches us to see the value of tonicity and atony from a more nuanced perspective, not as being absolute, but as being relative to the situation. This is how we must assess age, sex, the demands of daily life and professions. As we have already seen, atony dominates in the very young as assimilation is very important for growth. Levels of tonicity also vary according to sex; men have greater tonicity than women. In the male sex, it means dynamism, aggression, an independent spirit, the struggle for power and a logical mind. Relative atony is found in the female sex which explains her receptivity, softness, tenderness, the tendency for conciliation and intuition (Ill. 80, fig. 1 and 2).

These differences in tonicity influence aptitudes and, consequently, one's professional path. However, we can't categorically contrast masculine professions, which require strong tonicity, with more feminine professions which are compatible with an element of atony. Combinations are very common: when closely studied using morphological analysis, it is apparent that many professions requiring physical strength also require elements of atony which correspond to the valuable qualities of receptivity.

This receptivity is crucial in all professional activities that come into contact with nature, whether animals or plants. A strong tonicity creates a drive to act upon people and things, to manipulate them, even to the point of aggression, while atony leans more towards non-violence, to an accepting and sympathetic attitude. It cannot be denied that, for example, country labourers, no matter the physical vigour required of them, must not try to force nature's natural rhythm; once the seeding has been completed, they must wait for the harvest. This also applies to livestock farmers in their contact with animals. It is surprising to see the importance of a feminine component that is very frequently observed in seafarers as they adapt to the sea's rhythm. A strong tonic jaw with atonic eyes, showing a dreamy expression, creates contrast in their facial structure.

A certain amount of atony is also useful in those professions that require personal contact with others. In the social sciences, particularly psychology, it is necessary to have a certain empathy with others which strong tonicity would tend to suppress. This is why psychology, and particularly morphopsychology, is practiced much more by women than men. The practice requires a feminine element integrated into the personality.

This quality of feminine receptivity is also necessary in the arts. In order to transmit a message, one must first receive it and allow it to soak in. Naturally, a musician must know how to play his instrument, which indicates active qualities, but at the same time he must allow the soul of the music to enter him.

The same applies to actors. Every morphopsychologist will say that even though a male actor may play roles that require masculine virility and physical robustness, the great majority have some aspect of atony, particularly in the eyes (drooping eyes as in the style of Greuze). In the same way, female actresses, no matter how feminine they may be, will often have a quite strong jaw with pronounced angles, indicating a masculine component (Ill. 81 fig.2). You would be correct to think that, as much one for the other, a certain sexual duality forms an integral part of the plasticity necessary for acting.

Illustration 81. – I. COMBINATIONS OF ATONY

While total atony signifies passivity and helplessness, partial atony, as seen in the above portraits of two women, can soften the tonic elements in the face and carry with it, along with an element of dreaminess, artistic abilities. The actress, Lily Palmer, represented here (fig. 2), drawn by Annie Bret, demonstrates a morphological style that is frequently visible in creative people, noted by the contrast between the dream-like expression in the eyes and the dynamic ability for implementation in the jaw.

The value of combinations

In the Homogenous morphopsychological type where each part of the face has the same degree of tonicity, such as the man and woman in illustration 80, it is easy to identify its significance, as a function of active and receptive abilities which are required for any particular situation or profession. However, the situation is more complex where the combination of tonicity and atony are distributed across different zones. In his analysis, the morphopsychologist must pay attention to this distribution across the zones in order to understand the influence it has on the subject's psychology. He must establish what tonicity or atony brings to each zone and then, as is always necessary, summarise, attempting to establish if the subject has been able to integrate the combination of tendencies and generate additional value out of them. If not, it would instead qualify as a weakness.

For example, in the *instinctive zone*, a powerful tonic jaw indicates a very active personality motivated by a strong need for action that, in fact, could be enslaved by it. It is also dominated by ambition and the morphopsychologist must establish whether the structure of the other zones supports the aptitudes required to justify this ambition, otherwise it would operate in a vacuum. There are also subjects with a strong jaw and a forehead that is barely or not at all differentiated: their ambition may be to fulfil an important role in society, thus making a great intellectual effort in the acquisition of knowledge and qualifications, as the saying goes 'by dint of hard work' rather than through any natural talent.

On the other hand, where atony predominates, we will see a blurred jawline angle, a soft chin covered in flesh, an exceedingly soft mouth, loose even, indicating a lack of aggression, and a desire to resolve problems through reconciliation–qualities of tenderness and patience often resulting in easier social relationships. We might ask what it takes to be the head of a business and the first response is that a lot of tonicity is necessary. It's true, especially early on in the career as success requires a great deal of dynamism and corresponds to the following morphology: dilation combined with lateral retraction and frontal retraction. What frequently happens as the subject matures is that the morphology evolves and becomes fatter, particularly around the jawline area which becomes heavier, fleshier and acquires some atony (especially a double chin), which indicates less aggression, a less enterprising spirit and a tendency to prefer the status quo in the business that he manages. It also indicates greater warmth in human relationships. All of these attributes could be considered strengths or weaknesses depending on the situation. How the zones are integrated also provides insights on the subject's qualities. For example, if there is also atony in the cerebral zone, there is a lack of stimulus for active thought and action may be paralysed (Ill. 81-II).

In the *affective zone*, strong tonicity is expressed by firmness in the cheeks, a clear line of the cheekbones and an aquiline nose with an angled ridge and nostrils that vibrate. These are all signs that, in the affective area, the subject prefers to dominate others and impose his authority, not only in his professional life, but also his personal life. In order for this to be viable, this authority must be reflected in the other zones. However, atony can be identified by a rounded facial shape, cheekbones that disappear into plump cheeks and a concave nose, turned-up and plump. These are all signs of tenderness, passivity and a need for love and protection from others.

This kind of nose is especially common in women: it has the particularly childlike quality of passivity contrasted with a strong, angled masculine jaw. This style is nowadays particularly common in women who pursue a profession. Marielle Clevel did a detailed study of this which was published in the *Revue de Morphopsychologie* (1985, Ed. 3). From a psychological standpoint, it indicates the internal conflict between a desire to be independent, to be fulfilled, and an affective need of dependence and for protection. I personally have noticed that this is particularly common in actresses (Ill. 81-I).

In the *cerebral zone*, strong tonicity is present in a forehead that is not particularly large, with a firm shape, the eyes set in a little, closely outlined by the eyelids giving the impression that the eyes are quite small and at the same time giving them an intense, penetrating expression. These are all signs of an active, practical and logical mind. Atony manifests itself in a completely rounded forehead and globular eyes that stand out in the style of Greuze with a soft, almost droopy expression, which are signs of passive receptivity and intuitive intelligence.

However, the tonicity of the eyes is even more significant in another way. This sensorial zone, directly liaising with the brain, controls the activities of the two other zones in certain respects. For example, eyes that are strongly tonic are very selective and block the route of feelings or impulsive instincts which results, as we know, in a very objective and scientific thought process.

On the other hand, atony in the eyes indicates a slackening of control and therefore gives free rein to impulses. It is worth mentioning that this freedom is virtually indispensable for creative work. To be fulfilled, dancers, writers, musicians and painters must be able to let their deepest, wildest impulses loose in a kind of ecstatic Dionysiac fashion.

Illustration 81. – II. COMBINATIONS OF ATONY

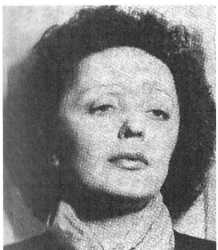

The portraits of the two men represent the increased atony that comes with age. But there is a very clear contrast between the first, where the atony is localised in the instinctive–affective zones and the expression remains lively, and the second, whose lazy eye indicates a weakening in the nervous system. This same weakening can be seen in the great singer, Edith Piaf; the lack of control over her passions indicates that she gave herself completely and without reserve to her passion to sing, and to the drugs that ruined her life.

262

This lack of control also has negative effects as this same freedom often leads to a life that is out of control and all kinds of self-abuse which weaken the subject's equilibrium. We may feel the right to criticise this lack of discipline in the lives of many artists, imagining that if their life were under better control that they would be able to make even more of their talent than they do. However, this way of thinking is erroneous and is inspired by a moralistic concept of how one should live, considering Good and Evil immutable. In reality, there frequently seems to be a mysterious connection amongst very talented people between their talent and the chaos of their life, which often leads to premature death. As already demonstrated, amongst others, in the study I made of Edith Piaf[3] I emphasised that she gave everything to her singing and at the same time she allowed her tumultuous passions to spin out of control, with the result being that she wasted her vital energy and became addicted to drugs. This situation is quite common and without a doubt explains why this weakening in the nervous system is frequent in particularly talented people (Ill. 81-II).

10 / COMBINATIONS OF EXTREME RETRACTION (ILL. 82)

As we have already seen, extreme retraction is a self-defence system that exists to protect against situations considered life threatening. However, the almost complete paralysis of any potential expansion, as this retraction implies, also has its negative effects on the development of the character and intellect, unless there is a compensatory factor. This type of compensation can be seen when a zone escapes retraction, allowing the subject's vital energy the opportunity to express itself and contribute to the accomplishment of action. The morphopsychologist must be observant and detect expansion zones within faces that have a dominant extreme retraction.

Balanced combinations

When this pronounced retraction combines with dilation and lateral retraction, as a foundation, they almost balance each other out, giving the morphology a certain harmony. The face, instead of being gaunt, is fleshy

---

3: Edith Piaf, 'Poésie et névrose', *Revue de Morphopsychologie*, 1982, 2.

(dilation), but is refined with delicate features (retraction). The receptors, in the same way, are quite open with a little bit of flesh within a delicate structure. The skin is delicate but not withered and has some colour (Ill. 82-I).

Illustration 82. – I. COMBINATIONS OF EXTREME RETRACTION

In the above portraits of two young women, we can see a retraction coexisting with a combination of dilation and lateral retraction, observable in a very refined facial shape and receptors. This refines their reactions and especially their feelings. Their mind is agile but tends toward frivolity.

Psychologically, these two opposing tendencies offset one another. While extreme retraction greatly limits the possibilities for adaptation, it is important to note that it leads to openness while in their preferred surroundings. Nevertheless, it co-exists with a delicate emotional sensibility, ensuring that one does not develop a rapport with others too quickly, being careful to avoid hurting others and trying to take their feelings into account. They are not very warm people, they hate passionate impulses and they express themselves delicately. Whatever their relationship with another person, they always remain reserved, wishing to preserve their individuality, which often leads others to consider them egocentric. They are never directly aggressive, preferring to be indirect and very diplomatic. They are more epicurean than sensual and avoid getting deeply involved. We could certainly apply the moralist Chamfort's words in his definition of love of his era to them: '*Love is the exchange of two fantasies and the contact of two skins.*' In them, nuance is everything, and their impulses are never violent, always tempered by the fear of getting too involved.

Illustration 82. – II. COMBINATIONS OF EXTREME RETRACTION

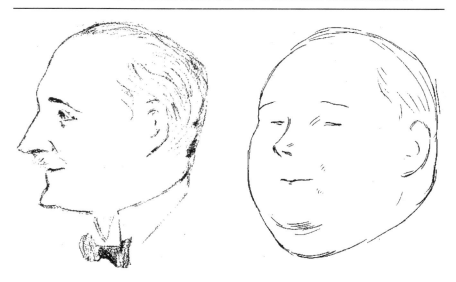

The first of these two men is a happy combination of dilation, lateral retraction and frontal retraction with expansion in the cerebral zone. Added to that, a slimming of the receptors adds an element of refinement, diplomacy and a sharp intellect but without any deep connection. The second is almost caricature-like in the extent of the contrast between a dilated frame and very small receptors. He resembles the concentrated type described in illustration 52 but with a hard heart.

Their intellect combines a certain openness with a need for finesse and precision, which gives them good taste and makes them difficult to please. They like material things but only of quality which indicates they have an aesthetic side. They are very acute and perceptive, more subtle than deep and more calculated than spontaneous. They are analytic and pay attention to detail; however, they are unable to see the big picture. They don't have much imagination or much creative talent.

They are adept and work with sensitivity and finesse but their emotions are sometimes an impediment.

Their will to act lacks strength; it is based on skilfulness and flexibility. They have good self-control and the element of dilation prevents the element of retraction from having an inhibiting effect.

Professionally, it is necessary to take the respective parts of dilation and extreme retraction into account. When dilation is predominant, the range of professional possibilities is quite large as the retraction simply increases the need for quality and greater sensitivity in relationships and greater vulnerability to the knocks in life, which means that they must remain in their preferred environment and, out of preference, in sedentary positions. They can be found particularly in administration, notary work, legal professions, embassies and secretarial positions. If the element of retraction is predominant, the down-to-earth qualities, so useful in commerce and industry, are less well developed and so relationships with others are more difficult. The most appropriate work is solitary, in offices and laboratories, and they are not at all suitable for professions where they must work with raw material such as in the country, farming or any work that requires a great deal of social contact.

Imbalanced Combinations

When dilation and retraction do not exist in a harmonious balance but are in juxtaposition, particularly in the case of a dilated frame associated with a small face in extreme retraction, the result is a struggle between the profound need for vital expansion and the drive for action on the one hand and a great difficulty in human relationships, which can lead to inhibition, on the other. It could be said here that individualism takes priority over belonging to a social group, as much in sentiments as in intelligence.

They are very sensitive but this doesn't make them at all sympathetic. It is essentially a defensiveness made up of the slightest deficiency in their surroundings and their egocentricity. They come across as cold as they are distant, silent and secretive.

They are not sensitive people as they lack intuition. Everything is based on strict logic according to their own criteria, applying a rigorous logical process to every problem, albeit with their own preconceived opinions.

Professionally, they don't handle practical problems well and are not comfortable in commercial professions that require being on good terms with people. They are most apt for solitary positions as technicians and jobs that require precision. They are more comfortable working on a computer than with people. They are sometimes the sole inventors of things that are based exclusively on their own ideas.

CHAPTER IX
BISEXUALITY

During the course of this work, I have made several references to the morphopsychological differences between man and woman and highlighted the frequent combinations. Traditionally, there was a clear-cut definition between what was considered a man and what was considered a woman. When a combination of sexes was seen in the same person, it was regarded as an anomaly, a perversion, even.

Of course, it can't be denied that there are significant differences between the sexes. As already mentioned, the morphology of females is closer to dilation while males are closer to retraction. This can be explained by the different processes of maturity: in the female sex, puberty starts earlier and the body blossoms in the post-puberty phase, corresponding psychologically to mature adaptation which females reach before males. The habitual female temperament, according to the humoral concept of the ancient Greeks, is *sanguine–phlegmatic*, which is typically a blend of elements of the nervous system which mature into greater sensitivity.

In the masculine sex, the path to maturity is a more complex process, creating specific defence systems which, at first, mean a poorer adaptation to family and social settings. The body type is usually a combination of *sanguine* and *choleric*.

The shape of the facial frame is different between the two sexes. Even though tonicity is present in both, it is more limited in the female sex and strong tonicity forms part of the male morphology.

Each time a morphopsychologist studies a woman's face, he must take into account the variety of distinguishing marks–those which are equally present in both sexes–which, in the female, will always have a base made up of dilation and medium tonicity from which the other traits are developed. In particular, the indented–retracted facial shape, generally considered to be of the male domain due to the strong tonicity of the indents and reliefs, gives the overall face a very varied landscape. This facial shape suggests an intense vital movement, thus creating a passionate character. The same interpretation applies to the female form; however, the indents and reliefs are less pronounced and the feminine elements of softness and tenderness offset the passionate spirit.

As mentioned earlier, some individuals are not clearly either man or woman but are a blend of the traits of both sexes. *Androgyny* has always existed; however, opinion on it has evolved. In the past, bisexuality was considered abnormal and contrary to societal order, and those individuals who had strong elements of the opposite sex were condemned. For example, Marcel Proust's very virile father couldn't, in the early 20th century, but be offended by having a son with a strong feminine side.

Beings evolve over time and come to appreciate that the concept of male and female is an extreme idea and a limited notion. Such thinking can only be maintained by highlighting the dominant sexual factor, that which defines each one of us, and systematically neglecting that of the opposite sex.

It is not only opinions that have changed but societal mores, too, which have followed the evolution of society, notably as women gradually gain their equal rights. This physiological and psychological evolution is also expressed in morphological changes. Nowadays, it is well established that all men, as well as their dominant masculine component, have a feminine element, and that all women possess, along with their dominant feminine component, a masculine element.

This bisexuality is particularly present in adolescence, in the post-puberty phase, which is well known to be a period of immaturity, or rather a quest for maturity and therefore a time of personal upheaval.

This combination of the traits of both sexes is generally more obvious in boys than girls, although it can be observed in both sexes: there are many boy-girls and girl-boys. Their psychology has been described often, particularly by novelists, so I shall not devote time to it here.

In cases like this, the morphopsychologist must be careful not to draw any quick conclusions regarding the current state and what the future might hold for the subject; transformations may happen years later which are likely to affect the balance in the personality. This is when we see very girlish male adolescents acquire a strong virility and reciprocally, very boyish girls become more feminine as they evolve over time.

The core issue relating to these combinations is to know whether the component belonging to the opposite sex will integrate into the sexual side that dominates. There is a very broad range of situations.

Sexuality might be altered by the other component, resulting in sexual attraction to the same sex. *Homosexuality* exists principally amongst men but also amongst women. For some psychologists, it is a normal stage in sexual development which a person may or may not grow out of, and there are others who consider it a perversion.

It is also common for subjects to reject the opposing sexual component as being incompatible with the socio-cultural norms of society. The subject then inhibits his behaviour, even to the point of blocking it from his consciousness. The result is what psychoanalysis refers to as *suppression*. The forbidden tendency is hidden in the depths of the subconscious which may furthermore cause problems. In one group, there are those who see the tendency as an alien part of them and as a result they feel terribly inferior: the man believes his feminine part represents passivity and judges it incompatible with his virility while the woman feels her masculine part to be an attack on her femininity. However, in general the situation is more easily accepted by women than men, due to the fact that it appeases a woman's need to feel equal to men.

In another group, the conflict between the self and the tendency judged as alien creates neurosis. By a recognised mechanism, the subject projects his tendency onto someone else and condemns it as if it were truly external to him. To give an example, a man who has repressed his homosexual component and has projected it onto others may believe that he is surrounded by homosexuals trying to 'convert' him.

Another type of reaction to the rejection of the alien component which is particular to the male sex is that of *overcompensation*. The subject sees his feminine component as inferior and attempts to compensate for it, even to the point of overcompensating through provocative demonstrations of virility that overstep the subject's bounds. It can reach the point of senseless acts of violence that are not a response to any external acts of aggression or in proportion to the aggression. Rather, they are triggered for no apparent reason and with a level of violence that is disproportionate to the provocation. Some delinquent or even criminal acts may be explained by this semi-unconscious act of overcompensation in situations where the motive isn't at first very clear.

There is the case of a nine-year-old child who was brought to see me by his mother for a consultation as he wasn't progressing in school. The mother was very masculine and, as sometimes happens the son was very meek and, in the projective tests that we had him take, in each he self-identified as a girl. He was sent to see me two years later by the juvenile judge due to the following incident. On leaving school, he was taunted by some of his classmates: 'You, you're nothing but a wimp. You couldn't even beat up that small boy'. Our Paul, red with humiliation, crossed the road and beat up the small six-year-old child, hurting him, from whence came the complaint and intervention by the judge. The child's behaviour has all the characteristics of a subconscious act of overcompensation for his feminine component. This act was not the result of external provocation but an internal sense of humiliation (the humiliation of being considered a 'wimp') and he attacked the first thing he saw even though the victim had done nothing to provoke him. From a morphological point of view, Paul had a very soft face due to his feminine element and his aggressive action was surprising as it didn't correspond directly with his morphology.

Amongst other examples (there are many), there is the case of the man called 'the mad shooter of Vendée'. In the region of Vendée, an unknown man would open fire on all passing cars after nightfall. He hadn't yet managed to injure anyone but, as he repeated this act every evening, panic spread across the entire region. He was finally arrested thanks to a cool-headed driver who was able to give a good description of the shooter's car. It was then discovered that it concerned a young man aged twenty-two years old, a good worker and loved by those around him. However, he was timid and reserved. He had never dared approach young girls, out of fear, as he said, that they would make fun of him. When the police asked him why he did it, his response was astounding but typical: 'I wanted to show them that I'm not an idiot'. He later confessed that each time he pulled the trigger he felt sexual pleasure. This confession enlightens us to the possible psychoanalytic meaning of weapons as a phallic symbol. Even though this young man was well built and sporty, his face was more feminine than masculine and therefore he represents a typical example of overcompensation.

Lastly, although I could have put this at the beginning, the best solution for adaptation to this conflict of the sexes is integration, whereby the principal dominant sex remains at the nucleus of the personality but is joined with the secondary dominance, having acknowledged that it adds value. So, in a man, the feminine element makes the character more sensitive, adds greater tenderness and a more intuitive understanding. The masculine element of a woman makes her more assertive, more dynamic and gives her greater ambition for self-fulfilment in an independent life.

This can be observed frequently in certain professions. If you examine a number of photos of both male and female actors, this bisexuality can almost always be detected in the traits and expressions on their faces. In actresses, within an overall feminine face, there are signs of masculinity such as a tonic jawline with clearly defined angles which has two important effects: on the one hand, this structure makes the woman more assertive. It also adds an element of dynamism and stamina, which proves indispensable in a physically demanding profession. On the other hand, the duality of these sentiments is an advantage as it lends itself to the ability to play different roles. The same thing can be said of male actors:

whatever the strength and virility in their facial expression, this structure adds some feminine elements and in studying photos from Westerns, where at first sight it appears that virility is the key element, you can see that the structure and expression on their faces is often more feminine than masculine.

It should be highlighted that notably, and very significantly, the feminine component of a man is most often situated in the cerebral zone (for example, the eyes of the actor Jean Gabin and of the great physicist Einstein). Meanwhile, the masculine component in the woman is most frequently based in the instinctive zone (as in the actress Audrey Hepburn). One could draw analogies with certain artists, writers, painters or musicians. It is clear that the artistic disposition which is made up of receptivity, sensitivity, plasticity and imagination is more feminine than masculine. This explains the frequency with which male artists have typically feminine facial traits.

Even more so, it has often been pointed out that practically all men who are geniuses have a strong feminine component and, in parallel, particularly influential women have a masculine component. This makes sense if we accept that complementary abilities further enrich each personality.

Illustration 83. COCO CHANEL AND AUDREY HEPBURN

The facial traits of Coco Chanel are delicate and marked by retraction, combined with a strong, angular jawline that gives her a masculine quality.

The same heterogeneity is found in the actress Audrey Hepburn. The contrast is even greater between the delicate feminine aspect of her face and the angles of her jawline.

Illustration 84. JEAN GABIN, ROBERT MITCHUM AND ALFRED EINSTEIN

Jean Gabin, actor   Robert Mitchum, actor   Einstein, at the age of 30

Illustration 85. ALFRED EINSTEIN

This is a photographic composition where the face of Einstein's wife, Mileva, has been superimposed on his own. She was a Serbian student who also trained to teach physics. They were together from 1903 to 1914, having two children before separating.

It is interesting to note that there is an almost infallible rule that a man who has a very strong feminine component is attracted to a woman with a strong masculine element. This masculine component is clear in Mileva's facial traits, particularly in the forehead and eyes which are marked by an asthenic retraction.

275

The morphopsychologist is frequently confronted with the issue of bisexuality and must avoid limiting himself to only identifying the traits that make one sex dominant. Instead, he must unearth the additional traits that nuance the subject's facial traits and confer on it aspects of the opposite sex. These portrayals above are significant. It is always surprising, when focussed, to see a soft expression in the eyes, in the style of Greuze, in the actor Gabin, in contrast with the strength of his face, particularly in the area of the jawline.

In the same way, in the two portraits of Coco Chanel, the renowned couturier, and Audrey Hepburn, the well-known actress, we can see tonicity in the jawline with very pronounced angles that contrast with the femininity of the rest of the face.

We have seen that the masculine component confers a logical mind which is more suitable for science than art. Of course, there are always exceptions and, in someone with a very large intellect, it is no longer easy to distinguish between their scientific and artistic abilities. The great physicist Einstein is an excellent example of that: within the genius, the influence of a strong feminine component can be detected. As can be seen from the portrait of him at thirty years old, this influence is clearly visible in the structure and expression of the eyes in the style of Greuze.

In the second portrait taken of Einstein at full maturity, the contrast with the face of his wife is striking as her face clearly shows masculine assets. It is well known that Einstein's great discoveries in atomic physics were, according to specialists, more inspired by intuition than through long and patient calculations based on a rational approach.

CHAPTER X
EQUILIBRIUM, ADAPTATION AND VULNERABILITY

In the course of this work, I have warned the reader of the potential errors that may be made in the process of analysis if the face is analysed as if it were simply a mosaic of juxtaposed traits. We should never lose sight of the fact that a face belongs to an individual, or in other words, 'an indivisible being' that feels, acts and thinks, not with one part of his being but with the whole.

Thus, as noted on various occasions, it is necessary to take a *comprehensive* point of view to ensure that we consider the subject's potential vital force in relation to the personality as a whole. At the same time, as each element cannot be isolated, it raises the question of whether or not the subject himself has been able to realise this potential in his own life. This integration is effectively testimony to his *equilibrium* which determines not only his ability to *adapt to the world* and his *efficacy* but, as a result, his *vulnerability*.

The study of morphopsychology affords us the opportunity to understand this equilibrium and, consequently, the opportunities to adapt to the world. Vulnerability can be therefore inferred as is a manifestation of potential weaknesses in equilibrium and adaptation. This three-pronged study reveals the subject's *qualities*.

CONDITIONS FOR EQUILIBRIUM

In studying the *Mixed Types*, the combinations of dilation and retraction have shown us that they create the best conditions for achieving equilibrium as they combine both the reactions of expansion and of conservation, making adaptation easy in a changing environment. For this reason, Mixed Types have few weaknesses and their qualities are particularly valuable in the professional domain.

Extreme Types, on the other hand, regardless of whether the most prominent feature is dilation or retraction, are subject to a precarious equilibrium, resulting in an adaptation which can only happen within the conditions of their preferred environment and, even then, if these conditions are not met, their weaknesses may manifest themselves and affect their overall efficacy.

DILATED TYPES

At first sight, the predominantly Dilated Type gives the impression of being well-balanced, comfortable in his own skin, well adapted and lacking weaknesses. It is simply that, as their field of expansion is so wide and they are not sensitive to change, as long as their environment remains more or less stable, their sound integration makes life easy and apparently effortless. In reality, as already mentioned, their equilibrium is precarious as they lack the introspection they need to have a solid base. They are vulnerable and only happy in a group environment. If they lack company, are deprived of contact and find themselves alone, they suffer from a malaise which can result in anxiety. This lack of equilibrium, due to the exclusive predominance of expansion, is manifested by certain signs that we must learn to recognise so that we may understand that it puts the subject's core vitality in danger, even when in the guise of good health. When the Dilated Type is out of balance, he eats a lot and gains weight (particularly the Atonic Dilated), or throws himself into activity (particularly the Tonic Dilated). Generally, he lacks self-control and is attracted to all kinds of abuse (promiscuity, overindulgence and drug abuse).

The quid pro quo for this lack of introspection is that the Dilated Type is incapable of protecting himself and is therefore always in need of external protection, such as from the family and social circle. Consequently, they are only able to maintain their equilibrium in the environment of their youth, where they grew up. For example, a farmer will maintain his good health into old age if he is wise enough to remain on the farm. But if he goes to live in a city and opens, say, a small business in this new environment which is unhealthy for him, he won't have the defence systems necessary to maintain good health.

The older the Dilated Type is, the harder it is for him to adapt to new environments. It has often been mentioned that retirement is a death knell for many men of this type. As hard workers thriving in their work environment, upon retiring they suffer due to the loss of support from this environment. Despite the fact that retirement supposedly brings health and wellbeing, on the contrary, they decline both physically and psychologically and the following years bring serious health problems or depression.

In the case of bereavement (in the broadest sense of the word), where they aren't able to compensate for the loss of outside support through their inner life, in order to maintain their expansion, the Dilated Type looks for an alternative outside environment, whether through the comfort of others, an alternative occupation or consolation in food or drink. If they don't succeed in finding this alternative, without outside support and lacking an inner world, the Dilated Type loses direction and their health fails as a result. Age is a determining factor. It is often seen in elderly couples of this type that if one dies then the partner follows within a year.

In the same way, considering that the Dilated Type can only maintain equilibrium within their own environment, it is therefore not surprising that failed businessmen, in cases such as financial ruin, may commit suicide even though they may be in their prime.

The situation changes somewhat according to the degree of tonicity. The *Tonic Dilated Type*, due to their great tonicity, has such resilience that their response to being exposed to a toxic environment is increased activity, a euphoric and optimistic thrust towards the future. This provides a deceptive impression of their capacity for adaptation for quite some time. However, there comes a moment, if the toxic environment persists, where their expansive response can no longer maintain the equilibrium necessary for good health. The decline can be brutal, even to the extent of sudden death.

The *Atonic Dilated Type* doesn't have this capacity for active response. Their reaction to changes in their environment is to stubbornly maintain their habitual surroundings that have sustained their equilibrium up to that point. As it is practically impossible to maintain the status quo, they tend to regress to childhood, particularly to the oral stage of food or drink. They, too, are in a grave state and often the only way they can escape from their depression is through alcohol or drug abuse, which may be life-threatening. It is the same with the Atonic Dilated characters already covered in this book: the priest from Tours or Brûlebois, searching for a means of maintaining the status quo and afraid of the smallest of incidents which may affect his equilibrium (see Bk II, chapter IV).

Dominant expansion

When dilation is localised in one of the zones in the face, known as *Dominant Expansion*, the situation is fundamentally the same but more complex.

The complication comes from the fact that the zone in expansion is largely open to the environment and therefore, to maintain equilibrium, there needs to be a lot of interaction. When absent, the subject falls into a state of serious privation and may have a breakdown.

It is vital that the morphopsychologist takes the equilibrium in the three zones into account in order to understand the situation. If there is harmony between them and there is equilibrium in the hierarchy between the zone in expansion and the other two in relative retraction, and these two are sufficiently open to provide the organism with whatever the zone in expansion can't, they counterbalance each other. This compensation results in the ability to adapt. However, if the retraction in these zones is very pronounced and the organism does not receive the nourishment it needs in the zone in expansion, nothing is provided as a substitution from the other two zones. As a result, the personality exists in a depressive and potentially fatal state.

In the case of a *Double Expansion*, that is, where two zones are in expansion and the third is in retraction, in the instance of a lack in one of the dominant zones, the other acts as a substitute and contributes to the transference of certain qualities from the zone in privation to the other. *I will give examples of these two contrasting situations.*

Imagine a child with an exclusive expansion in the cerebral zone denied all possible intellectual interaction, deprived of books or lacking time to read as he is obligated, for example, to work all day in a monotonous manual job (as in the case of Charles Dickens, the British novelist who, at eleven years old had to stick labels on boxes for fourteen hours a day). Or the case of a child with a predominant affective zone who has no one who loves him nor anyone to love (for example, a child rejected by his family, or a child who has been hospitalised and without family visits, and the nurse visits only when administering medical care). Or a child with a dominance in the instinctive zone who is either deprived of nourishment (famine), deprived of movement (a baby tied into his pram who is neither rocked nor taken for a walk; or a child whose mother is so anxious that she keeps him confined to the house).

The same applies to adults, such as in the case of someone with an expansion in the cerebral zone who is deprived of the opportunity to cultivate his intellect (Dostoyevsky while imprisoned in the labour camp bitterly complained about his inability to get hold of a book) or the case of someone with expansion in the affective zone who is frustrated in all affective interaction (for example, a grandmother whose children never visit or someone where the child that she'd tenderly cared for during his entire infancy has been taken away) (see Ill. 86). Or, in the case of a person with an expansion in the instinctive zone who has a large appetite but is subjected to famine or deprived of movement (the case of a prisoner confined to his cell who can cope as long as he maintains hope of escape but who may have a breakdown if this hope is dashed).

In contrast, the second situation to consider is when there are other facial zones in expansion whereby the vital energy might flow away from a zone that is deficient, shifting to another zone where it can be liberated. This is the case of the double expansion Type who, for this reason, is better adapted and therefore less susceptible to weaknesses. So, someone of the Affective–Cerebral Expansion Type who experiences a blockage in the affective zone due to some prior emotionally painful event may find solace in reading or listening to music or writing a personal journal. It has often been noted that for artists who fall into this category, emotional rejection is often the driving force for their creativity, meanwhile their artistic productivity is suspended for a period of time when they are happily in love.

Illustration 86. A TYPE OF VULNERABILITY

This is the face of a female Dilated Type where atony has been accentuated by age. She has the dominant affective zone of a Dilated Type (observable in the concave shape of the nose which projects forward). She is therefore very vulnerable to emotional impacts and, as is often the case, tends to push the effect of any emotional trauma into the subconscious. She is unable to find solace in action due to the atony in the chin, nor via the cerebral zone due to its retraction (small, flat forehead). As a result, she tends to get stuck on fixed, depressive ideas leading up to a breaking point where she sinks into depression. This is visible in the lacklustre expression in the eyes.

RETRACTED TYPES

The equilibrium of predominantly Retracted Types is also precarious. Outside their preferred surroundings, the slightest provocation will result in withdrawal and a turning inwards in a process of retraction.

A key cause of vulnerability exists precisely in their inability to deal with whatever circumstances arise within their environment. We are aware that they are fearful of the world and of groups and environments that the Dilated Type is at ease in: anything from routine gatherings to large, formal events. They aren't comfortable in situations that do not conform to their preferred surroundings, to the point of choosing solitude.

As a result, they appear to be more vulnerable than the Dilated Type. In reality, it is of a different nature: it manifests itself in the need to preserve their individuality by rejecting the calls to or obligations of community life. Their vulnerability is therefore more psychological than physical and so they are not exposed to the health problems suffered by the Dilated Type.

However, we should highlight that the degree of tonicity can make a significant difference. In the *Tonic Retracted Type*, the rejection of expansion in a specific area represents an active resistance, a voluntary rejection of the rules of community life, customs and the perceived wisdom which could even lead to the life of a revolutionary living on the fringes of the law, predisposed to action which is aimed at the destruction of the established order.

In the *Lateral Retracted Type*, there is an inability to accept the status quo and the irrepressible need for movement and change. Vulnerability is expressed through an all-or-nothing attitude, a break with routine and evasion of any potential difficulties.

Conversely, the *Frontal Retracted Type* obstinately imposes their preferred surroundings regardless of circumstances. For example, in religion or politics, they refuse to submit to official doctrine and wish to apply their own personal doctrine. Vulnerability resides in fanaticism which is a refusal to concede to circumstances and a preference to fly in the face of the community rather than make concessions.

The defensive reaction of the *Atonic Retracted Type*, although more passive, is no less significant. Subjects of this type aren't capable of making the smallest effort required for expansion regardless of how light the demands are, for example, the most natural of sentiments such as love and friendship. The typical reaction of the Atonic Retracted Type in the face of love is characteristic of a fear of expansion. While the Dilated Type seeks out love as a means of satisfying instinctive and affective needs, the

Retracted Type often considers it a dangerous extroversion threatening the integrity of the self and, as a result, protects himself against it. The novelist, Marcel Proust, an Atonic Retracted Type, wrote that *'Others can be no more to us than a source of emotional disappointment and disconnection from ourselves.'*[1] The poet, Baudelaire, another Retracted Type, defines love as *'a dreadful game where it is obligatory that one of the players loses command of his self.*[2] Another example, Jacques of *The Thibaults*, who has been cited on a number of occasions here, is in love with Jenny and is planning a trip with her, but the project is cancelled and the novelist, commenting on the young man's reaction to this rejection, says, *'The suffering and disappointment which coloured his attitude were real; however, they were superficial. The last attachments were broken! He was leaving! Cut ties! Leaving by himself! Everything had been simplified!'*[3]

We have also seen in Book II, Chapter V, that when Salavin, an Atonic Retracted Type, establishes a friendship with a Dilated Type, he quickly tries to pull away and the novelist shows us that for Salavin, all of the expansive emotions—happiness, joy and success—are sources of suffering that he tries to avoid.

As we have already seen, the Retracted Type, particularly the Atonic Retracted Type, takes refuge in solitude, alone with himself and his thoughts. This is the case of Prince Munchkine, a character by Dostoyevsky whom I've already spoken of, who is shown to be completely inept in social situations which he finds, for being so sensitive, painful. The novelist says of him, *'Sometimes he wished to go somewhere, anywhere, to completely disappear; he desired a sombre and solitary refuge where he could be alone with his thoughts and where no one would be able to find him'.*[4] (Ill. 48, 2)

Already vulnerable to the most ordinary of situations, the Retracted Type is even more vulnerable to shocks, for example, in suffering a loss (in the broadest sense of the word). The retreat into himself is even more pronounced as it is in the form of a rejection of the situation, refusing food, not trusting anyone, not speaking, all which may lead to a complete blockage and, of course, a constant desire for solitude.

1: Unpublished translation.
2: Unpubl. trans.
3: Unpubl. trans.
4: Unpubl. trans.

It is worth mentioning that the Retracted Type's vulnerability is often expressed in the form of fatigue, which should be considered more like a 'sensation of fatigue', meaning that the forces of expansion have been temporarily exhausted. It is true that simple fatigue is a banal symptom when it appears naturally after a period of strenuous activity and should not be considered a sign of vulnerability. However, the Retracted Type, particularly the Atonic Retracted Type, suffers from a type of particularly intense fatigue known as 'asthenic' fatigue, characterised by a persistent tiredness occurring even prior to activity and certainly completely disproportionate to any effort made. This astheny, which is considered by medicine to be an illness which must be treated with energy-giving tonics, is in reality a defensive reaction of the instinct for conservation of those exposed, who, if they were to maintain their expansion, would suffer serious health consequences. The asthenia therefore provides a useful function and the morphopsychologist, in analysing an asthenic's face, must search for signs of the imbalance that generates this defensive reaction in order to provide the appropriate advice.

Predominant retraction

In those with partial expansion, due to their hypersensitivity, the retracted zones are more vulnerable than the dilated zones in the sense that they react to the smallest disturbance in the environment. Through their morphology, we can appreciate how they have to manage their life in order to maintain equilibrium, particularly in the area (the zone in retraction, in this case) where changes in the environment will be most felt and have the most destabilising effect.

Retraction in the instinctive zone means that the subject does not adapt well to dietary changes and in particular to the excesses to which he is accustomed. He tires easily if he has to make some kind of effort that he is not used to. Retraction in the emotive zone indicates a dislike of social situations and interaction with strangers. We have already seen the example of Jacques Thibault who, in certain situations, reaches the point where he is unable to tolerate even the presence of loved ones. Retraction in the cerebral zone means that intellectual work is very tiring and cannot be sustained over long periods if he is not accustomed to it, which is why he is better adapted to specialised work.

What is remarkable is that, given their inherent connection, the retracted zones may feel and be affected by environmental impacts at the same time as the dilated zones even though they are not directly implicated. They may react first and energetically, which seems surprising. In fact, everything depends on the balance that exists between each of the three stages.

So, someone with expansion in the cerebral zone who is overwhelmed intellectually, or has problems that he is obsessing over, has a vulnerability in this zone that may be expressed in the form of a migraine or some mental weakness. If there is a major structural asymmetry, such as extreme retraction in the instinctive zone, his problems may physically manifest in this zone through digestive issues (known as the Retracted Hypersensitive Type) and suffer from anorexia, constipation or spasms related to poor digestion.

In the same way, someone with expansion in the instinctive zone who abuses food and drink or consumes food that has spoiled may suffer indigestion with vomiting. Or, if he overdoes some sporting activity, he may suffer from intense muscular pain. However, in the case of a pronounced retraction in the cerebral zone, the reaction is most likely to manifest itself in the form of a migraine or mental exhaustion.

In the case of the woman with depression in illustration 86, the morphological study tells us that the exceedingly open affective zone (a dilated face with dominance in the affective zone through the open and projected nose) has made her very vulnerable to emotional rejection. As a result, a traumatic experience has paralysed her ability to love, which had previously fulfilled her. As her cerebral zone is very retracted (small, narrow forehead), she is unable to find a means of evading or coping with it; on the contrary, she has become fixed on the notion of her unhappiness which has only added to her depression.

Lateral–nasal retraction

A particularly important case is the type of affective retraction which I have called the *lateral–nasal retraction*. This is the unusual combination of expansion and retraction in the same zone. The vulnerability comes from the internal conflict between extroversion and introversion in the emotive life. The solution to this conflict, a gauge of equilibrium, depends on the overall morphological structure. Connection between the different zones provides the solution. As I demonstrated in Chapter VII, the affective life, which is in part repressed, may transfer its vital energy to the zone in expansion, either the cerebral zone or the instinctive zone, thus establishing a new equilibrium.

Taking the three types of lateral–nasal retraction—*inhibiting, dynamising* or *productive*—into consideration is very useful as this transfer of vitality has a positive effect if the retraction is either dynamising or nourishing. Meanwhile it is impossible in cases of inhibition and repression, as it often manifests itself in an emotional imbalance and potentially a grave inability to adapt. The examples given in illustrations 68, 69 and 70, which demonstrate the rule, should be studied carefully.

In the same way, we can deduce that, where there is a functional difficulty to adapt, the remedy does not lie in the systematic treatment, as tends to happen, of the zone where the illness manifests itself. Instead, it may lie in the zone where the problem has originated, even though it may not appear so at first.

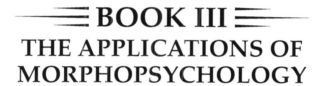

BOOK III
THE APPLICATIONS OF
MORPHOPSYCHOLOGY

The field of application for morphopsychology is vast as there is nothing in the human being that it does not encompass. In my opinion, there is no question that it should be a unique science with its own domain and specialists. However, if we continue to investigate and go further into all that we already know about the human, morphopsychology can add a new dimension to our knowledge.

As a medical professional, it has contributed a considerable amount to my knowledge of the ways in which organisms react, in healthy or sick states, and it has helped me to understand the truth of the ancient doctrines about temperament, sadly abandoned in the present day due to a medicine that has become too technical. As a psychiatrist, thanks to this knowledge, I have been able to penetrate, in the way that Dr. Kretschmer in Germany has, the psychology of the mentally ill and understand the constitutional factors relating to their inability to adapt. In the fields of education and child psychiatry, the study of faces has enabled me to deepen my knowledge of children, both the requirements for good physical health and psychological adaptation. Through a decades-long collaboration with Paul Planus, a specialist in organisational issues, I have been able to establish a proven professional method which constitutes one of the most useful applications of morphopsychology. Morphopsychology is not simply a method of selection by aptitude; more than anything, it gives each person the ability to better understand themselves so that they can maximise their innate abilities. This also provides a base for couples counselling with respect to the formation of couples. Its use in the field of theatre and cinema in the selection of the most suitable actor for a role is all that remains to be demonstrated.

Lastly, from a cultural standpoint, I have been able to re-examine those great men of the past and reveal the true reality of their faces, consequently gaining a better understanding of the profound relationship between man and the work that he has created.

CHAPTER I

BECOMING A MORPHOPSYCHOLOGIST

As I have demonstrated throughout this work, morphopsychology is a science in the sense that facial forms and personality traits obey laws. This is derived from a combined study of *morphology* and *psychology*. But above all it is based on the *relationship between the physical form and the psyche*.

Our analytic tendency leads us to study the facial traits that are visible to us separately from the character traits revealed to us through intuition and then attempt to synthesise the two. But this method of analysis is too static. I have previously demonstrated the importance of always taking into account the *fundamentally dynamic character* of these relationships, the life that flows throughout the whole being, shaping the physical form as well as determining the functional processes. One must assimilate the idea that the physical form and the psyche are not separate entities in the eyes of the morphopsychologist but that, on observation, the *psyche becomes visible and can be interpreted through its physical form*.

The dynamic point of view is also intimately tied to the *demand for synthesis* as the personality forms a whole where everything is interrelated. As a result, isolating one process from another nearly always leads to erroneous conclusions. It is often said that the forehead is a sign of intelligence, yet it is absurd to isolate the forehead. As a humourist once commented, 'Have you ever seen a forehead walking down a street on its own?'

At first, due to the difficulty presented by a morphopsychological study, we must break down the individual parts and deal with them separately, but this phase of the study must be as short as possible.

We must *learn morphology*, that is, learn how to examine and describe the facial forms. A few may have a natural aptitude but most must acquire this talent through consistent practice. However, this doesn't mean a brief glance at the face of the person in front of us as one would do in a normal social situation. It is not a question of simply seeing; one must *learn to observe*. Some will easily appreciate the overall whole of the face while others are better with detail. It is necessary to study both. I recommend drawing the face and for those who have no talent for drawing to at least try to make a sketch as a means of concretising the image you have in front of you.

Portrait artists know from experience that we cannot be completely objective no matter what we do as we always tend to project certain traits of our own personality on the model and as a result distort it a little. It is impossible to eliminate it completely as our temperament affects everything we see. We must at least be aware of it and minimise projection in order to have as objective a viewpoint as possible. With the assiduous practice of morphopsychology, it is possible to gradually improve.

To *learn psychology* is to learn about the tendencies, emotions and interests that make up the human personality and, of course, to familiarise ourselves with the most appropriate vocabulary to describe what we are talking about. It is very useful to do psychological studies and to read books on the subject. However, studies that are too abstract aren't very useful. Psychology is the study of life, of living situations, and it is necessary to make a consistent effort to formulate the character traits that one discovers in a person in straightforward language in order to make them a concrete reality.

The great writers provide us with a good example as their work shows that through their observation of their surroundings, and of themselves, they have created real characters and they see them as a whole in the intimate connexion between their outward appearance and their profound psychology. Through their natural intuitive ability, they have practiced morphopsychology before the science existed. I have always thought that it would be extremely useful for university literature faculties to learn psychology through reading the great literary works. And I have demonstrated in my work on the morphopsychological Types in literature that the observations within their works provide us with a rich seam of morphopsychological information as instruction on the method for interpretation according to the basic parameters of our science.

To *learn morphopsychological relationships* is to learn how to connect the facial forms with character traits and intelligence aptitudes. The laws of morphopsychology, particularly the law of dilation–retraction, help us a great deal in our study with the understanding that the source of these relationships is biological; that the same vital movement, as we have seen, determines on the one hand, the facial form, and on the other, the character traits. At first sight the application appears simple and I have demonstrated in this work that the foundational types, given a simple morphological identity, provide precise psychological analyses.

However, most humans are complex and constitute an amalgam of traits which are often unconnected and borrowed from different foundational types. To understand them, *they cannot simply be juxtaposed, they must be understood as a whole* where every part combines to create a living unity. The morphopsychologist is assisted in his analysis by the rules described in this book and, as we have already seen, starting at the simplest Type and moving to the more complex Types, we finish by pulling together these traits that form the peculiar originality of the human beings that one encounters in daily life.

Nevertheless, having scientific knowledge is not enough. The application of this science is an art, an art which is not acquired without a great deal of practice over time and which requires this curious aptitude which we call *intuition*. Many naturally possess intuition and can interpret faces without learning the rules. However, scientists object to the use of intuition, claiming it to be too subjective for it to be considered a science. This is true and especially considering what we have seen above, that everyone has the tendency to project some of their own facial traits on the morphology of the person that they are studying. Likewise, a similar projection plays a part in intuition and may misrepresent the personality studied. I have already shown examples in this book by demonstrating that the antagonisms within the different Types lead to an erroneous understanding of character traits that don't actually exist in the individual. I believe that intuition is indispensable for morphopsychological analysis; however, innate intuition must be trained and made more precise through the rational application of the rules of our science in which the two opposing intellectual mechanisms, intuition and logic, are united in a common purpose.

Vitality

Logic breaks the object under study down into its component parts in order to make a detailed analysis. Intuition perceives the whole, often in a confused fashion, and can't offer a clear conclusion without the use of logical analysis. Nevertheless, intuition is closer than logic to the dynamics of vitality and provides a better understanding of living beings.

Whichever method employed for the study of a face, we must never lose sight of, as stated above, this essential element which is dynamism, the vital flow which runs through beings and controls their destiny. The morphopsychologist must distance himself as far as possible from the static viewpoint of the personality which usually prevails in psychology. In this book, I have specifically criticised the abuse of the concept of symmetry. Morphologically I have underlined that the harmony of a perfectly symmetrical face is a long way from being, as if often thought, a sign of value. Asymmetry, as long as it is moderate, indicates an active vital flow and constitutes a sign of vitality while total symmetry corresponds to weak vitality. From a psychological standpoint, I have also criticised the typologies that focus on extreme contrasts, attached above all to value judgements in which the psychologist tends to project his own subjectivity, such as when a Dilated Type pejoratively judges a Retracted Type and *vice versa* (see Book II, Chap. III). The morphopsychologist must avoid classical *Manichaeism*, the schematic opposition of Good and Evil, as these opposing values come from a common origin in the biological dynamism, a point of view which leads to a more nuanced understanding. One therefore understands that the personality may be nourished from every source and grow from a base of the most contrasting tendencies. We find within that the requirement for synthesis which, as I have stated, must be the foundation of all morphopsychological studies.

Determinism and free will

One of the most common arguments put forth by those that disagree with the concept of morphopsychology is that it may lead to determinism. In this view, character traits would depend entirely on the morphological structure and could not be modified, in the understanding that once growth has been completed, the structure is definitively set in stone.

We could respond by stating that if the shape of the facial forms is hereditary and is therefore, to a certain degree, fixed from birth, denoting innate aptitudes which will later define the personality, this fixedness is a long way from definitive; we know that over the course of growth the face will change a great deal and, as a result, the character (see Book I, Chap. VI).

However, our understanding of morphopsychology drives us to refute psychological determinism in the way it is usually presented. We don't regard the character as the sum of a series of elements. It is a *composition* of dynamic elements which react one with another and which, through these reactions, change and evolve. We have seen this particularly in the chapter which deals with antagonisms (Book II, Chap III). Due to this evolution, the end result is what counts above all else, not the original components. Freedom resides in the way in which this composition of elements functions. It is not, despite what is often said, the ability to do what we want without considering the biopsychic conditioning of our actions. It is, through the strength of character that we possess, the ability to discover the best point of equilibrium, which allows us to access our potential. *Liberty is therefore not the opposite of determinism; it is the use of determinism for a higher purpose.*

The honest man and the sincere man

I am borrowing this comparison of opposites between the *honest man* and the *sincere man* from Jacques Rivière who, in his work '*De la sincérité envers soi-même*', poses a problem which is exactly that of morphopsychology.

According to Rivière, the honest man is one who models his personality according to the demands of his social life, of the current social mores, while the sincere man ignores these societal demands and tries to live only according to his own personal, most authentic inclinations. The honest man is someone who only wants to think permissible thoughts; the sincere man has the courage to think anything. The honest man is not a free man, he is conditioned by the standards of the world he lives in and in which he has been steeped since infancy, and from an early age a mask of good behaviour, and later of respectability, has been installed in his subconscious. His must project an image of himself that is stable and straightforward in terms of his strengths and weaknesses. Considering his strengths valuable and his weaknesses failings, he tries to eliminate them.

Morphopsychology teaches us that man is in reality not at all simple, that he is composed of different tendencies which are often antagonistic. However, it does not limit itself to examining these tendencies as opposites. It shows us that the vitality which creates them corresponds to a double movement—expansion and retraction—which is found in the various expressions of behaviour. It also teaches us that we must not be attached to these partial movements but to the end result which is the expression of the complexity of the character.

Morphopsychology establishes a radically different approach to the traditional psychology that we are accustomed to; it always takes us back to the source of the character and engages us in the essential vital movements from which, as we have seen, all is derived. At this profound level, there are neither qualities nor faults, nor Good or Evil, only vital tendencies which prove favourable or unfavourable depending upon the environment in which they are manifested. This outcome also depends on the knowledge we can gain of our own abilities and it is our responsibility to integrate them so that we may understand what they offer us.

In the same way, morphopsychology teaches us to value the sincere man, the authentic man, one who places no limits on himself, who wishes to *'garder tout en composant tout'*,[1] according to the writer Montherlant.

The honest man (according to Jacques Rivière) refuses to recognise morphopsychology. He thinks it is dangerous as it lays bare the soul and therefore may call into question the equilibrium he has attained in the wearing of a mask. We have seen, for example, that the contrast

1: 'to put his entire being into creation of anything and everything'

between the sexes, upon which social life is based, is often at the core of an individual's personality: an essential component of the opposite sex can be central to the personality, whether male or female. This component, which makes the subject androgynous, is considered an anomaly by society that should be repressed. It is even viewed as such by the subject himself who, to maintain his sex, *the fiction of his sex*, rejects everything in him that he believes belongs to the opposite sex and suppresses it to avoid having to acknowledge it. The sincere man accepts this anomaly, clearly understanding how it could bring positive and negative aspects to his life and therefore makes an effort to integrate it. Starting from the initial contact with the subject, morphology immediately reveals this androgyny. It provides an authentic point of view that enriches our understanding of the subject and the subject of himself.

CHAPTER II
PARALLEL BIOTYPOLOGIES

Human science has perpetually wished to define the human being by his *essence*, that is, by the physical and mental traits that are central to his character. On the other hand, there has been a need to differentiate each human being by describing their particular individuality. Then, between these two opposing poles, *general essence* and *individual existence*, there lies an intermediate point whereby men are similar to one another through the defined traits of homogenous groups also known as *Types*, which are racial types.

To create a *typology*, it is necessary to define the dominant traits that characterize the group, meaning the traits which allow us to identify a subject as belonging to a particular group. The selection of these dominant traits is dictated by the ideas of the greatest authority in any particular era and, in comparing the different typologies, we can evaluate the progress that has been made from one era to the next through the way we understand the living organism. In this way, each typology brings its own collection of original observations which can enrich our knowledge of man. However, the problem lies in being able to synthesise all of these observations in order to study the different doctrines' viewpoints and be able to make comparisons. The danger lies in making comparisons which are only superficial juxtapositions and to confuse juxtaposition with synthesis. *In reality, synthesis aims to achieve unity by going to the source from which all typologies emanate, that being the core structure of the human being.*

I am going to attempt to classify the different typologies according to the ideas of life from which they were inspired and how their authors used it in practice.

HUMORAL TYPOLOGIES

The four temperaments of the Ancients

In antiquity, there existed a sole notion of science which considered man an element of nature, united with everything that constituted it and subject to the surrounding cosmic influences. In this science, which was not yet distinct from philosophy, the world was made up of four elements which counterbalanced each other in pairs: hot and cold, humid and dry. Warmth and humidity being the principles of life, the reproduction of human beings operated through their union (warmth being a masculine principle and humidity a feminine principle). Cold and dry were principles of destruction, of death.

Climates and seasons were characterised by the specific distribution of these elements: Winter, cold and humid; Spring, warm and humid; Summer, warm and dry; and Autumn, cold and dry.

These same elements are found in human organisms and particularly in the human being in the form of 'humours': the lymphatic system is cold and humid; the blood, warm and humid; bile being warm and dry; and black bile being cold and dry.

Parallels were drawn between the predominance of the humours during the various stages of adolescence. The lymphatic system is predominant in the infant where the tissue is waterlogged and the function that regulates temperature is still weak (phlegmatic temperament). As the child grows, blood replaces the lymphatic system and all areas of activity, particularly the regulation of temperature, begin to develop (sanguine temperament). As an adult, catabolic activity which is connected to the function of the biliary system becomes predominant (choleric temperament). In old age, tissue cools and dries out (nervous temperament). We can't go into depth here about the close ties which, according to the Ancients, existed between the external and internal effects of the elements and how, for example, through these actions they interpreted the influence of the seasons on the human being and the states of health and sickness.

The dominance of any one of these elements defined the temperaments: a balanced temperament was that in which the four elements were equally balanced; and specific temperaments were characterised by the unequal development of the elements. There were therefore four temperaments: *Phlegmatic, Sanguine, Choleric* and *Nervous*. However, it is worth highlighting that, from a comprehensive view consistent with the integration of man in nature, the Ancients also had to consider man equal in all parts of his entire being and therefore that the physical and mental aptitudes, as well as external physical appearance, were connected and simply represented different aspects of the same living reality.

Each one of the dominant temperaments indicated the way in which the individual reacted in health or sickness, physically as well as mentally. In addition, how the functions expressed themselves in the morphology of the body, the 'look of a hustler', was sufficient to identify a type from which a number of conclusions could be drawn about hygiene, the diagnosis, prognosis and treatment of illness.

The doctrine of the four temperaments has been attributed to the medical doctors Hippocrates and Galien and reigned for almost two millennia before being replaced by typologies which are more in line with modern physiological discoveries.

This four-pronged concept created by the Ancients, despite being discredited, still had its resolute followers in the 20th century who remained faithful to the notion of the temperaments. Dr. Carton is a doctor of complementary medicine who adopted this doctrine in its integrity and created a number of therapeutic remedies that made him famous. Dr. Allendy, a homeopath and psychotherapist, also adopted the doctrine by reinventing it in an original concept based on the notions of plasticity and tonicity (which I will come back to later).

Alchemists and homeopaths

Inspired by the idea that man was connected to cosmic influences, the alchemists, notably their leader, Paracelse, created a new typology in the 16th century based on the same essential elements as the Ancients but represented them with material symbols. The key principles of the functions of the organism were: warmth, represented by sulphur, which burns; humidity, represented by mercury, a liquid despite its high density; and cold and dry, represented by salt which gives the chemical body stability and is therefore not conducive to chemical reactions. From this, they deduced three types of temperaments: *sulphurous*, *mercurial* and *saline*. In the 17th century, the homeopath Grauvogl reprised this typology but with new denominations: *oxygenoid*, *hydrogenoid* and *carbo-nitrogenoid* which are, respectively, equivalent to sulphurous, mercurial and saline.

TYPOLOGIES OF THE MAIN FUNCTIONS

Developments in physiology have brought to the fore the notion of the organ and its function, thus replacing the humours of the Ancients. However, the majority of investigators have understood that a temperament cannot be characterised by the functional importance of a particular organ in isolation from the rest of the organism. The basic premise of the typologies is to contemplate the organism's combined reactions by groups of organs which act in concert, that is, in systems: the musculoskeletal system, the nutritional system, the circulatory system and the nervous system.

The original investigators who demonstrated the combined reaction of the organs remained faithful to Socrates' doctrine and attempted to draw parallels. Richerand, followed by the illustrious Cabanis, characterised the Phlegmatic temperament by the significant development of the digestive organs, the Sanguine temperament by the development of the heart and blood vessels, the Choleric temperament by the liver and the Melancholic temperament by the development of the nervous system.

More recently, others have wished to create a typology based on the development of the *embryonic layers*. At the beginning of the 20th century, the Frenchmen Polti, Gary and Encausse attributed the Phlegmatic temperament to the hyper-development of the *endoderm*, the Sanguine temperament to the development of the *mesoderm* and the Choleric and Nervous temperaments to the development of the *ectoderm*. At around the same time, this thesis was backed by the German Carl Huter. More recently it provided the theoretical base for the American Sheldon, who by observation, anthropometry and the photographing of three types of men (he never studied women, I wonder why!), he created three types which he defined as endomorphs, mesomorphs and ectomorphs, from which he studied the corresponding psychology in depth.

It should be highlighted that embryological study adds nothing to our understanding of the types and that, in the process of demonstrating their theory, the typologists did not overlook the use of empirical evidence based on simple observation.

I mentioned above that these typologists regularly focused on synthesis in the sense that they didn't take individual organs into account, only groups of organs. The Italian Pende placed great importance on the internal secretional glands and described the *Predominant Endocrine Types*, not considering a gland in isolation but studying the combined action of several similar glands. In parallel, Gaskell, in associating the endocrine glands with the nerves of physiological systems in their combined action, described two opposing temperaments which he denominated *vagotonic* and *sympathicotonic*. Knowledge of these adds completely original elements to our knowledge of the processes.

MORPHOLOGICAL TYPOLOGIES

To differentiate the types, Hippocrates, Galien and those that followed used the morphology of the body and face as a base. The tradition continued until the experimental period where anthropometry emphasized measurements, often to an excessive degree. Relying on the descriptions of the Ancients, I have, with my friend Pazzi, drawn the Hippocratic temperaments, which medical practice presents every day (Ill. 87). When the study of the organs and groups of organs was popular, it was natural that the characterisation of these types was based on the shape of the naked body, made easier by the fact that the majority of typologists were doctors.

In the 18th century, Husson, then Hallé, and later in the 19th century, Thomas, focused on morphological traits which made it easy to distinguish between the different temperaments. They described three main types: *Cranial* (predominantly in the cranium which envelops the central nervous system); *Thoracic* (predominantly in the thorax which envelops the heart and lungs); and *Abdominal* (predominantly in the stomach where the digestive system is found).

Illustration 87. THE HIPPOCRATIC TEMPERAMENTS

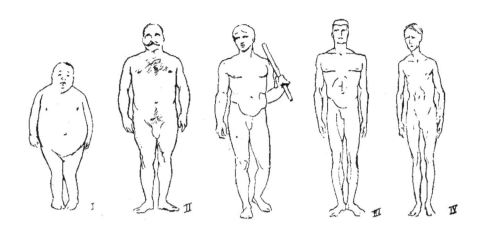

Illustration by Pazzi

In the beginning, Sigaud was without doubt inspired by this classification when he described the three types—*Cerebral*, *Respiratory* and *Digestive*— to which he added *Muscular*. (We will see later on that there is another Sigaud, that of the law of dilation–retraction, which in my opinion is much more important.) The doctor from Lyon confined himself to a description of the temperaments without illustrations and it is very surprising that his short book *La Forme Humaine*, which describes the foundation of his doctrine, doesn't include a single illustration. On the other hand, one of his disciples, Dr. Thooris, in his remarkable work, *La Vie par le stade*, applied the doctrine of temperament to the study of sporting abilities and included very detailed illustrations.

The body forms also constitute the basis of Sheldon's typology who appears to have ignored the Hippocratic classification by reducing the number of temperaments to three, as we have already seen, and re-establishing the complexity of the individual types through combinations of these three components.

All of the investigators, being doctors, limited themselves to the study of the body, unwittingly neglecting the study of the face. Only the German psychiatrist Ernst Kretschmer integrated physiognomy into his system. Taking a purely empirical view, based equally on direct observation and measurements, he also described three types: the *pyknic*, *athletic* and the *leptosomic*. It is easy to make comparisons with the temperaments of the Ancients. The pyknic is a combination of Phlegmatic and Sanguine, athletic is Choleric and Leptosomic is Nervous or a combination of Nervous and Phlegmatic. Kretschmer's greatest virtue is that he completed extensive studies on the connections between the three types and the mental illnesses particular to each one. However, as he himself appeared to be a pyknic type, he wished to focus on a purely empirical analysis and, hostile by nature to theories, he never constructed any.

MORPHOPSYCHOLOGICAL SYNTHESIS

In these functional typologies, we try to characterize the temperaments as a general way of reacting to the external world. This approach, as we have seen, already existed in the Hippocratic doctrine of the humours but a more functional approach has taken its place and truthfully does not have the same universal character as the doctrine of the Ancients.

And so, in the 17th century, Stahl and later on Hoffmann focused mainly on the structure of tissue fibres and contrasted *laxum* with *strictum*, which is atony and spasm, and described temperaments according to these contrasting qualities.

In the 18th century, Rostan revisited a similar idea as a means of explaining the Phlegmatic Temperament of the Ancients. He focused on the *inertia* of the functions in the Phlegmatic Temperament, stating that 'if the lymphatic system, fleshiness and fat predominate in the phlegmatic constitution, it is due to inertia in all bodily systems and functions'.

In a different way and in the same era, Haller, followed by Broussais, adopted *irritability* as the key element in the organs. A bit later on, the celebrated Bichat, who renewed all conceptions of physiology of his time, made this irritability which he called *sensitivity*, associated with *contractility*, one of the primordial qualities of life. Bichat reasoned as a physiologist and the theory that he elaborated was as applicable to the healthy as to the sick; however, most typologists reasoned as doctors and based their doctrine on temperament on the dominance of this or that function, considering the pathologic status. For example, the doctrine of the strictum and the laxum, which relates to tonicity, is seen in its extreme forms: strictum means spasm which is a morbid state, and laxum is the complete relaxation of tone which is also extremely unhealthy.

Dr. Allendy elaborated on the subject, as we have already seen, with a doctrine on temperament inspired directly by the Hippocratic doctrine and attempted to explain it using the most up to date information from pathology. Plasticity is the tendency of the organic processes to spread, for example in the form of the fatal growth of tumours, while tonicity is the tendency to react with energy to other factors, for example, in the form of aches or fever. The equivalent in the Hippocratic temperaments is the following: the Phlegmatic Temperament is atonic-plastic; the Sanguine Temperament is tonic-plastic; the Choleric Temperament is tonic-aplastic; and the Nervous Temperament is atonic-aplastic.

SIGAUD'S DOCTRINE

The first original aspect of Sigaud's work was to give *sensitivity in the organism's defence system* a key role, not only the active response to stimuli which is characteristic of the nervous system which Bichat focused on, but overall sensitivity, understanding here what is called cenesthesia, which is the sensitivity of the internal organs which plays an important role in their protection.

The second original aspect of the doctor from Lyon's work was to have observed that this sensitivity is different in each individual and that these differences are visible in the body's morphology. Revisiting the comparisons between fat and thin, which exists in every typology, taken from this new perspective he discovered that the fat are characterised by *hyposensitivity* and the thin by *hypersensitivity*. In his view, each type's defensive reaction to illness essentially depends upon these different types of sensitivity.

One of the most important ideas which had been missed by prior investigators is that, according to Sigaud, the slimming down of forms so the subject becomes 'lean' does not represent atrophy but rather *an active defensive retraction* which the organism activates as a means of extracting itself from external aggressions.

Continuing with Sigaud's work, I was able to establish that the morphological processes of dilation and retraction correspond to the two essential movements which are the instincts of expansion and of conservation, combining their actions in different ways according to the demands of the vital defence system.

If you add the law of tonicity to this law of dilation–retraction, by combining these two factors, we have at our disposal four combinations which, if based on a strong scientific foundation, provide a rational explanation for all of the other typologies.

Morphopsychology therefore allows us to build a bridge between the theory of the Hippocratic humours and the doctrine of the main functions of the organism. It is therefore easy to establish a very precise relationship between the temperaments of the Ancients and our foundational types.

The Phlegmatic is an Atonic Dilated Type; the Sanguine is a Tonic Dilated Type; the Nervous is an Atonic Retracted Type; and the Choleric is a Tonic Retracted Type.

These characterisations in terms of dilation–retraction and tonicity–atony correspond remarkably well to the attributes applied to the four temperaments of the Ancients. These attributes, taking inspiration from the type of person that one comes across every day, provided my friend and artist Pazzi with the elements required to create very expressive drawings of these temperaments (Ill. 87).

The science of morphopsychology also helps us explain other typological doctrines and consequently establish rational parallels between them.

In passing, it is worth noting that these parallels are more easily visible when the body types in discussion are illustrated. For example, no one can dispute the connection between the Sanguine Type of the Ancients, the Pyknic Type of Kretschmer and the Thoracic Type by Sigaud (in the first sense), which all correspond precisely to the Tonic Dilated Type. In the same way, it is easy to show that the Endomorph of Sheldon is a combination of the Phlegmatic and Sanguine Types which correspond to a Dilated Type with pronounced atony. The Ectomorph by the same author is the same as the Choleric Type and the Leptosome by Kretschmer corresponds to our Atonic Retracted Type.

It should nevertheless be highlighted that as almost all typologists are doctors, their characterisations of the types are always based on the morphology of the body, and on only that. With the exception of Kretschmer, who was as much a psychologist as a doctor, nobody thought to represent the faces as well nor thought to consider the meaning of this part of the body in the creation of their doctrine. Moreover, Sheldon not only neglected the face, he negated it and made no mention of it. Sigaud didn't include it either and when I integrated his ideas into my understanding of the human being I had to add the final details to the description which I found incomplete.

As a result, all of these investigators (again, with the exception of Kretschmer) failed to understand the crucial importance of the face, on the one hand, as much in that it represents different parts of the body in miniature, and on the other hand, that the face is the part of the body which holds the vitally important sensory receptors—powerful tools of communication.

CHAPTER III

MORPHOPSYCHOLOGY AND CHARACTEROLOGY

As we have seen in the previous chapter, the Ancients' doctrine of the four temperaments was established in an era where the human being was thought to be a single *unit* and the mind and body were interconnected. In addition, the morphology of the body was linked to the main functions to the extent that the description of a type of temperament was composed of three elements: physical, mental and morphological, none of which were ever dealt with separately.

Later, the idea of developing a more rigorous science came about, advancing from the synthetic to the analytic and entrusting the study of man to different disciplines: physiologists and doctors studied the body while psychologists studied the psyche. In the process, we lost sight of their close relationship, even to the point of negating it.

The great French thinkers had a taste for categorisation, which culminated in Descartes' philosophy and accentuated this separation further. As a result, personality types were described according to their intellectual capacities without taking the body into consideration. There is consequently a tradition of intellectualism in our universities which manifests itself particularly in the science of character: Characterology. This science has been the source of various studies in which the personality was frequently analysed according to its two basic components: *sensitivity* and *activity*, which were considered to be the foundation of the psyche and human conduct. More recently, Characterology came back into fashion when two Dutchmen, Heymans and Wiersma, thought to add a third component: *resonance*, defined as the speed of response to environmental stimuli. *Primary resonance* is when the reaction is immediate; *secondary resonance* when it is delayed. Character types are therefore defined according to the respective value of these three components. Their different combinations make up a total of eight character types whereby four of them are associated: E (sensitivity or emotivity) and A (activity), to which is added the value of resonance (P or S). The philosopher René Le Senne popularized the concept in France through his excellent work *Traité de caractérologie*, wherein he clearly describes the eight types, particularly in the way he used them in his study of great men.

The greatest weakness in characterology is that it completely ignores the body and its functions and, when describing aptitudes, it is as if they emanate purely and simply from the psyche. Morphology has consequently been ignored and never used as a means of differentiating the different types. As a result, and remaining in the purely conscious and rational psyche, characterologists have defined each of the eight types according to the responses given by the subject himself to a behavioural questionnaire. This is a very fragile foundation and prone to error since the subject has to some extent written his own characterological diagnosis through his responses.[1]

It is easy to understand that the three components of character cannot be considered as purely originating from the psyche. They are all derived from the depths of the vital source, specifically the subconscious, the dividing line between the psyche and the body. This is obvious for sensitivity and activity which are equivalent to the traits of irritability and contractility in all living organisms, as understood by the physiologist Bichat (see previous chapter). This is also true of resonance which the investigators describe as cerebral even though the specific reaction depends upon the organism as a whole.

One of the most interesting applications of morphopsychology is the

---

1: I explained this concept along with the reservations that can be made, in my work *Caractérologie et morphopsychologie*, PUF, 1983.

ability to substitute the questionnaire method with the direct observation of character based on facial traits. In 1955, in a work entitled *La Synthèse des caractérologies*, I demonstrated that we can apply the corresponding morphological indicators to the three components of character (Ill. 88): *Sensitivity* is expressed by a delicacy in the traits, a slender facial frame, refined receptors and a lively expression; *Activity* is expressed through tonicity in the facial contours; and Primary *Resonance* is expressed through dilation with open sensory receptors while Secondary Resonance is expressed through retraction with an accentuated closure of the sensory receptors.

All that is left is to combine these indicators to conceptualize each of the eight types from a morphological viewpoint. For example, the Nervous Type is formulated by E.nA.P., and characterised by a slender face (E), contours that lack tone and a slightly long face (nA) with very open receptors (P). This corresponds to the Reactive Type that I have already described in this book.

Illustration 88 shows the morphology of the eight types in the female sex. (The same table could apply to the male sex.) For anyone with experience in the morphopsychological reading of faces, there is no doubt that the diagnostic of a character type through close scrutiny is faster than any obtained by the questionnaire method. It is also more reliable when the subject cannot be directly queried (such as historical figures) and therefore must be based on other elements, for example, the daily routine of the subject or his work, which might result in multiple errors. To illustrate my criticism, I have used the example of the writer Balzac, which Le Senne placed in the Choleric Type—EAP— which, at a first approximation, morphopsychology confirms as an asthenic Dilated considering his corpulence and large nose. However, closer observation reveals the superposition of this facial feature by a contrasting forehead (frontal retraction), supported by passionate and ardent eyes. Illustration 73-II demonstrates this duality very clearly, showing Balzac as a combination of the Choleric and Passionate types (EAS).

Illustration 88-I. THE CHARACTER TYPES OF HEYMANS-LE SENNE

Nervous E.P.nA

Sentimental E.S.nA

Choleric E. P. A.

Passionate E. S. A.

By applying the rules of morphopsychology, we are on solid ground when it comes to identifying the eight characterological types. Here they are grouped in twos (of women). It is easy for the reader to find the morphological indicators that correspond to each type.

Illustration 88-II. THE CHARACTER TYPES OF HEYMANS-LE SENNE

Sanguine A.P.nE

Phlegmatic A.S.nE

Amorphous P. nA.nE

Apathetic S.nA.nE

JUNG'S TYPOLOGY

As I have demonstrated in my work,[2] the morphopsychological method has an excellent application in the analysis of the typology developed by Jung, the Swiss psychiatrist.

One of the most original features of this great psychologist is the contrast that he established between 'extroverts' and 'introverts'. He is not the first to have identified these two elements that make up the human: the *external being*, whose interests and activities are entirely directed towards the surrounding environment; and the *inner being*, the heart of the individual, the 'I'. However, he had the advantage of exploring this contrast in depth while developing the corresponding character traits.

However, as already mentioned in relation to the contrast between primary and secondary resonance, the error that arises in characterological systems is that they often establish fixed contrasts that don't exist in real life. According to Jung, extroversion and introversion are extreme opposites; one is either an extrovert or an introvert and cannot be both at the same time.

In 1928, he wrote (*L'inconscient*, Payot): *'Without doubt, these movements of extroversion and introversion harmoniously constitute the rhythm of life. However, it would seem that, in order to achieve this rhythm, a superior level of living is necessary, either totally unconscious, or conscious at a higher level. It is true that this superior conscience would make our condition in life voluntary with the awareness of the fundamental questions of life, and constitutes a superhuman ideal but which one can nevertheless propose as an objective.'*[3]

Jung has shown himself here to be more flexible than Le Senne in that, at a later date, he revised his original opinion by adopting a more accurate point of view. After having defined extroversion and introversion as types of attitude, he wrote: *'One's type of attitude, being a general phenomenon, cannot be the result of judgement or conscious intention. Without doubt, it owes its existence to instinctive unconscious reasoning. The opposition of these types, a generally psychic phenomenon, must in some way have biological antecedent s... Extroversion corresponds to increased productivity while the individual's defensive force and life duration remain relatively*

2: *Synthèse des caractérologies*, Ed. Stock, 1957.
3: Unpublished translation.

unsubstantial ... Introversion corresponds to an individual equipped with a variety of means of personal conservation but with low productivity.'[4]

If Jung had been a morphopsychologist, he would have immediately understood that extra–introversion reflects, through behaviour, the double movement of life—expansion and conservation—which manifests itself in every one of us. The way in which he has characterised extroversion and introversion in the text above—by highlighting the processes of *'increased productivity'* and *'equipped with a variety of means of personal conservation'* — resonates in morphopsychology. As commented on by his biographer Le Lay, he did not explore this point of view by going to the biological source of the process. Morphopsychology fills this gap and, at the same time, provides us with the means of recognising the predominantly Extrovert and Introvert Types, that is, dilation and retraction. It enables us, too, to identify the types with whom extroversion and introversion are associated, whether through a balanced combination such as the Frontal Retracted Type or through a conflicting combination such as the Indented Retracted Type.

The cognitive functions

Extroversion–introversion concerns the organism as a whole. However, Jung considered partial functions whose predominance characterised other types, and each one could exist under either extroversion or introversion. Here again, in my opinion, he was too fixated on the need for symmetry, as he established extreme functional oppositions which are not wholly justified. He distinguished four essential functions—*thought, feeling, intuition* and *sensation*—and contrasted them in pairs. He declared that the thinking and feeling functions were incompatible and consequentially could not be dominant at the same time in the conscious personality of the same subject. Again, I think that if Jung had been a morphopsychologist, he would not have been so categorical and he would have been aware of the frequently observed combination of thought and emotion, particularly in the cerebral–affective expansion Type (see Book II, chapter VII). In the same way, extreme opposition between the functions of intuition and sensation, apparent when intuition is placed on the elevated plane of spirituality, of spiritual clairvoyance, is not such a contrast when you

---

4: Unpubl. trans.

consider the type of intuition known as the sixth sense which is much closer to sensation and a long way from being in opposition.

With regard to the four functions, the morphopsychological method helps us to recognise each one of Jung's predominant types. The three functions (thought, feeling and sensation) correspond to the expansive development of the three zones of the face, while intuition is understood in its superior form as Jung understood it, indicated by the 'spiritualisation' of the traits with a notable expansion in the cerebral zone where the qualities of imagination are predominant.

CHAPTER IV

MORPHOPSYCHOLOGY AND PLANETARY TYPOLOGY

Placed first amongst the numerous systems that establish the relationship between facial features and character traits should be what some call *planetary* typology and others *mythology*. Some authors postulate that the stars have an influence on the formation and evolution of the human being. Others see the gods of mythology as the incarnation of the principle human tendencies. I have never been able to discover the origin of planetary or mythological typology but it can be assumed that it is very ancient.

Without referring to the underlying theories, I will confine myself to an empirical format, that which is the result of observation and unreservedly adopting the terminology in current use. The most important point is to demonstrate that the application of morphopsychology in the study of the planetary typology attests to its accuracy.

Its greatest advantage, in my view, is that it is *all-encompassing* as it represents each type with general traits that correspond to those that can be observed in daily life. I used it a great deal for a number of years before developing morphopsychology as a science. It seemed, at that time, important to classify these planetary types in opposing pairs: Mars–Venus; Jupiter–Saturn; Earth–Mercury; and Moon–Sun. I presented this classification with Gervais-Rousseau in 1930 in *Visages et caractères* (Ed. Plon).

During this period, as I mentioned at the beginning of this book, I was fortunate to have been instructed in Claude Sigaud's doctrine and was quite shocked to discover the similarities between the Jupiter–Saturn opposition and that of Dilation–Retraction. All that was left to do was to transpose Sigaud's morphology on to the study of faces, which up until that point had been reserved for the study of bodies, in order to establish the bases for that which I have called morphopsychology.

It is still possible to use planetary typology to determine a subject's personality on two conditions. The first is that the psychology that corresponds to each of these eight types must be well understood. Secondly, it is necessary to have mastered the art of interpreting all of the possible combinations across these types, which are varied and reflective of the complexity of human nature.

However, what we need is a clear guide that adds precision to our evaluations. The application of morphopsychology to this planetary typology provides us with this guidance by following these simple rules:

Mars is a very tonic Lateral Retracted Type with a strong instinctive–affective expansion.

Venus is a Dilated Type with medium tonicity and expansion in the affective–instinctive zone.

Jupiter is a balanced Dilated Type with a slight frontal retraction in all three facial zones.

Saturn is a Dented-Retracted Type whereby the strong retraction is distributed evenly across the three zones.

Earth is a heavy Dilated Type, tonic and with pronounced expansion in the instinctive zone.

Mercury is an Extreme Retracted Type with open receptors and expansion in the cerebral zone.

Moon is an Atonic–Dilated Type with sometimes an expansion in the cerebral zone.

Sun is a combination of extreme dilation and retraction with expansion in the cerebral zone (Ill. 89-I and II).

The reason for the current interest in morphopsychology is that it is impossible to provide a precise analysis of the personality in complex cases where there are double or triple combinations of the planetary types. However, the application of the laws of morphopsychology provides complementary and conclusive information.

This application gave me the opportunity to update my study of foreheads. In planetary typology, the Jupiter, Mercury, Moon and Sun Types are considered to have a strong forehead development. The notion of facial contours, which is primordial in our science, has added important elements which I will briefly address here. For example, that the forehead of the Jupiter Type is rounded or, frequently, wavy, indicates frontal retraction combining two very different types of intelligence: spontaneous, practical intelligence and reflective and organised intelligence. However, the greatest problem arises when we are comparing the large forehead of the Moon to the large forehead of the Sun Type. It could be said that the Moon Type has a high, dome-shaped forehead while the forehead of the Sun Type, not quite as high, is broader and more compact. However, this overall view is open to error. What can we say about a large forehead? Is it a Moon or Sun Type? This also leads us to the issue of intellectual qualities, which, despite what is generally thought, are not proportional to the volume of the forehead.

Through morphopsychology, I have been able to come to two conclusions that answer this question with the necessary precision.

Firstly, very large foreheads, due to the predominance in the imaginative zone, and their complete roundness, are connected to the Moon Type with its keen ability to assimilate information, its powerful memory, passivity, a disposition towards dreaming and invention but lacking the ability for realisation or critical analysis. On the other hand, the forehead of the Sun Type is notable, less for its largeness (although it is to a certain degree quite large), and more for the harmony in the contrasts and its nuanced contours which correspond to a better adaptation to reality, a more precise vision with clearer ideas and the ability for synthesis and organisation that the Moon Type doesn't have. (For example, see the forehead of Pascal, Ill. 64.)

Illustration 89-I. PLANETARY TYPOLOGY

Contrasting Mars and Mercury

Contrasting Mars and Venus

Illustration 89-II PLANETARY TYPOLOGY

Contrasting Jupiter and Saturn

Contrasting Sun and Moon

Secondly, the expression in the eyes isn't the same. If there is any doubt about the interpretation of the shape of the forehead, I would advise the morphopsychologist to study the expression. In the Moon Type, it is unfocused, vague and unfeeling, and the expression is atonic and dreamy, indicating limited self-awareness and the tendency to give free rein to the instinctive tendencies (read artistic). The Sun Type's expression is clear, bright and warm, which indicates acute self-awareness and an understanding of the limits of the imagination.

In this way, the morphopsychologist can use planetary typology to provide him with a general impression; however, he must always be prepared to confirm the results by applying the rules of our science to ensure that he doesn't commit any errors.

CHAPTER V

MORPHOPSYCHOLOGY AND PSYCHOANALYSIS

We have seen that characterology postulates the existence of innate abilities in every human being which are inherited from our parents and which remain fixed over the course of our lifetime. I have argued against this viewpoint in favour of a dynamic vitality, emphasizing— through morphopsychology—how much the notions of change, contrast, conflicting tendencies and evolution must take priority over a static and rigid view of the personality.

It is worth mentioning that, as far as morphopsychology is concerned, every individual has natural aptitudes which are the foundation of the personality. However, these aptitudes evolve, partly because of the interior life force (the vital flow) and partly due to environmental influences. The concept I therefore propose is a blend of the two which is generally rejected by psychoanalysts who tend to negate the existence of innate aptitudes, only wishing to see the pure and simple result of educational and sociocultural influences in the personality. We have, therefore, two contrasting viewpoints: that of the characterologists and that of the psychoanalysts with morphopsychology residing in the middle.

The morphopsychologist should never reject any doctrine that may help to enlighten and deepen his knowledge of man. He must be aware of any psychoanalytical information that may be of benefit to him. Similarly, the underlying biology of our science aids us in understanding the variety of reactions that psychoanalysis studies.

The stages of evolution, as described by psychoanalysis, are consistent with the morphological process of development. One of the key elements of psychoanalysis involves the maturing process of the child as he develops into adulthood and effortlessly passes through the different stages of evolution. Any obstacles in the process of maturation are responsible for neurotic disorders, meaning that the sick individual remains stuck in a regressed stage, a stage that he should have already gone through.

This same process of evolution sees the human being transition from dilation to retraction and, if there is a blockage, a regressive fixation. In most cases, we can connect this to the subject's morphology. In a Dilated Type, particularly those with atony, it represents a kind of passive oral fixation while the Retracted Type represents an anal fixation. If the conditions of a neurosis come together in either a Dilated or a Retracted adult, we can assume that this neurosis will be marked by oral or anal tendencies.

The psychoanalytical notion of the repression and inhibition of instincts is also very important. We know that this repression of tendencies is expressed in a process of retraction. However, the element of tonicity is crucial. Dilated and Retracted Types with strong tonicity have a powerful vital expansion which keeps them moving forward. As a result, they can comfortably overcome the obstacles of regression. However, the atonic Dilated or Retracted Types have a strong tendency to regress towards their past point of fixation if they come across an obstacle.

In psychoanalytical therapy, tonicity is important as it allows freedom from the repressed tendencies, their reintegration into the subject's conscious personality and the return to a normal life, free of the neurosis. Morphopsychology can be a useful support for the psychoanalyst in bringing to light the strength or weakness of the 'I', the strength of progression of the personality or its weakness, which leads to regression.

We may wonder to what extent regression determines if the individual has overcome the oedipal stage, that period during which he detaches from the adoring fixation on his parents, which is part of infancy, in order to reach sexual maturity. I hasten to add that there is no single morphological sign that reveals the Oedipus complex as it is a combination of factors. It does not occur when there is a harmonious balance between the vital forces of dilation and retraction.

The dynamic nature of morphopsychology also resembles psychoanalysis in an important area: neurotic conflicts. A powerful instinctive tendency, whether aggressive or sexual, and which is overly powerful, is censured, thus having an inhibiting effect on the subject. It is furthermore repressed into the subconscious. In addition, we know that to maintain this repression, the conscious 'I' creates a completely opposing tendency which is 'a reaction to' the excessiveness of the instinct. For example, a subject who is extremely aggressive adopts a mild and conciliatory behaviour, or potent sensuality is replaced by extreme prudishness. This is where the morphopsychologist is in danger of making a mistake. For example, a subject whose facial structure is retracted and asthenic, combined with a powerful jaw, should logically demonstrate a great potential for aggression. But the exact opposite may occur and the structure of the jaw combines with an almost total absence of aggression, for example, the manner of verbal expression is very soft. The dynamic analysis of this situation helps us to understand that the powerful aggressive impulsions probably provoked censure in the subject's youth, resulting in inhibition and a reactive attitude. However, underlying this reactive attitude, all of the initial aggression remains in the deepest part of the individual. If the morphopsychologist rightly notes its existence in his analysis, he may deduce that, to create equilibrium in the personality, the subject must free himself, at least partially, from this aggression by either diverting or sublimating it.

The dynamic point of view of morphopsychology also helps us to understand the changes that may be produced in an individual's personality as a result of successful psychoanalytical treatment. We know that a suppressed neurosis is usually accompanied by a tendency towards retraction, resulting in emotional difficulties in adaptation and accompanied particularly by sadness. When treatment cures the repression, sadness is replaced by joy which can change the facial traits. This modification, however, when it is long-lasting, may not be restricted to only one expression but can change the morphology of the face in the sense of an expansion in the facial frame and sensory receptors.

In conclusion, while a solid knowledge of the evolution of psychoanalysis can be very useful in the training of a morphopsychologist, I would be so bold as to advise psychoanalysts to learn morphopsychology. They cannot reasonably pretend that human beings are not born with certain aptitudes which later mark their personality and which particularly constitute a possible predisposition to neuroses. As discussed earlier, and summarizing in a few lines what I have said in Chapter IX about the vulnerability of the different morphopsychological types, psychoanalysts could also find useful indicators about the viability of being able to re-establish an equilibrium. A significant example lies in the case of subjects with a facial structure of extreme retraction and atony wherein the zest for life is consequently very weak. They are therefore unable to overcome the passive oral stage and we can be certain that it will be extremely difficult to free themselves from their inexhaustible need for protection and to forge an independent personality that will allow them to lead their own lives.

CHAPTER VI
HEALTH AND EDUCATION

Morphopsychology also explains the evolution of human beings by age and the connections which exist between body structure and functions at different life stages.

Here, too, I will limit myself to explaining only the essential to demonstrate the accuracy of the laws of morphopsychology. As we have already seen with the four temperaments of the Ancients, the development of the human being follows a defined course which can be summarised as a progressive journey from dilation to retraction. In the very early stages of life, the demands for nutrition and growth require the consumption of abundant nutrition in an atmosphere of passive receptivity. This corresponds to the Lymphatic temperament and atonic dilation. However, the weakness in this structure—hyposensitivity, as noted by Sigaud—is that it lacks a defensive reaction. This lack of defence constantly exposes the very young infant to sickness, thereby explaining its fragility. Special protection must be provided to protect the child from external morbid influences.

As the child develops, the body gradually becomes more tonic as it passes from the Lymphatic to the Sanguine stage. The protected environment is gradually replaced by a natural environment that includes everything, both good and bad. In order to survive, the child must absorb the good and reject the bad. This is where tonicity appears; it correlates to an improved defence system.

The progression from the Lymphatic to the Sanguine stage, from Atonic–Dilated to Tonic–Dilated, is a function of youth. However, as the human being ventures into life and becomes more exposed, he must increase his defensive reactions. This is the role of retraction, particularly that of frontal retraction, which corresponds to the Choleric temperament with its strong tonicity.

There comes a time when vital force diminishes or expansion stops and where, in order to maintain life, the defence system must be developed to the maximum. At this point, retraction dominates exclusively, which is visible in the morphology, and tonicity is very limited. This retraction is characteristic of the majority of the elderly.

This is the most common evolution and is in line with good adaptation.

However, the advantage of the science of morphopsychology is that it allows us to interpret anomalies in this evolution and suggest the most suitable regime to assure an appropriate adaptation. For example, an Atonic–Dilated Type in adulthood indicates the persistence of a stage of infant physiology, indicated by an insufficient defence system and determining a particular pathology. This also conditions the character traits. From a health point of view, this requires a protective environment. We have studied examples in this book where, instinctively, subjects of this type force themselves to remain in such an environment. (See, for example, the characters of the priest of Tours and Don Abbondio.)

In contrast, a premature retraction, which gives the infant the look of an old man, indicates, according to the laws of morphopsychology, that the child has had to defend himself from the aggressions of the environment (pre- or post-natal) from a very young age. This has stymied his development (and, as a result, expansion) and all of his vital strength has been dedicated to purely and simply staying alive. Because of a precipitated Nervous Temperament, pathological nervous reactions are keen. As a result, his youth is punctuated by episodes that are pathologically painful even though they are not serious. The character is also affected.

I won't go into detail about what morphopsychology brings to the understanding of the physiology and character of children, having covered it in a book dedicated to this subject (*Connaissance des enfants par la morphopsychologie*, PUF). I would simply like to highlight parenting style, the most appropriate subjects to study and health practices to follow both in sickness and in health.

THE CHILD AT HOME

Individuals are born with a morphological structure that is inherited, which is why no two infants are alike. The differences can sometimes be so pronounced that the morphopsychologist can make a confident assessment of how the child will behave, from both a physical and moral point of view, during his lifetime.

It is well known that children of the Dilated Type, having a facility for adaptation, raise themselves, as they say. However, we should be aware that resistance to illness presumes a progressive evolution towards retraction and that this retraction should be reinforced through an appropriate health education. More specifically, this involves teaching the child to protect himself against what could hurt him and to practice self-control.

Vice versa, a child belonging to the Retracted Type will not only have health problems, frequently falling sick, but will also be unwell in the sense that their hypersensitivity often makes it difficult for them to adapt to the family environment. An understanding of morphopsychology helps to avoid making mistakes in child-raising. We have already covered the concept of preferred surroundings and, in a situation where the child is understood by his caregivers, the opportunity exists to create the conditions for better adaptation.

Another example: A child may, from birth, have a dominant expansion localised in one of the three zones. We can immediately tell that he will have the tendency, in whatever he does, to develop abilities evident in this zone in expansion. From an educational standpoint, we must not hinder this development: a child with expansion in the cerebral zone should not be deprived of reading material and instruction; a child with expansion in the affective zone should not be deprived of the human or animal contact that he needs; and a child with expansion in the instinctive zone should not be deprived of sufficient nourishment and movement.

Raising a child is much more complex for those with a dominant expansion as the sub-dominant zones also need to be educated. If the dominant zone is too pronounced, it will tend to affect the equilibrium of the organism's physical and mental health. The child should have a variety of different influences in his life which is often difficult to administrate. How, for example, do you ensure that a child with expansion in the cerebral zone doesn't spend his entire time studying or reading? How do you get him into the fresh air, spend time with his friends and be active? How do you ensure that a child with expansion in the affective zone doesn't always react emotionally to circumstances which inhibit his ability to objectively judge the situation so that he is not then exposed to disappointment? How do you ensure that a child with expansion in the instinctive zone doesn't react with irrational impulsions, for example, if he can't control his need to be constantly in motion and that he should learn to think before acting? A good understanding of the morphopsychological structure of the face will help the caregiver to resolve all of these problems.

THE CHILD IN SCHOOL

The school teacher that has some training in morphopsychology knows from experience that not all children are equal, neither emotionally nor intellectually, and that in class teachers must adapt their teaching methods according to the particular need of each of their students.

Morphopsychology allows us, as we will see in another chapter, to understand the intellectual aptitudes of each individual and their facility for assimilation and memorization, their speed of comprehension and reaction, their preference for the tangible or the abstract and their talents for reflection and imagination.

However, in the relationship between teacher and student, teachers believe that affection motivates students. The ease of ability to adapt in children of the Dilated Type makes them good students: docile, with a good memory and the ability to express themselves easily. On the other hand, the difficulties that the Retracted Type faces in adaptation may result in wilfulness, blockages and inhibited expression. The notion of the preferred surroundings is crucial here and if the teacher had been aware that for a student of this type he needs to create the conditions for expansion, the child can completely transform from the class dunce to a good student.

The morphopsychologist must be particularly aware of the passionate Indented–Retracted Type and their intense affective reactions. They are also able to excel in school when their passionate tendency is satisfied, whether through a good affective relationship with the teacher or by teaching a subject that he enjoys learning about.

THE ROLE OF THE DOCTOR

Health and education, as we have seen, are related. The teacher and the doctor have a joint role to play in child development. They would both benefit from being able to lean on the knowledge of morphopsychology. The interpretation of facial traits helps them to understand each child's particular way of reacting and therefore apply the most appropriate educational and health practices for each situation.

In addition, they must understand that morphopsychology is not a typology: it is not static, rather it is dynamic and, in reading faces, they can imagine the future of each subject, for example, the difference in childhood between a Dilated Type and a Retracted Type. To give a more significant example, through morphopsychology a doctor learns not to give the same importance to symptoms of sickness when they arise in the state of hypo-excitability of a Dilated Type and the hyper-excitability of the Retracted Type.

With the return of holistic medicine balancing out the current overly technical medical practices, from now on morphopsychology will find its place as an indispensable tool for any doctor who considers individual temperament to be important.

CHAPTER VII
EVALUATING INTELLIGENCE

As demonstrated earlier in my account of the abilities of each of the morphopsychological types, intelligence is the highest mode of expression of one's understanding of the world and is closely tied to adaptation. Establishing intellectual aptitudes is of primordial importance for the morphopsychologist, particularly when he aims to give advice on someone's life choices, and especially their career choice.

This evaluation of a person's intellectual abilities is two-fold in that it is both *quantitative* and *qualitative*.

It is *quantitative* when we want to understand a subject's degree of intelligence in comparison with others, formulated by 'he is more or less intelligent than this or that person'. Or when we want to measure the level of intelligence in reference to a norm established within a given population, formulated by 'more or less intelligent than the average'.

There are a number of tests that have been invented to this effect, resulting in what is known as the *intelligence quotient*. However, previously, the quantitative evaluation was based on the child's or adolescent's academic performance which, when consistent, provided a sufficiently precise idea of what could be expected in terms of the subject's intellectual abilities.

Nevertheless, in many ways this quantitative evaluation is disputable and it would seem to be much more important to admit that intelligence is *qualitatively* different from person to person and that the different intellectual aptitudes are unequally developed across the different human types. However, by being partly subjective, this understanding is open to error. In this book, we have seen that each morphopsychological type has a tendency to value his own type of intelligence above others. Consequently, a Dilated Type places greater value on the intelligence of his fellow Dilated Types than that of the Retracted Type and vice versa. In the same way, those with expansion in the cerebral zone, very common in our universities, have always and still tend to exaggerate the value of their own academic intelligence. They thereby minimise the importance of practical abilities of those with expansion in the instinctive zone, unable to see its utility. Every morphopsychologist must, from the very start, adapt his subjective understanding to take into account the value of each type of intelligence. And we have already seen that the mixed types, with their balanced combinations of dilation and retraction, are in a better position to judge as they find themselves in the middle of the road with a clear view in all directions.

We know that the *dynamic character* of morphopsychology will always give greater weight to the qualitative than the quantitative.

As far as intellectual abilities are concerned, the different kinds of adaptation to different situations are much more important than their sum total.

To approach the problem in a clear and straightforward fashion, I have established a classification system consisting of three levels. Note that the word 'level' does not imply a value-based hierarchy.

Level 1: Intelligence is at the service of instinctive or affective tendencies and, as a consequence, closer to intuitive flair than rational intelligence.

Level 2: Reason and instinct are balanced. It is the most flexible in terms of activities where the practical and theoretical work together.

Level 3: Academic intelligence dominates, where intellectual notions drive behaviour.

Level 1 belongs to those with dominance in the instinctive or instinctive–affective zones. The forehead is small or medium in size, particularly broad and projecting in the zone above the eyes. It proffers a real-world, down-to-earth type of intelligence with a sense of the practical. These are the qualities necessary for manual labour, the technical professions, construction, commercial activities and, in a more general sense, all scientific or artistic activities which connect man directly with objects or real-world situations. It does not exclude inventive abilities whereby the invention comes not from an idea but rather from a certain flair or manual ability (he is 'handy' rather than 'inspired'). It lends itself to management positions where authority is derived from practical knowledge.

Level 2 belongs to subjects with the three facial zones in equilibrium and a combination of dilation and retraction (particularly frontal retraction). The intellectual ability is a combination of both the concrete and the abstract at the same time, necessary in many professions: technical, commercial, administrative, social, freelance, artistic, educational or in either subordinate or management positions depending on the situation.

Level 3 is where the subjects have a dominant cerebral zone and, to be precise, according to the fundamental rule previously described, this dominance must not be evaluated solely according to the size of the forehead but also by its contrasts and harmony. These aptitudes are suitable for intellectual careers, freelance work, education and some types of art, in research and conceptual inventions. He may also have leadership qualities.

The value of intelligence

Again, we all have a tendency to value intelligence in relation to the level in which we find ourselves, as defined above. However, this subjective viewpoint can lead to serious errors if it is not adjusted to give a more objective evaluation. We should think of intelligence as having a useful function which helps us to understand the world we live in, to adapt to it and to act accordingly. This is why basing every evaluation of intelligence on academic performance and other tests doesn't show us the extent to which intellectual demands are different. To make an intelligence quotient the only criteria of intelligence can only lead to errors, the most notorious being to believe that a subject with a very high IQ (known as genius level) is capable of resolving all problems, no matter what they are. It has come to the point where, for example, it has been proposed that a group of scholars, eminent in their speciality, should be consulted to find solutions to the social, economic or political problems that exist in their countries, as if there were a general intelligence that proffered an all-encompassing ability.

The problem should not be approached in this way. Whoever is able to resolve the problems that exist in a particular sector of activity should be considered intelligent. The key for the morphopsychologist counsellor is therefore to be aware of the requirements for a particular type of life or profession and, from that, be able to determine if the subject possesses the necessary abilities.

It is at this point that it is crucial to take the three zones of the face into account, already comprehensively covered in this book. We can say that there is instinctive intelligence, affective intelligence and cerebral intelligence. It is indisputable that in the same sector of activity there are those who are more intelligent than others. This brings us back, after this detour, to the quantitative point of view, but in a completely different way from that in usage in schools or in the test methods.

Dynamism and harmony

Morphopsychology teaches us that intelligence cannot be measured by tests (such as psychometry and anthropometry) but depends on non-measureable factors such as *dynamism* and *harmony*.

Dynamism is a function of sensitivity, of tonicity, which can be seen not only in the cerebral zone but also in the instinctive and affective zones. It is an essential function as it is the expression of an individual's vitality. *Harmony* is a result of the equilibrium that exists among an individual's strengths, meaning between his instinctive, affective and cerebral lives. This demand for harmony is primordial. The equilibrium between mixed types, as previously mentioned, combinations of dilation and retraction, greatly assist in the fair assessment of problems.

Back to the three levels. Despite what is often thought, intelligence is not a matter of the level in which an individual is positioned; rather, dynamism and harmony are determining factors within each level.

Let's take levels 1 and 3 as an example. In each one, the morphopsychologist can identify the signs that will help him assess an individual's intelligence.

Imagine someone with a very strong expansion in the instinctive–affective zone and a very pronounced reduction in the cerebral zone in a kind of combination of dilation and lateral retraction. This means that impressions in the environment provoke an immediate response in the zone that has the highest degree of expansion; meaning, this man reacts instinctively and without prior reflection. Therefore, he has a lower level of intelligence (see Ill. 62, I).

To give an example of level 3, an individual has a strong imbalance between cerebral expansion (as shown in a large forehead) and a very pronounced retraction in the other two zones. This structure lacks both dynamism and harmony. Thought is predominant but proves to be mediocre when it comes to accomplishing tasks (see Ill, 60, fig. 1).

We can make our assessment according to the role that dynamism and harmony play in each one of these two groups, excluding extremes. In doing so, the morphopsychologist must assess all three zones of the face according to these two elements. I will give a few examples.

In level 1, the individual's degree of intelligence is greater than the volume of the forehead which is the sub-dominant zone, although it is smaller in size if we compare it to the instinctive zone. If, in this case, the forehead is harmonious, we could say that it means that he has some common sense within his intuitive instinct. The illustration shows images with different degrees of intelligence, allowing us to see the role of this harmony in different situations.

The first example demonstrates a disproportionate difference between the superior and inferior zones given that the forehead is small, narrow and not very differentiated. We can therefore conclude that thought is very limited and comprised of routine ideas. Initiative, when implemented, is more related to the spontaneous instinctive activity of a man used to resolving all problems through action. This person does think but within the limited sphere of his activities. He has what we would call common sense (Ill. 55, 4).

The second case is based on the great businessman, Raymond Berthault, who was not a reflective man but rather a man of practical initiatives. The forehead, being lateral retracted, is the source of a powerful dynamism; as soon as an idea arises, he acts upon it (Ill. 63-I).

The third case is that of the Armenian Napoleon Bullukian who was an important figure in the field of construction. He was characterised by his energy and tenacity. The forehead, quite narrow and differentiated across the zones, has a pronounced brow bone. This is a forehead of concrete and practical ideas which always operates in support of and never as an impediment to action (Ill. 63-I).

The fourth case is that of the Bishop Romero who was not a theologian but someone of social action whose ideas were simple but practical (Ill. 90).

Illustration 90. – ROMERO

The Salvadorian Bishop was murdered by hired assassins because of his impetuous dynamism as a Lateral Retracted Type. He had a passion for working in the service of the masses (Dilated Type) to improve their social situation.

Illustration 91. – FOREHEAD STRUCTURES

The three types of forehead structures illustrated here are represented by three eminent men of science. The first is Dr. Chassaignac, a renowned surgeon and an ingenious inventor of instrumental techniques. His forehead is not big; it is that of a pragmatic lateral Retracted–Dilated Type. It is the forehead of a technician. The second is Louis Pasteur who, as we know, revolutionised modern medicine through his discoveries. His forehead is large, differentiated across the three zones and straight due to the frontal retraction. It is the forehead of an observer and an experimenter. The third, Father Claude Bernard, was both a great physiologist and a philosopher. He has a very large forehead with a dominant imaginative zone which demonstrates his aptitude for great synthesis.

The fifth case is that of the renowned surgeon Chassaignac who also has a balanced face with a dominant instinctive zone and a sub-dominant cerebral zone strongly marked by dynamism. This equilibrium, achieved through an overall frontal retraction, explains his great practical ability. The technical inventions which made Chassaignac famous are the product of someone with a gift for the practical as opposed to theories and systems (Ill. 90).

The sixth case is that of the great physician Pascal who we can see has a high degree of harmony in which a strong affective–instinctive zone is supported by a forehead of average dimension but remarkable for its excellent differentiation. Pascal doesn't belong to the typical type of cerebral expansion which is most common amongst the great men. As I demonstrated in a work dedicated to him, morphopsychology is of extreme value here as it explains the practical character of Pascal's intelligence, where his discoveries, particularly in physics, are remarkable, not for their theoretical concepts, but for their spirit of experimentation. It is therefore not surprising that this great man was the first to introduce experimental science in physics (see Ill. 64).

Those who have an expansion in the cerebral zone tend to underrate those with practical intelligence due to their difficulty working with abstract ideas and theories. However, the examples cited above provide evidence that the degree of intelligence does not depend on having a large forehead.

At the other extreme is level 3 where we find examples of expansion in the cerebral zone. Overall harmony also plays a very important role in the development of the lower two zones, these zones which I refer to as *the zones of contact with reality*. If there is harmony, intellectual abilities become part of real life; they are stimulated by the affective impulse and put into action through the instinctive zone. On the other hand, if these zones are deficient, then thought remains detached from reality, residing in pure abstraction, rumination and theories that are never brought to fruition. On this point, it is remarkable to note that most great men, those who have produced a work of value, if they have a large forehead, also have a solid structure in the two lower zones with a large nose and mouth.

The Swiss writer Amiel is an excellent example. In illustration 48, you can see the dominant expansion in the cerebral zone on a base of extreme retraction. The size of the forehead is poorly supported by deep-set eyes and by the relative deficiency in the two lower zones, inhibiting creative thought which would have appeared to exist at first glance. At his own admission, he recognised that he was incapable of anything other than the eternal rumination of his own problems (in the extensive personal journal which is his only notable work) and his inability to come out of himself and take action, thus wasting his greatest talents.

Harmonious structures

What we learn from morphopsychology in this area is crucial: It teaches us that equilibrium, harmony, in the different zones of the face is the principle factor for creativity. If the forehead, which is the seat of intelligence, suggests creativity, it must be supported by sufficient development in the instinctive and affective zones. There are many examples we can choose from.

Wagner is an example of productive lateral–nasal retraction (Ill. 70). His large composers' forehead dominates a face whose almost earthly heaviness reveals his powerful vitality and which is, effectively, the orchestral talent which characterises his musical genius.

Returning to our comparison of the three levels, I have chosen men of high intellectual qualities and compared them: Chassaignac, Pasteur and Claude Bernard. Chassaignac is notable for his technical and inventive intelligence (level 1); Pasteur, whose forehead is harmoniously differentiated and in balance with the rest of the face, has an intelligence that is both concrete and abstract, resulting in countless practical inventions and original ideas (level 2); and Claude Bernard has a much larger forehead but it is well supported by the other parts of the face, demonstrating a higher degree of intelligence that is both experimental and philosophical (level 3) (Ill. 91).

Given all of this, concentrating on the larger picture is primordial in morphopsychology as an understanding of the world does not depend on isolated abilities that could be considered intellectual faculties. Rather, it is the result of the activities of the entire being, open to all of the impressions that he receives. Morphopsychology provides us with not only a practical method for understanding intellectual aptitudes but, above all, it informs us, better than traditional psychology, as to how we create our presence in the world—how we adapt—through the convergence of the multiple functions of our organism.

CHAPTER VIII
MORPHOPSYCHOLOGY AND CAREER COUNSELLING

The morphopsychologist can't avoid, whether he has considered the idea or not, finding himself faced at some point with the issue of career choices. After all, it is one of the most important and useful applications of morphopsychology. In addition, it should be noted that career counselling is one of the best uses for knowledge acquired in this field as it forces the morphopsychologist to be very precise in his evaluation and to avoid using abstract or vague psychological language, instead expressing himself in a concrete and practical manner.

Guiding someone towards the best profession for them is an issue of adaptation. It depends on being able to achieve the best pairing of the person's abilities with the demands of the work at hand.

The best adaptation is where the subject is the most efficient in his chosen profession and, in addition, where he finds the greatest satisfaction in his accomplishments. We can deduce that the subject is less fatigued by work that he enjoys (efficiency) and it is said that this adaptation is the best guarantee for maintaining good health. If a subject is not suitable for a specific job, it 'gets on his nerves', according to common opinion.

We have seen numerous examples in this book that demonstrate that career counselling is based on the aptitudes that we are aware of in each foundational type and, for the reader's information, I have demonstrated, case by case, how it was established based on strictly logical rules.

However, you must not assume that we can establish a universal table of relationships between the aptitudes of each foundational type and any particular profession, requiring a simple equation to choose the profession. A static view such as this is prone to error. We must adopt a dynamic view not only concerning the subject's aptitudes but also those required by a particular profession. A subject's aptitudes cannot be determined in a rigid fashion; they evolve and above all they combine with each other, and the result of this combination is the most important factor to take into account.

The aptitudes required for different professions are often complex and one subject will be more adept than another. If you compare several subjects who are successful in a particular domain, you will find that they aren't successful in the same way; the process of compensating factors means that they can use particular qualities to compensate for the lack of others. For example, if dynamism and patience are required in order to be a good salesman, some may be successful because of their dynamism even if they lack patience and others for their patience even if they lack dynamism. Clearly, everything depends on the demands of a particular position to be filled and any decision should be made based on these demands.

As we know, professions evolve over time and to maintain the same level we must be *flexible and adaptable*. This is an essential point that the morphopsychologist must understand.

Enough has been said about the variety of aptitudes required for the different professions. It is best to simply explain how to proceed from a practical perspective. The best method is to make a morphopsychological diagnosis of the subject who has applied for a position, working with him as closely as possible. Talk to him about what morphopsychology reveals about him, listen to his response, perhaps even his objections and, based on this exchange, devise as precise an analysis as possible of these aptitudes.

This method has the advantage of also being a teaching opportunity as it helps the subject to understand his true talents and therefore help him to make the best choice for himself. The ideal is not to reject someone through a simple 'no' but to be positive so that, if the subject doesn't get the job, he can then be directed towards another which is in line with the aptitudes that we have discovered in him.

CHAPTER IX
UNDERSTANDING THE GREAT MASTERS

Understanding those men and women renowned for an original work of art, in any domain, rests essentially on the study of the work itself. This may seem at first to be a banal observation, however we must recognise that the study of the piece is not at all easy. It is not about, as many would imagine, applying the rules of common sense to a masterpiece. To appreciate its originality, we have to attempt to rise to its level. As Balzac said, 'Knowledge is the great equaliser'.[1]

It has often been thought that the superior creative genius is essentially based on the degree of intelligence and that the other values that are part of the personality—the physical, instinctive and affective aspects—which all play an important role in daily life, have no part in the creation of original works. We know, for example, that in the past it wasn't polite to inquire about the sex life of a great master and it required Nietzsche and Freud in a more recent era to go into depth in this area of psychological research to understand its importance.

The issue is that we have to break with our habit of analytical thought and our tendency to think of intelligence in an abstract manner, separate from all vital attachment with instincts and feelings. An overall view of the human personality shows us that the great masters create their works

---

1: Unpublished translation.

with their entire being, body and soul together. Moreover, the personality traits which one might consider defects and wish to suppress are likely to play an important role in the originality of the genius, contrary to what is often asserted in the name of the limited opposition of Good and Evil.

This synthetic vision is also part of morphopsychology. The practice of this science has helped us to understand that the personality of the great masters and their work form a whole. From this, we can deduce that we are able to have a better understanding of their work by studying every aspect of their personality. It is one of the most successful applications of morphopsychology which I have demonstrated by studying numerous exceptional personalities from this perspective.[2]

Reading literary works

As highlighted on a number of occasions, good writers make use of morphopsychology 'without knowing it' as their intuition enables them to experience their book or theatrical characters completely authentically. I demonstrated in *Types morphopsychologiques en littérature*, and on numerous occasions in this book, that the morphopsychologist can learn a great deal by studying the great literary works. Literature will help him to better understand the everyday reality of the types described in our science based on logical foundations. As a result, morphopsychology allows us to approach literature differently as, right before our eyes, it reveals the characters of the work's heroes with a particularly expressive sense of reality.

On the other hand, an authors' intuition would gain a great deal by making use of a sound knowledge of morphopsychology. In the same way, theatre and cinema directors would benefit from selecting the faces that best fit with the role's character when choosing actors instead of being influenced by, as is often the case, celebrity names.

2: I have studied a number of characters that differ greatly from one to the next, including Andersen, Balzac, Bergson, Giraudoux, Colette and Pascal in the *Revue de Morphopsychologie.*

Biography

Louis Corman (1901–1995) is the creator of Morphopsychology.

He studied medicine at the prestigious Sorbonne University in Paris with professors such as Marie Curie.

Working as head of medicine in the psychiatric department at Nantes Hospital (Brittany, France), he founded the department of child psychiatry. To gain a better understanding of children with comprehension difficulties, he studied the relationship between facial and psychological traits. In 1937, he established the foundations of morphopsychology with the writing of *'Quinze leçons de morphopsychologie',* (Fifteen lessons of morphopsychology) in which he established the laws which can be applied to every living being, based on the fundamental law of Dilation and Retraction.

As the author of numerous works, he founded the *Société française de morphopsychologie* in 1980.

For more of our books, visit www.guid-publications.com

28240865R00206

Printed in Great Britain
by Amazon